BCIM: Economic Corridor
Chinese and Indian Perspectives

Editors

Swaran Singh
Zhu Cuiping

ADROIT

Adroit Publishers
New Delhi

BCIM: Economic Corridor Chinese and Indian Perspectives

ISBN : 978-81-87393-37-5

First Published in 2017

Published by

ADROIT PUBLISHERS

4675/21, Ganpati Bhawan, Ansari Road,

Daryaganj, New Delhi-110 002

Phone : 011-23266030

Distributors

AKHIL BOOK DISTRIBUTORS

email: akhilbooks@yahoo.com

akhilbks@gmail.com

Typesetting—Gaurav Graphices, Delhi.

E-mail: gauravsingh1908@gmail.com

Printed at Reliable Infomedia, New Delhi.

Dedicated

to the vision and efforts of all the participants of the first BCIM Conference that was held in Kunming (Yunnan, China) in August 1999

Contents

Foreword

BCIM sub-regional cooperation has been close to my heart for over two decades ever since I was heading the Institute for South Asian Studies at Kunming. Starting from year 1999, various scholars from Bangladesh, Myanmar China and India had been exploring and examining BCIM cooperation which has lately achieved its first formal conceptualisation of BCIM-Economic Corridor. Their constant endeavours have produced remarkable research outcome in many forms. After each conference for the Forum of BCIM Regional Cooperation, the Yunnan Academy of Social Sciences would collect and translate conference papers and publish these as a volume of BCIM Forum paper collection in both Chinese and English. In these series, the BCIM-EC Report (2014) was published by the Press of Chinese Academy of Social Sciences as the first such book after the China-India Joint Statement signed by the two Prime Minister in 2013 in which BCIM-EC initiative was for the first time officially recognised by both China and India.

In my knowledge, however, this book BCIM-Economic Corridor: Chinese and Indian Perspectives, presented first study on BCIM-Economic Corridor from the perspective of both Indian and Chinese experts in the field. Moreover, it clearly stands out in presenting a rather balanced and very academic analysis of not just the historical evolution of the regional cooperation but also its cultural moorings and social groundings that provide the promise for realisation of the BCIM sub-regional cooperation which is where this book locates the BCIM Economic Corridor narratives and initiative. Most of its chapters present extensive research in highlighting various specific areas of cooperation and present detailed examination of their mutual and multilateral weaknesses and strengths to suggest its likely future trajectories and what could be its pragmatic pace of progress. Second, this is also the first book on the subject of BCIM Economic Corridor and it provides an equal space and freedom to well-known Chinese and Indian experts in the field. I have known most of these experts and also followed works of some of them rather closely. And, of course, this is also the first book to be simultaneously published both in Chinese and English which promised to widen its dissemination and reach. No doubt, its publication is going to not just make value addition to the literature on this critical theme but also provide a push to the very idea of BCIM sub-regional cooperation that several of us have held dear and worked tirelessly towards its realisation over the years.

Few words about editors of this book would also be in place. I have known Professor Swaran Singh for about two decades now, since we first met during my first visit for a conference in New Delhi in 1997. I had the chance to meet him again at the inaugural conference of BCIM sub-regional cooperation on 15 August 1999 which is where delegates had adopted the ambitious 'Kunming Initiative' document working late in night. I had much better chance to know him when he accompanied our delegation on a road trip of India's northeastern region to revisit the legendary Stilwell Road during December 2000 and I have followed his works with interest ever since. Likewise, I have known Prof. Zhu Cuiping, the Deputy Director of Research Institute of Indian Ocean Economies at Yunnan University of Economics and Finance for many years. I had the pleasure of attending the launch ceremony of the RIIO in 2011 and have also joined some of the annual international conferences. Prof Zhu is a well-known expert on South Asian issues and Sino-Indian relations. In recent years, she has written extensively on Indian Ocean Regional Cooperation and BCIM, on Indian economy and investment policy issues, and on economic relations between India and China.

I admire this collaboration of my two long-time friends in producing this excellent publication and wish them all the very best for their continued academic cooperation in further promoting BCIM regional cooperation which remain the need of hour for these four countries. With my best wishes,

Professor Ren Jia
President
Yunnan Academy of Social Sciences
Kunming, Yunnan, People's Republic of China

Preface

Since the year 1999 when delegates from Bangladesh, China, India and Myanmar (BCIM) held their first conference of the Regional Economic Cooperation Forum at Kunming, and signed the *Kunming Initiative*, various people and institutions from these four countries have worked hard to promote the BCIM sub-regional cooperation and they have also achieved several milestones. However, compared with the vast economic and developmental potential of these four countries and even compared to their perspectives on sub-regional cooperation, their actual momentum has been slower resulting in only tentative new mechanisms and smaller-scale investments. For instance, after long drawn parleys, in February 2013, the first BCIM Auto Rally was successfully organised, indicating the feasibility of their physical connectivity. Same year also saw Chinese Premier Li Keqiang paying a visit to India in May and the two countries signed the China-India Joint Statement where the two prime ministers agreed to consult with the other parties as they set up a joint working group and promised to strengthen the regional connectivity to boost the bilateral economic and trade cooperation and cultural exchanges. And, the most important of all, their Joint Statement also proposed to build the BCIM Economic Corridor which is the theme of this volume where experts from China and India examine various facets of this proposition from both Indian and Chinese perspectives.

The proposal for building a BCIM Economic Corridor was again discussed during visit to China by Prime Minister Manmohan Singh in October 2013, and their Joint Statement on the Future Development Vision of China-India Strategic Partnership once again underlined their shared commitment to the building of the BCIM Economic Corridor and the two also agreed to maintain communications and consultations on this matter with Bangladesh and Myanmar. Finally, on the 18th and 19th day of December in 2013, the first meeting of the Quartet Joint Working Group for BCIM Economic Corridor was held in Kunming China, where anointed experts and representatives from all four countries conducted in-depth discussions on development prospects, cooperation priorities, cooperation mechanism and other matters, marking the BCIM Economic Corridor. This means that the BCIM sub-regional cooperation has already moved from Track-2 to Track-1, and over the last three year, after this 'upgrading', we have found that there is much clearer consensus on how its 'effective promotion is of great significance.' The real challenge, however, lies in implementing these ideas and to start actual construction process which, in spite of enormous potential, has continued to be engulfed in certain amount of empathy and skepticism amongst its stakeholders.

It is also pertinent to underline the strategic significance of this sub-region. The proposed BCIM Economic Corridor covers an area of 1.65 million square kilometres and has a population of about 440 million. However, the total trade volume between the four members of the sub-region accounts for only 2 per cent of their total volume of the foreign trade. This is because the enormous development potential of this sub-region has remained underutilized. Currently, all three, Bangladesh, India, and Myanmar, have formidable trade deficit viz-a-viz China. For example, in 2014 the China-India bilateral volume of bilateral trade amounted to $ 71.6 billion but India's trade deficit with China stood at whopping $ 44.96 billion. The China-Bangladesh bilateral trade volume of $ 12.55 billion had deficit with China worth $ 11 billion. And, China-Myanmar bilateral trade volume of $ 9.05 billion had deficit of $ 1 billion. To expand their bilateral and multilateral trade and resolve trade deficit, the most pressing issue is to cut trade costs and enhance the merchandise export capacity of India, Bangladesh and

Myanmar. There is also enormous potential for expanding Sino-Indian economic cooperation, because China has achieved cutting-edge technologies in manufacturing and infrastructure building, especially in power generation and telecommunications as also in project contracting, and it has the strength and abundant experience in infrastructure-building which is fast emerging as major requirement for India's infrastructural development.

Indian Prime Minister Narendra Modi has been campaigning for 'Make in India' which has resulted in China promising over $52 billion investments in India which will also involve technology transfers. India has adopted this innovative approach to open up for China's investments to address its persistent trade deficit with China. This opening up to China's investments and technology transfers is also expected to boost India's lagging manufacturing industry and boost India's export potential. At the same time, India is seen as relatively well-developed in terms of the information and communication technologies, software-outsourcing, pharmaceutical and other service industries, where India has a competitive advantage and these sectors of India can make investment in China. If both sides can work in cooperation with a due division of labour and know-how for their niche sectors based on their comparative advantage and mutual market demand and explore appropriate institutional arrangement for trade facilitation, such cooperation will not only help reduce India's trade deficit with China, but will also create more job opportunities and enhance the bilateral capacity to achieve sustainable economic development. This will also create positive climate for enhancing their border trade and sub-regional cooperation including pushing their BCIM Economic Corridor project further forward.

Although China and India currently also have to address problem areas like their long and disputed border, it is equally important to discern how their people in these peripheral border regions have suffered from rather complex socio-economic, political environment and harsh geographic conditions. The people of their sub-region lack basic infrastructure like rails or roads available to directly connect to main hubs of these two rapidly emerging economies. As a result, their border trade has not pick up and much of their bilateral trade depends on ocean shipping which has become increasingly exposed to maritime dangers of piracy and terrorism. With Kunming, Mandalay, Dhaka, Calcutta and other cities as the bases, with the interconnection of the infrastructure including railways, highways, aviation, oil and gas pipelines as the link, the BCIM Economic Corridor promises an alternate network for free flow of all kinds of goods, services and resources materials as also jointly developing these remote border regions inhabited by restless minorities of all four nations. Potentially, BCIM Economic Corridor can also facilitate building of industrial parks and border trade zones, so as to effectively reduce transportation cost and time, trade and transaction costs, and also enhance the added value of products as also export capacity of local commodities establishing a potent model of sub-regional economic cooperation with complementary advantages as well as labor-division.

In September and October 2013 respectively, the Chinese President Xi Jinping proposed his larger vision to build the "Silk Road Economic Belt" and "21st Century Maritime Silk Road" with the aim of seeking close cooperation with neighbouring countries in economy, culture and national security to promote the realisation of China's national development goals. Here again, BCIM remains an important link where economic integration network is sought to be formed through "policy communication, road connection, trade facilitation, currency circulation and people interaction", which is inevitable for ensuring sustainable development in the context of globalisation. At present, all the member states of BCIM Economic Corridor have unanimously agreed that Economic Corridor Construction will not only strengthen the sub-regional economic cooperation and promote the networking of the regional cooperation mechanisms between South and Southeast Asia, but will also serve as an effective means to obtain economic benefits through cooperation and as a powerful approach to reduce conflicts through connectivity and cooperation.

China and India are the two large size economies and major emerging powers and their slow pace of mutual cooperation has had direct impact on the pace of progress and participation of Bangladesh and Myanmar though they also have their domestic limitations. The slow progress of the China-India bilateral cooperation is undoubtedly a key factor in the BCIM Economic Corridor just as development of their mutual understanding on this subject has also provided it a boost to overall BCIM sub-regional cooperation. The perennial problems of trust-deficit between China and India has always seen security considerations overriding development imperatives. However, their increasing interface in regional and global multilateral forums has provided some positive spin to their mutual policies and perceptions. While vigorously promoting the China-India inter-governmental and non-governmental exchanges, both China and India have been trying to strengthen contacts and exchanges of intellectual elites between the two countries to help reduce "self threat" caused by suspicion and distrust.

In 1947 India gained its independence from British colonial rule, and People's Republic of China was liberated and founded in October 1949. Since then, the two countries have been confronted with the same development issues; how to produce adequate grain to support such a large population has been most basic amongst these questions. India and China made market-oriented reforms respectively from 1978 and 1991. Benefiting a lot from such an open-door policy, the two countries have achieved rapid trade-led economic development, and today they stand at the forefront of the developing world. But they continue to face their old dilemma: how to resolve their mutual problems and contradictions. China and India are the two emerging market-economies and also world's most populous nations. In terms of GDP, China and India are ranked, in purchasing power parity (PPP) terms, as the largest and third largest economies of the world yet, both remain at very low in terms of per capita income and consumption levels. India remains still far behind China in several economic parameters starting from the size of China's economy being more that four times that of India.

Data from International Monetary Fund (IMF) indicates that the GDP per capita in 2014 was $ 7,589 for China and $1,626 for India, which are ranked 77th and 140th in the world respectively. China and India have a poverty-stricken population of 70 million and nearly 300 million. The urgent challenges facing China and India are how to increase employment, alleviate poverty and improve people's livelihood by means of accelerated economic development. The 2.5 billion population base of China and India means a huge potential market for rest of the world. However, after the outbreak of the global economic slowdown since 2008 and the debt crisis in Europe, experts have been exploring possibilities to achieve mutual benefits and win-win situations. Meanwhile, China and India have continued to grow rapidly and world has stakes in ensuring that their close physical proximity and the "closeness effect" implies nothing but an enormous potential for the cooperation. It is premised on their confidence that in spite of differences and disputes China's and India's policies remain focused on their national economic development, resolve the thorny issues in the development process and constantly enhance the economic strength so as to play a more positive role in the international arena. After all, the political and military power depends on economic strength.

Indeed, both China and India are home for several important points on the ancient Silk Road roadmap and there are obvious complementary features in their current economic structures. In the case of the opening of its northeastern region, India first needs to focus on building roads which is most effective way for India's northeast to get rid of its economic backwardness. Over the years, the northeastern region of India has been strongly advocating the opening and construction of 'Stilwell Road' which is linked to Yunnan in China and had been built and used during World War II. No doubt, in 2013 these four countries successfully held their first auto rally, strongly evidencing the feasibility of the land route connecting the southwest China with the northeast India, New Delhi has had security concerns about possible negative effects of mutual openness between the northeastern India and the southwestern China. In addition to the differences brought about by their historical experiences, the important reason for this are the insinuations on how the strategic competition between China and India can take shape after they rise as emerging powers.

However, these differences have not affected their processes of reforms and opening-up and the two economies have experienced sustained high growth rates for several decades now. If the two may set aside their bilateral disputes for the sake of their shared interests it will help them to continue their high economic growth rate, it can be even expected that in the next few decades both China and India may return to the historical pinnacle of being the major production houses as also centres of learning that they were till the 18th century when industrial revolution made Europe as centre of modern history. However, there is still a long way to go. At present China and India are at a turning point in their development trajectories and there are two options available for them: one is that they will do their utmost to reduce poverty and bridge the gap of wealth through effective reforms, continue to benefit from the globalisation and economic integration processes and play a more positive role in the multilateral trading system; the other is that they will implement trade protectionism, conduct military expansion using 'threat' as an excuse, upholding assertive foreign policy and contend against each other. Obviously, the latter option would result in vast losses and tremendous negative impacts on both China and India as also to the entire Asian region and even the rest of the world.

To sum up, as emerging economies of Asia, China and India must ensure their peaceful coexistence and build mutual cooperation to ensure that their growth trajectories become locomotives of regional peace and development. At the ideational level, taking the peace and development path has always been the preferred national policies of both China and India and both have worked assiduously to evolve mutual understanding and trust. Peace and development is the main theme of the present era and China and India have a special responsibility in the making of a new global order. China and India should seize this historic opportunity and take important steps to cement their bilateral cooperation as also lead new initiatives in promoting sub-regional development models like BCIM-Economic Corridor. This promise to promote the cross-border economic cooperation through their development of their border regions and opening and connecting their transport infrastructure to release enormous economic potential of their remote land-locked regions inhabited by restless minorities.

The main purpose of this book is to present balanced and scholarly perspectives both from Chinese and Indian scholars to help understand how to promote the construction of BCIM Economic Corridor and especially how to achieve physical connectivity and other promotion mechanisms for enhancing their trade and investment, energy flows and refine their sub-regional diplomacy that could have lessons for others. Editors would especially like to thank all the contributors for their patience and perseverance in being part of this project. Editors also wish to record special thanks to Research Institute for Indian Ocean Economies (RIIO) of the Yunnan University of Economics and Finance (Kunming) for facilitating this project and making it possible. Editors remain responsible for all other limitations and omissions that may have escaped their eyes of understanding as of now.

Swaran Singh and Zhu Cuiping

New Delhi/Kunming, 2016

List of Contributors

ABOUT THE EDITORS

Dr. Swaran Singh is Professor for Diplomacy and Disarmament at Jawaharlal Nehru University, New Delhi. He is president of Association of Asia Scholars, general secretary of Indian Congress of Asian and Pacific Studies and Guest Professor at Research Institute of Indian Ocean Economies, Yunnan University of Economics and Finance, Kunming, Yunnan, China. He has published articles in *Journal of International Affairs* (Columbia, US), *Security Challenges* (ANU, Australia), *Journal of Indian Ocean Region* (Australia), *African Security* (South Africa), *BIISS Journal* (Bangladesh) and several Chinese and Indian journals of repute. His recent books include *Transforming South Asia* (2014), *India and the GCC Countries, Iran and Iraq* (2013), *On China By India* (Cambria, NY 2012), *Emerging China* (Routledge 2011)

Dr. Zhu Cuiping is a Deputy Director of Research Institute for Indian Ocean Economies (RIIO), Yunnan University of Finance and Economics (YUFE), Kunming, China. She is the Editorial Director of *Indian Ocean Economic and Political Review* and *Annual Report on the Development of Indian Ocean Region*. She has written articles on Indian Ocean Region, India's Foreign Policy towards China, Indian Ocean and the Sino-Indian "cooperative Dilemma" (2014), Maritime Strategy of the United States and India (2013), Indian Ocean Strategy (2012), Sino-Indian Relations (2012), India's Enterprise Investment and Policy (2011), China and Myanmar Relations (2012) and also published books: *Indian Ocean and China (2014)* and *Institutional Analysis on Economic Growth (2010).*

ABOUT THE AUTHORS

Dr. B R Deepak is Professor, Centre of Chinese and Southeast Asian Studies, School of Language, Literature and Culture, Jawaharlal Nehru University, New Delhi. He is Managing Editor of *Think India Journal.* He is formerly Post-Doc Fellow at University of Edinburgh (UK) and Asia and Nehru Fellow at Chinese Academy of Social Sciences (Beijing). He has published extensively on China-India relations including his most recent autobiography *My Tryst with China: 'Our' Footprints on the Sand of Time* (2016).

Dr. Binoda Kumar Mishra is Director, Centre for Studies in International Relations and Development (CSIRD), Kolkata. He is a Ph.D from Jawaharlal Nehru University, New Delhi. He was formerly Fellow at Maulana Abul Kalam Azad Institute of Asian Studies, Kolkata and taught Political Science under Burdwan University, West Bengal. Dr. Mishra serves as the Secretary General of the only Sub-regional Civilian initiative between India and China, namely Kolkata to Kunming (K2K) Forum.

Dr. Liu Peng is a lecturer in Research Institute for Indian Ocean Economies (RIIO), Yunnan University of Finance & Economics and a Ph.D. in School of International Studies, Jinan University. He is also a certified Economical Analyst of banking and visiting scholar of Washington University in St. Louis (2015-2016). His research interests include research of Sino-India relations, Indian Ocean region and Oversea Chinese Studies. His research papers have been published in different journals both in Chinese and English.

Dr. Satyabrat Sinha is Assistant Professor, Department of Political Science, Presidency University, Kolkata, West Bengal, India. He obtained his PhD from Centre for Interantional Politics, Organisation and Disarmament, School of International Studies, Jawaharlal Nehru University, New Delhi. He is formerly of Institute for Chinese Studies as has was Assistant Editor, *China Report.* He also taught at

Sikkim University and has deep interest in security issues especially with regards to China and South East Asia.

Dr. Li Yanfang, received her Ph.D in Economics from Sichuan University, she is Master tutor of Yunnan University of Finance and Economics. Her current research interests include world economy, International Trade, Sino-Indian economic relations and sub-regional economic cooperation. In recent years, she has published about 20 academic papers in *South Asian Studies, Asia-Pacific Economic Review, South Asian Studies Quarterly* and a book named *A Study on Development of Indian Service Outsourcing.*

Dr. Manan Dwivedi is Assistant Professor at Department of Interantional Relations and Interantional Organisation, Indian Institute of Public Administration, New Delhi. He is PhD from Jawaharlal Nehru University, formerly of Gujarat National Law University (Gandhinagar), Shaheed Bhagat Singh College, University of Delhi and Bhawani Mandi Government College, Univeristy of Kota, Rajasthan.

Dr. Liu Wu is an associate professor in Research Institute for Indian Ocean Economies (RIIO), Yunnan University of Finance & Economics (YUFE) and a Ph.D. in Institute of International Relations, Yunnan University. His research interests focus on Sino-Myanmar relations, History of Southeast Asia. His research papers have been published in many journals such as *Journal of Contemporary Asia-Pacific Studies, Journal of World Peoples Studies, South Asia Studies, Southeast Asian Studies.* He has published a book named *Myanmar's Nation-building since 1988.*

Dr. Yang Yishuang is associate professor, Research Institute for Indian Ocean Economies (RIIO) of Yunnan University of Finance and Economics. She received her Ph.D. from Institute of Asia-Pacific Studies, (CASS, Beijing) in 2011. Her research focuses is regional and institutional cooperation in South Asia. She has published several papers as “The influence of the informal institution on growth: India and China’s comparison”, in *Economic Persepectives*, (2013). Her research interests also include cultural, religious, and political history of India.

Dr. K. Yhome is Research Fellow with Observer Research Foundation’s Regional Studies Initiative and formerly Editorial Assistant, *Indian Foreign Affairs Journal.* His research interest include India’s regional diplomacy, China and Southeast Asia and the BCIM sub-regional cooperation.

1

Introduction

Swaran Singh and Zhu Cuiping

World's largest and the third largest economies, located in emerging Asia – namely China and India – have had but only a limited economic engagement. This has been both the cause as also consequence of rather limited socio-cultural interactions amongst these 2.6 billion people on both sides of their Himalayan frontiers. Even their political interactions have remained sporadic, restricted, and prey to deep-rooted and persistent skepticism from both sides. Their economies though, especially the Chinese economy, have been growing at impressive rates for several decades, and their bilateral trade did experience substantial rise during the 1990s when it was called the most reliable as also most agreeable pillar of their *rapprochement* since early 1980s.[1] But, even this economic relationship has witnessed stagnation in recent years. For over a decade now, their bilateral trade has been stymied by a persistent formidable trade deficit that hovers around half of their total annual bilateral trade figure. This has triggered search for alternative strategies to revive and expand their economic partnership. Strong economic relations has always been seen as key for creating positive atmospherics for resolving their complex political equations that remain mired in colonial and cold war legacies. End of cold war and the resultant paradigm shift from Europe and North America to Asia-Pacific and Indo-Pacific presents China and India with a unique opportunity to resolve their complicated bilateral ties as that can empower these two Asian giants to play their critical role in determining the tenor and trajectories of the 21st century.

At the very outset, it is their up-in-the-face trade-deficit that has not just stagnated their economic initiatives but also coincided, and even triggered, frequent political tension-escalations. This has further entrenched their perennial and deep-rooted trust-deficit which calls for urgent attention from both sides. Indeed, both China and India have been trying hard to explore alternate strategies for expanding their bilateral and border trade as also exploring mutual investments and third country joint ventures. The argument for expanding their border trade was presented as the key in early 1980s. It was then seen as an innovative strategy to directly build confidence between their border communities. This was expected to facilitate their border management and help resolve their long-standing boundary dispute. But, their persistent mistrust meant that their border trade did not pick up any momentum and border communities remain disconnected, underdeveloped and restive. More recently, the two sides have tried to expand their mutual investments and third country joint ventures like in oil and gas explorations in *Al Furat* in Sudan. But it has remained a singular initiative. During September 2014 visit by President Xi Jinping to India, China agreed to invest $20 billion in India, primarily in automobile and power sectors. This was followed by China promising additional $22 million during Prime Minister Modi's visit to China during May 2015. This is projected to herald a new chapter in their bilateral relations and energise their other initiatives. Chinese investments in India's manufacturing sector are expected to reduce India's need for imports from China and not just address problem of trade deficit but also provide momentum for India's 'Make in India' campaign on strengthening its local manufacturing industry.

But most innovative and interesting in the long run has been their efforts at building economic relationship via a framework of sub-regional multilateralism called the Bangladesh-China-India-Myanmar Forum or BCIM Forum which has since evolved a new BCIM-Economic Corridor initiative. This vision had first germinated as the Kunming Initiative in 1999. This period has also witnessed that in their increasing interactions in various regional and global multilateral forums where China and India have experienced an unprecedented bonhomie driven by their shared perspectives.[2] Especially the success story of India's Look East Policy since early 1990s has seen China and India participating in several ASEAN-centric and other forums that can be seen as precursors for the BCIM Forum and its Economic Corridor initiative. BCIM Forum has helped participating countries to highlight their strong mutual complementarities that make their sub-regional framework far more promising than what their persistent bilateral political differences have allowed them to achieve. While smaller partners like Bangladesh and Myanmar hope to benefit from the economic rise of China and India, these two rising Asian giants remain equally in need of these two smaller neighbours that are replete with not just markets but also with energy and other mineral and hydrocarbon resources, so critical for development trajectories of Beijing and New Delhi. Therefore, starting from the Kunming Initiative of 1999, their sub-regional multilateralism has gradually evolved from generic BCIM Forum to specific BCIM-Economic Corridor initiative that promises multi-pronged positive outcomes to help them resolve their complicated political ties. Moreover, Southwest of China and Northeast of India – which form the core of BCIM sub-regional cooperation framework – have remained the most underdeveloped parts of their respective countries and are inhabited by their minorities with strong cross-border links that need to be revived to ensure their sustained socio-cultural and economic development and thus to ensure peace and stability in this larger region.

It is in this promising backdrop that this volume examines the idea of sub-regional cooperation and locates the origins and emerging contours of their BCIM-Economic Corridor from both Indian and Chinese perspectives. While there are distinct shades of interpretations with regards to specific details, experts from both sides see this sub-regional format as one most interesting, innovative and acceptable proposition with enormous long-term positive implications at both macro and micro-levels. At present it seems full of challenges yet most experts believe that BCIM-EC presents multiple advantages especially for people living in border regions of all four participating countries, and in the long run promises to facilitate the overall understanding and cooperation between China and India as also amongst other stakeholders in this sub-regional cooperation of these four countries.

Unfolding Multiple Connectivity

To begin with underlining the inherent strengths of BCIM sub-regional multilateral framework, this sub-region has historically enjoyed a strong tradition of socio-cultural and physical connectivity in terms of both their infrastructure and socio-cultural interactions. Though creation of new states at end of British imperialism led to creation of disputed boundaries and to travel restrictions yet till early 1960s their interactions had not really shrunk the way they did following China-India tensions from late 1950s and especially following their short war of 1962. Indeed, during the later part of World War II, the Axis powers' had helped China to fight Japanese in the Far East theatre which had involved building of dozens of airfields for Superfortress B-29 bombers in today's BCIM sub-region.[3] Especially, the building of Stilwell road during this period had marked the peak of building physical connectivity which had persisted but piecemeal since ancient times. However, the formation of post-colonial territorial sovereign states with each seeking to protect the sanctimonious demarcated boundaries resulted in creating artificial divides amongst various overlapping communities inhabiting these frontier regions.

Especially between China and India the boundary dispute was to complicate matters for their smaller neighbours as well. So much so that after decades of official parleys under various official mechanisms — from Joint Working Group to Special Representatives —concluding several joint statements and few agreements at the highest level, nothing has yet managed to resolve their border dispute or address their persistent trust-deficit problem. Their trade deficit is but only a symptom. Even after several years of having set a target of taking their bilateral trade to $100 billion they have remained stuck to around $70 billion. Persisting trade-deficit of about $30 plus billion for over last five years has seen Indian exports shrink substantially; often reaching not even one-thirds of China's exports to India which has made their bilateral trade increasingly one-sided and therefore stagnant. This marks the backdrop of BCIM Economic Corridor where both sides are exploring alternative strategies to revamp their bilateral trade.

Even their border trade – that was once hoisted as the key to creating humane atmospherics across these disputed border regions and to cut on their costs on military deployments and thereby to help resolve their long-standing boundary question – has lost its initial shine. Instead, it is the growing frequency of their military incursions and military standoffs that seem to threaten their time-tested thesis of maintaining tranquility in border regions. Border trade has not only failed to grow but declined over years and security considerations for opening new border trade have become far more overbearing. Similarly all talk of creating a China-India Free Trade Area have evaporated over period of time. All this has clearly allowed various persistent political irritants to repeatedly disrupt their mutual understanding and trust building so assiduously evolved over the years.

This downtrend in their bilateral trade has also impacted upon their growing mutual understanding and cooperation in various regional and global forums, especially on future challenges like terrorism, energy security, climate change etc. Rise of China followed by sustained high economic growth rates in various nations has triggered the debate about emerging economies. Despite their differences, these emerging economies do have a distinct understanding and responses to various global and regional challenges. Recent years have witnessed various new formations like IBSA, BASIC and BRICS providing an effective platform for both China and India to rediscover their shared worldview and evolve broad shared strategies with regard to most of their security and development concerns. This multilateralisation of China-India ties was beginning to show some positive spin on their bilateral deliberations but sustained stagnation of their bilateral trade has impacted their camaraderie even in these multilateral platforms and can potentially undermine their ambitious initiatives.

All this calls for innovative solutions and strategies to rejuvenate their core economic engagement with the aim of expanding their positive vibes into various other segments of China-India economic relations like expanding their border trade, mutual investments, and third country joint ventures, technology transfers, shared R&D initiatives and BCIM Economic Corridor. It is in this context that given their bilateral, regional and global frameworks not providing much relief, one can attempt recasting them by locating these in their least developed adjoining sub-regional peripheries. These relatively low-profile context could allow China and India to take the lead in formulating new sub-regional strategies. Also by seeing this not just an initiative in resolving their bilateral economic relations but as an approach to address their turmoil ridden peripheries to ensure their national development can be both a cause as also consequence of improved China-India relations.

This book locates itself in this larger context of both Chinese and Indian leaders being convinced of the need as also their ability to expand their economic partnerships and to use this to create atmospherics for resolving their complicated political and historical issues that have continued to retard their potential to make their mark and to contribute to the 21st century world order. The onus this book believes lies primarily on China and India though contributions from Bangladesh and Myanmar remain no less critical. While this chapter outlines various drivers for these regional partnerships it also contends how BCIM-EC offers a potent tool to achieve a positive spin in their complicated equations. While various chapters of this volume address some of the following themes from varying perspectives their focus remains on the framework of the BCIM Economic Corridor and on pros and cons in making it effective tool of stakeholders' foreign policies.

Transport and Communications Networks

Liberalization, privatization and globalization (LPG) has been the buzzwords for all the BCIM nations, or at least they see no escape from these influential trends. Amongst others, this calls for multilateralization of their production and services in order to cut costs of their growing consumption levels as also make their exports competitive and mutually beneficial. The national liberations of these former colonies starting from late 1940s saw these nations preoccupied with their territorial sovereignty, emphasising on their distinct identities rather than common connections. Their evolving widely distinct political cultures and cold war dynamics only further re-enforced their divergences making minorities inhabiting this sub-region deprived, disinherited and their distrust of their rulers and neighbours resulting in making of these turmoil ridden and underdeveloped peripheries.

The very foundations of BCIM sub-regional cooperation since late 1990s was, therefore, premised on the argument that development of these peripheries call for revival of their age old cross-border interdependence and connectivity. However, in most cases, it took really long time for this thesis to move beyond academic circles. Partly, it was the rapid rise of China that was to make others – especially India – relatively circumspect in turning down these counterproductive barriers not just into buffers but bridges for combined strategies and initiatives for shared development and security. The BCIM-EC, which was finally endorsed by prime ministers of China and India in 2013, symbolises this expanding connectivity through regular and multiple-destination flights, car rallies, rail and road networks as also real time video conferencing and data transfers. China and India both have Asia's largest road and rail networks with a potential of linking them and turning these remote regions as thriving hubs of transshipment thereby bringing new opportunities and employment to these remote communities.

Energy Security

Energy security has been the other buzzword of BCIM-Economic Corridor. This coincides with rise of China and turmoil in the Persian Gulf region since the early 1990s. The fact that energy security debates are driven by deficit between rising demand and uncertain and limited supplies of primarily petroleum products has resulted in tremendous focus on alternative sources and suppliers of energy. Also, the robust climate change debate has circumscribed this search for alternatives with qualifications of being environmentally friendly and reliable in terms of regular supplies and without too much fluctuation in prices etc. Bangladesh and Myanmar emerging as providers of gas fields for Chinese and Indian investments makes their relationship so complementary, also little competitive. This makes their cooperation in new sectors like hydropower, solar power, wind and nuclear power equally attractive and makes the BCIM-Economic Corridor as very attractive framework for exploring cooperation in power generation and helping each other in evolving more environmentally friendly, sustainable and efficient consumption patterns to overcome their impending energy crisis.

Water Sharing and Navigation

It is being widely recognised that natural resources will be the fundamental triggers for all future international conflict or cooperation. Major national policies are no longer driven by territorial aggrandisement or even by boundary disputes, even issue of energy security belong largely to 20th century. Future conflicts and cooperation are expected to be triggered by scarcity of water which, unlike energy, has no substitutes to it. Over one-third of human population seems deprived from access to water which threatens to undermine all economic progress. This scarcity can especially worsen inter-riparian relations unless cooperative arrangements are evolved well in time. Water sharing involving China-India-Bangladesh remain disputed and these have not been resolved in spite of several initiatives. Here again BCIM-Economic Corridor provides an ideal framework for maximising better understanding and sharing of water resources amongst these dense populations with their exponentially growing consumption patterns. These and other issues have been addressed in this volume that follows the following outline.

In this book

Prof. B. R. Deepak in chapter two, titled "BCIM-EC: Evolution, Opportunities and Challenges" examines starting since ancient times, the deeper roots and historical settings of the germination of this idea of BCIM sub-regional integration. Contemporary deliberations for him seem quite rooted into various branches of ancient Silk routes and the resultant physical and cultural connectivity and interdependence of the peoples of this region. From this perspective, he examines the recent unfolding of China's new economic and foreign policy strategy of 'one belt one road' vision that aims to revive the ancient 'southern silk route' This chapter then locates the BCIM Economic Corridor in recent history, discusses its evolution in the context of China's aggressive economic engagement in this region, and the opportunities and challenges its efforts face in the region. From here, it evaluates the pre-BCIM-EC regional cooperation in terms of air connectivity, overland rail and road links, waterways, trade and commerce. Author believes that the BCIM–Economic Corridor would mean deeper integration amongst countries concerned, and will open new vistas for opportunities in many diversified areas including trade, transport, tourism, as well as cooperation in traditional and non-tradition security. Above all, some of the landlocked regions of the BCIM-Economic Corridor could be turned into nodal points of connectivity, enabling them to mitigate poverty and backwardness. Potentially this Economic Corridor can connect the Indian and Pacific Ocean and gradually realise the cause of regional integration.

Prof. Zhu Cuiping, co-edior of this book, in chapter three, titled "BCIM Economic Corridor: Building Future from Shared Past" also looks back at the history of Southern Silk Road and shared cultural heritage of the people of this region. She examines in detail four following questions: (a) the main progress that BCIM economic corridor has achieved so far; (b) what kind of common interests can China and India obtain from the BCIM economic corridor construction; (c) is there any consensus formed in the BCIM economic corridor construction between China and India; and (d) the main challenges in China and India jointly constructing BCIM Economic Corridor and their policy responses. Prof. Zhu sees BCIM-Economic Corridor as an important part of the ancient Southern Silk Road and also important part of the 'Silk Road Economic Belt'. As a sub-regional cooperation mechanism, BCIM-Economic Corridor has a critical role in the construction of 'Marine Silk Road' as well and this includes development of port cities to facilitate the promotion of trade and economic cooperation via the 'dual track' of land and sea. To promote mutual trust, especially between China and India, it is critical to promote common prosperity. China's western region and India's northeastern region could turn from 'frontier area' into the future 'open frontier' and promote balanced development of their regional economies. With the constant improvement in connectivity, trade and investment will expand thus narrowing regional disparities. BCIM-Economic Corridor can act as a breakthrough in regional economic cooperation. And finally, even when BCIM may not necessarily generate political trust as 'relative gain', it must be able to achieve win-win cooperation 'absolute gain' in economic terms.

Dr. Binoda Mishra's chapter four titled "India and the BCIM-EC: Functional and Sub-regional Approach" examines the idea of BCIM Economic Corridor in the official lexicon of India-China bilateral relationship, as the culmination of 14 years of Track II interaction among the four BCIM countries. Initiated as the Kunming initiative in the year 1999, this chapter shows how scholars and officials met annually in their individual capacities to explore possibilities of cooperation among the BCIM countries. Of the two dominant countries in the arrangement, China was much pro-active while India was viewed as the most reluctant partner. He believes that there were valid reasons for India's reluctance and these go beyond the generally perceived security reasons. The fear of relative loss to China in spite of absolute gains and the prospect of China using such relative gains against India in any future strategic bargain are seen as disincentive enough for India to consider when it comes to committing its most volatile northeastern region to new BCIM initiatives. Of late the realisation that engaging China can provide the much needed boost to the economic development of India's northeast has made India open to the idea of BCIM-Economic Corridor. The only way India can be induced to cooperate in this arrangement is through an incremental and graduated process that would begin with unilateral sectoral (read functional) incentives offered by the willing partner to induce the reluctant partner to reciprocate. India from her side can also initiate such moves at smaller scales to allay her own fears of relative loss. The difficult issues of disputes between India and China and the other security issues are not going to fade away any sooner even after the operationalisation of BCIM-Economic Corridor. But a combined commitment, much needed to address these issues, can be expected only when the parties to the arrangement experience the benefits from the arrangement.

Dr. Liu Peng in chapter five titled "Institutionalising BCIM Sub-regional Cooperation" examines various existing institutions in the BCIM to showcase their weaknesses and strengths. From this specific perspective of institutionalism, BCIM cooperation does not seem to change much even after its upgrading from Track-II to Track-I; and it still remains broadly only a platform for dialogue. These 15 years of institutionalisation of BCIM should now move to creating tangible bodies like secretariat and written agreements outlining standards, rules etc. According to Dr. Peng, using this broad definition of institution, although BCIM sub-regional cooperation have some international institutions of a certain sense, these institutions are very weak. The openness and inclusiveness of existing mechanism of BCIM has been a good start. At present, the development modes of BCIM sub-regional cooperation mechanism can have three types of models: the first is to institutionalise the BCIM economic cooperation mechanism and economic corridor into a sub-regional cooperation organisation, that is, "BCIM Sub-regional Economic Cooperation Organisation"; the second model is to construct the BCIM economic corridor into "BCIM Free Trade Zone"; and the third mode is to stick to the mode of "wading across the stream by feeling the way", not set specific targets, and gradually progress. No matter which route is chosen, its eventual execution will be a long and tortuous process. If we can make all four countries reach consensus on economic cooperation model, it will be a good beginning for this sub-regional economic cooperation.

Dr. Satyabrat Sinha in chapter six titled "Locating India's North East 'Region' in BCIM-EC" examines the strengths and weakness of the North East Region (NER) of India in the context of increasing and multiple Regional Trading Arrangements (RTAs) that enmesh these four countries. With particular focus on India's Look East Policy and the BCIM in particular, he makes an argument in favour of regionalism-from-below and seeks to locate the dissonances in the capabilities and strengths of North East

Region (NER) of India and the policy emphasis in the RTA's. Dr. Sinha also examines the contemporary understanding of India's NER as a region and the uniform policy prescriptions that aim at opening up the region without appreciating its diverse make up. At the same time, he also argues that land connectivity to South East Asia and China can only occur through North East India and it is important to put in place measures that would harness the strengths of the region for it to have a ameliorating effect on the socio-economic context. In order to make the NER as a stakeholder in the process of opening up, it is important to find means to align the national objectives with sub-national objectives and decision making and policy forums need more participation from the region.

Dr. Li Yanfang's chapter seven titled "Analysis of the Economic and Trade Relations in BCIM Sub-regional Cooperation" presents detailed empirical analysis showing how compared to their economic growth and total development level, intra-BCIM trade and investments have remained so low. Especially, when it comes to the core BCIM region – i.e. Bangladesh, Myanmar, China's southwest and India's northeast — the proportion of their trade and investment remain negligible. Apart from differences in their development levels, not only there are sectors where they compete with each other, there remains urgent need to calibrate their complex set of comparative advantages across various sectors. Analysed from the structure perspective, there also exist a certain competition among the intra-regional players. The structural changes can bring about comparative advantage in different commodities in the BCIM. From the perspective of rapid economic and trade growth, the trade structures amongst BCIM economies has both mutually competitive and complementary strands but the current intra-regional trade structures prove that the trade potential of this region has not been developed. The mutual trade, investment and the ability of attracting the investment outside this region (except for China) has been weak, indicating that the intra-regional market power and the whole attraction towards the outside world remains limited. The comparative analysis of time series data show that the dependence of four countries on the intra-regional trade and investment has been weakening goading them to construct BCIM economic corridor. Thus, what BCIM economic corridor construction needs to consider is not constructing a closed market driven by an endogenous power, but how to embed in the global integration of production system and the value chains. The lack of endogenous power also shows that the economic potential of BCIM economic corridor needs many technical conditions to support and realize. That is, when the internal market forces are fatigue, the regional development needs mechanism and other forces to intervene, which is one of the important reasons for that BCIM economic corridor need more external force and mechanism construction to promote.

Dr. Mannan Dwivedi in chapter eight titled "Energy dynamics of BCIM-EC: Connectivity for transactions", locates the ongoing piecemeal success of BCIM projects in the evolving developmental needs of all four countries but especially the growing needs of China and India that have pushed them in search of alternative sources, suppliers and strategies for cooperation. This chapter zeroes on the energy sector related connectivity and it alludes to immense potential that this sub-region has to emerge as energy trade hub for trans-shipments between regions of production and consumption of energy. Dr. Dwivedi provides a balanced analysis on each of the BCIM nations in the search of better energy security. He also details on how, apart from energy sectors like the nuclear, coal and hydro power projects, other resources such as wind and solar power can play a prominent role for ensuring development of this peripheral regions of these four nations. This has to be a combination of various strategies that, he believes, can unify this sub-region and inculcate a shared energy culture. He also deals with the role and responsibilities of both India and China in the BCIM regional energy dynamic. China's energy deals with Myanmar, India's energy ties with Bangladesh form a part of his narrative. The India-Bangladesh water sharing arrangements dwells with the idea of convenient energy connectivity. Finally, he uses the international relations precept of Robert Keohane's theory, namely, the Regimes, in order to draw a theoretical underpinning for the BCIM-Economic Corridor framework.

Prof. Liu Wu's chapter nine titled "Physical Connectivity of BCIM: China's Perspectives" brings forward what he sees as achievable infrastructure projects that can boost physical connectivity. Historically, when the maritime trade route had displaced the land route, it had greatly depressed trade between South Asia and southwest China. This was followed by newly independent states following policy of seclusion which further hampered their historic connections. Lack of physical infrastructure discouraged private investments in the peripheries which today stand in the way of regionalisation of production, consumption and market formation. China's central government and local government in Yunnan have been considering to jointly repair the abandoned 'Stilwell Road' between China and India. For China, the economic benefits of this route is far less than from the other route that runs through Myanmar from Ruili to Kyaukpyu yet, China is willing to repair and upgrade this connection. However, India and Myanmar have doubts about China's intentions. BCIM Economic Corridor involves foundational engineering and calls for comprehensive planning. In terms of capital, BCIM can obtain capital from the World Bank, Asian Development Bank and other international institutions. But most importantly, the degree of political trust is insufficient or absent. As first thing therefore, BCIM needs to promote wisdom and patience for long-term plans as any rush of thoughts and practice could backfire.

Dr. Yang Yishuang in chapter ten titled "Scope and Promotions Mechanism of BCIM Economic Corridor" examines the scope and promotion mechanisms of the BCIM. She points out that BCIM-Economic Corridor must surpass the frame of old and new regionalism. This economic corridor is located in the world's poorest zones, which must be distinguished from conventional regional integrations. This area is characterised by evident lack of infrastructure, fragmented markets that hinders flow of trade, capital and development. This region needs integration impetus not simply by mapping out BCIM economic corridor but to urgently provide institutional environment through development assistance and interworking etc. Cooperation in Frontier Economic Area will be the most critical link to boost economic corridor. Based on the directions and principles, achieving functional cooperation in two fields may be the simplest way to move forward for promoting regional cooperation and expanding cooperation zones through institutional innovation. These include the cross border cooperation in border region as well as the development and supply of public products in assistance, poverty relief, education and medical treatment, etc.

Dr. K Yhome in the final chapter eleven titled "Locating BCIM-EC in India's Sub-Regional Diplomacy" seeks to locate BCIM-EC in India's conceptualisation of its evolving neighbourhood diplomacy. This re-set, Dr. Yhome believes, has been triggered by the process of regionalisation (read federalisation) of India's domestic politics as also by the recasting of sub-regional geo-economics and geo-politics where smaller neighbours are engaging major powers to counter balance India's traditional sphere-of-influence thesis. This is seen as comfortable framework for engaging a powerful neighbour like China. It is with this change in approach to sub-regional diplomacy that New Delhi has come to the fore to provide official endorsement to the BCIM forum and the BCIM-Economic Corridor. This has build shared stakes for both China and India as both sides need stability and development of their peripheral regions of China's southwest and India's northeast. It also promises to build their mutual trust which marks a clear departure from the past. Another factor that has perhaps influenced New Delhi in accepting the BCIM-Economic Corridor thesis is that there exist mutual benefits for both sides. Politically, India and China can work together in the development of this sub-region that has been their soft under-belly and lately a breeding ground for various traditional and non-traditional security threats resulting in continued instability and underdevelopment. The BCIM forum and BCIM-Economic Corridor thus provide a new platform for them to collaborate in addressing these shared problems and challenges.

Endnotes

1. Swaran Singh, China-India Economic Engagement: Building Mutual Confidence, *CSH Occasional Paper No 10* (New Delhi: Centre de Sciences Humaines, 2005), p. 143.
2. Swaran Singh, "Paradigm Shift in India-China Relations: From Bilateralism to Multilateralism", *Journal of International Affairs*, Vol. 64, No. 2, (Columbia University, Spring/Summer 2011), pp. 81-82.
3. Leo J. Dougherty III, The Allied Resupply Effort in the China-*Burma-India Theatre during the World War II*, (London: McFarland and Company, 2008), p. 106; Richard Holmes, *World War II: The Definitive Visual Guide from Blitzkrieg to Hiroshima*, (London: Dorling Kindersley, 2009), p. 247.

2

BCIM-EC: Evolution, Opportunities & Challenges

B.R. Deepak

In May 2013, during the visit of Chinese Premier, Li Keqiang, point 18th of the India-China joint statement referred to development of Bangladesh, China, India, and Myanmar Economic Corridor (BCIM-EC). It made provisions for setting up of a Joint Study Group (JSG) on strengthening connectivity in the BCIM region for closer economic, trade, and people-to-people linkages. The statement also referred to the BCIM Regional Forum and said that the two sides appreciated the progress made in promoting cooperation under this forum (MEA 2013). Is the idea of BCIM an old wine in new bottle? How did India and China reach to the idea of BCIM-EC? And, what are the ins and outs of such a corridor?

Locating BCIM in History

It has been established from the Chinese as well as Indian records that Sino-Indian interface was always a two-way traffic and the two major elements of this traffic were material and spiritual-cultural exchange. This two faceted exchange was carried through the Central Asian Route or the so-called Silk Route; Assam-Burma (now Myanmar) and Yunnan Route or the famous Southern Silk Route; Tibet, Nepal and Bhutan Route; and the Sea Route or the so-called Maritime Silk Route. The Assam-Burma-Yunnan route was in fact the earliest route between India and China, and there are historical as well as archaeological records to prove that (Deepak, 2001:2; Ray, 2003: 65). The route, originated in the northeast of India, passed through the northern part of Myanmar, and entered Tengchong, Baoshan and Dali of Yunnan province and finally reached Chengdu in Sichuan province. It further ran through Bengal and then finally merged with the central Asian route.

Prof. Duan (2010), from Sichuan Academy of Social Sciences, posits that the Indus valley civilization vanished around 1500 BC. However, Sanxingdui (三星堆) civilization in ancient Sichuan was still at its prime, and from the remains of this civilization various products such as *cowries* from Indian Ocean regions (IOR), huge quantities of elephant tusks, willow leaf shaped bronze daggers, had definite connection with Assam in Eastern India and Myanmar. Especially the *Monetriaannulus* types of cowries that are only found in the IOR, these according to professor Duan has also been found in various burial graves in Yunnan and could be seen in the Yunnan Museum reflecting the continuity of these trading routes since ancient times.

The first reliable information about this route is provided by Si Maqian (BC 145 - BC 90?). This great Chinese historian in his masterpiece *Records of the Historian: Foreigners in the Southwest* (史记·西南夷传) narrates that Zhang Qian who was Han envoy in the Western Region (西域), returned to the court in 122 BC. He reported to Han Emperor Wu Di (BC 140 - BC 87) that while in Bactria, he saw clothes and walking bamboo sticks made in *Shu* (Sichuan). When he asked the local merchants they replied, "We bought these at *Shu* merchant's market in *Shendu* [Sindhu for India], a place several thousand *li* [1/2 km] in the southeast from here" (ISAS, 1994:4). It could be established that Assam-Myanmar-Yunnan route was already there in the 2nd century BC, and perhaps was the earliest route between India and China.

The Kamarup (present Assam) has been mentioned as *Panyue* (盘越国) or *Dianyue* (滇越) or *Jiamo loubo* (迦摩缕波国). Historical records such as *Records of a Historian: Dayuan Hisotry* (史记·大宛列传), *Three Kingdom Gazetteer of Wei* (魏略·西戎传), *Later Han Annals: History of Western Regions* (后汉书·西域传), *Liang History* (梁书) volume 54 etc. all mention about Kamarup, its location and that merchants from ancient Sichuan had often visited the place. Xuan Zang's (601-664) *Journey to the West during Great Tang* (大唐西域记), describes Kamrupa even better. Talking about the route he says that Kamrup was some 24000 *li* from Magdha. To reach the region, one had to cross the kingdoms of Iranaparvata, Champa (present Bhagalpur, Bihar), Rajanaghara and Pundravardhana. In the east of Kamarupa, mountains and mounds join together, which have no big national capital, and whose natural boundary is contiguous to the areas inhabited by the ethnic groups in southwest China, whose people seems to be savage tribes. While talking about the state, Xuan Zang says that it runs into thousands of kilometres, and the capital city is almost 15 kilometres in circumference; the people are short stature and dark in complexion, the language they speak is not very different from middle India (Ji Xianlin 2000: 794).

It is believed that the Chinese silk was imported to India through the Assam-Myanmar-Yunnan route. Kautilya (370 BC-283 BC), an official during Chandragupta Maurya (340 BC-298 BC), records in his classic *Arthashstra* (Treatise on Politics and Economy) that the silk is the produce of China (*Kauseyam Cinapattasca Chinabhumijah*). If Kautilya's statement is to be believed the Chinese silk was in vogue in India during the 4th century BC. Sichuan was one of the earliest places to raise silkworms in China. Being close to Yunnan, and Yunnan being the earliest gateway to India, silk as a matter of fact, became one of the earliest industries of northeast India. By the 7th century, Assam's silk industry had reached its pinnacle and perfection. Banabhatta (7th Century), the author of *Harshacharita* (Biography of Harshavardhana) records that Bhaskara Varma (600-650), king of Kamarupa presented Harshavardhana silken towels which was described as "silken towels pure as the autumn moon light...soft loin clothes smooth as birch barks (Ray, 2003:89).

During the Song, Yuan and Ming dynasties (960-1644) when trade replaced religion as the main career of cross-cultural currents, the route did not lose its relevance. About 600 years ago, Zheng He (1371-1433) of Yunnan led a large fleet to ports of Burma, Bangladesh, Indonesia, India and even Africa. Even in the 20th century, the Assam, Myanmar, Yunnan route came to the rescue of Allied Powers against the Japanese during the Second World War. It is only in the post-colonial period that nation states of the region decided to focus more on their disputed boundaries and distinct political cultures thereby disconnecting these historical connections of these peoples. The fact that China and India fought a war in 1962 and belonged to opposite sides of the cold war dynamics made these historical connections being seen with suspicions and none of the neighbours tried to revive this connectivity till very long time.

Initiatives towards the Revival of Routes

With the increasing globalization of the world economy, and increasing level of economic interdependence, various regional economic blocks such as Association of Southeast Asian Nations (ASEAN) in Southeast Asia, European Union (EU) in Europe, North American Free Trade Agreement (NAFTA) in North America, Mercado Común del Sur or Southern Common Market in English (MERCOSUR) in Latin America, South Asian Association for Regional Cooperation (SAARC) in South Asia and many more at sub regional basis have emerged all over the globe. Many more are on their way; for example, the Eurasian Economic Union (EEU) is ecpected to come into force from January 2015.

As regards Asia, the initiation of reforms and open door policy in China especially since Deng Xiaoping's south China tour in 1992, Indian economic reforms in 1991 especially its 'Look East Policy' (LEP); similar opening from Bangladesh in the 1990s and Myanmar in late 1980s has created favorable conditions for further regional economic groupings and triggered trends of integration. Notwithstanding the fact all these four are members of one or more economic groupings in the region all four together constitute a sub-regional group called BCIM after initials of all four nations. The BCIM has since launched a new idea of creating an Economic Corridor called the BCIM-EC which is more than being just another block in making in this sub-region.

China's aggressive economic engagement with the ASEAN has greatly benefitted its adjoining regions of Yunnan and Guangxi. Yunnan has a border line of 4061 kilometers, bordering on Vietnam, Laos, Burma in Southeast Asia and South Asia. A Free Trade Area (FTA) between China and the ASEAN further calls for building state of the art infrastructure in these relatively underdeveloped areas. The FTA has prompted China to invest heavily in Yunnan and Guangxi and connect these provinces with the ASEAN and turn these into logistical and trade centers. A 179.2-kilometer expressway between Nanning, the capital city of Guangxi and *Youyiguan* (Friendship Pass) had connected China with Hanoi in 2006. There are over hundred flight routes originating from Yunnan to various ASEAN and South Asian cities. A network of railways, highways and waterways to Vietnam is already in place, and construction of Kunming-Bangkok highway and Kunming-Singapore railway is under way.

Since Myanmar has become a member of ASEAN and can be reached by rail and road from India, China has been keen about initiating joint development of these links. It is in this backdrop that the scholars from Yunnan Academy of Social Sciences with all help from the provincial government had floated an Idea of BCIM regional economic cooperation in the late 1990s. Though Oberoi (2013:6) gives the credit of BCIM idea to Professor Che Zhimin (then Deputy Director of the Economic and Technological Research Centre of the Yunnan Provincial People's Government), who during his November 1998 visit floated the idea through his paper titled 'Proposition on Formation of "Sub-regional Cooperation Zone of China, India, Myanmar and Bangladesh"', however, Prof. Chen (2005:8) ascribe it to both the Chinese and Indian scholars. For example, in 1994 Prof. Tan Chung wrote an article titled "Prospects of integrating southwest China to south Asia and South east Asia from a trans Himalayan perspective", in vol. 3 issue 64 of the *Southwest China Studies* journal published in June 1994. In the same issue many other scholars from Hong Kong and Mainland like Huang Zhilian 黄枝连, Xu Kangming 徐康明, Wang Yiqian 王益谦, Chen Jidong 陈继东, Lei Qihuai 雷启淮 etc. also contributed articles on similar theme.

As result of China initiating its western development strategy, the Chinese scholars in Southwest China had begun to pursue various linkages of southwest China to South and Southeast Asia with new fervor. However, it is true that as the time progressed and also as Chinese government declared Yunnan as the gateway for its linkages with south Asia, and with the unfolding of China's 'Western Development Strategy', scholars from Yunnan with support from Yunnan provincial government took multiple initiatives in this direction. During their deliberations, they talked about rebuilding the old Stillwell Road that starts at Ledo in Assam (in India) and goes up to Mong-Yu in Myanmar. In Myanmar, it connects the Myanmar Road up to Kunming, the capital city of Yunnan. Of the total 1726 kilometers of the Stillwell-Myanmar road, only 61 kilometer is in India, 688 kilometers in Myanmar and 976 kilometers in China. The regions those are likely to benefit from revival of Stillwell Road include Southwest China (primarily Sichuan and Yunnan), Northeastern India (Arunachal Pradesh, Assam, Manipur, Meghalaya, Mizoram, Nagaland and Tripura) and Myanmar (Yangon, Mandalay and Myitkina).

Also, with the ASEAN, BIMST-EC, SAFTA, APTA, Ganga-Mekong Initiative involving India, Myanmar, Thailand, Cambodia, Laos and Vietnam etc. came into being as part of various regional and sub regional initiatives, the scope of economic and cultural relations in the BCIM regions widened further, and it was felt that the BCIM region must be integrated with these economic groupings. Having the full backing of their provincial government, the academics from Yunnan regularly frequent India, Myanmar and Bangladesh, and host scholars from these countries in various institutions in Yunnan. In the course of these exchanges they established cordial relations with the various top think tanks and academic institutions of these countries and successfully floated the idea of BCIM Regional Forum. Yunnan now hosts annual China-South Asia Expo and China-South Asia Business Forum meetings

From 'Kunming Initiative' to BCIM-EC

Three rounds of 11 rotational meetings in countries involved have been concluded ever since the idea of BCIM was floated. Primarily, the discussions have been around the so-called 3Ts (Transport, Trade and tourism), however, as the meetings progressed these have been diversified to other areas including traditional and nontraditional security and many other softer issues of economic cooperation in the region.

(i) The First Round 1999-2003

On 15-17 August 1999 the scholars from Yunnan convened First International Conference on Regional Cooperation and Development among China, India, Myanmar and Bangladesh under the auspices of Yunnan Academy of Social Sciences in Kunming. The conference was attended by 134 delegates from BCIM countries and signed the 'Kunming initiative.' Six major themes were discussed at the conference - Practical and strategic significance for the regional cooperation; feasibility of economic, trade and technological cooperation; study on the construction of communication channels and networks; prospects and basis for the economic cooperation; open-door policies and trade and investment environment; and framework for regional cooperation.

This 6-point Kunming Initiative (KI, 1999) "agreed that regional cooperation should be guided by the Five Principles of Peaceful Coexistence, emphasizing equality and mutual benefit, sustainable development, comparative advantages, adoption of international standards, and infrastructure development in order to enhance connectivity and facilitate the widest possible economic cooperation." It also proposed the establishment of a Forum for Regional Economic Cooperation, and created a two member country specific Working Groups that were supposed to bring the outcome of the conference to the notice of the respective governments, business and trade chambers

The **second meeting** was held in December 2000 in New Delhi, attended by around 50 delegates from BCIM countries. Issues such as transportation, overland trade, tourism, and exchange of information etc. were discussed. Beside, nontraditional security, narcotics smuggling and illegal immigration etc. issues were also put on table, thus broadening the scope of regional cooperation. The biggest outcome of the meeting was that the business charter flights between Kunming and New Delhi were initiated, thus connecting the ancient civilizations once again thus ending a long hiatus of self imposed separation. Shao Qiwei, Deputy Governor of Yunnan province led a 100 member delegation consisting of scholars' entrepreneurs, officials in this charter flight.

The **Third Forum** was held in Bangladesh's capital Dhaka in February 2002 under the auspices of the Centre for Policy Dialogue (CPD), a founding partner institution of the BCIM initiative. The meeting was grandiose in its scale with around 200 people from all walks of life participating in the opening ceremony. The meeting issued the 'Dhaka declaration' that proposed that the 'the track II' nature of the BCIM regional forum should move towards 'track I' (SEASAS 2014; Ren, Jia et.al, 2004 Please *add a Citation for this Dhaka Declaration*). It was in this meeting that 'Forum' was added to BCIM Regional Cooperation. The **Fourth Forum** was held in Myanmar capital Yangon in March 2003. The meeting issued its 'Yangon Statement.' The meeting also proposed to jointly establish a 'Forum' coordination office and smaller research groups pertaining to traffic, trade and tourism (Do not have much lead on it Any *idea what happened to this proposal? Please write a line on its fate*).

(ii) The Second Round 2004-2010

Fifth Forum was held in Kunming on 21-22 December 2004. The forum was sponsored by Development Research Center of Yunnan, Yunnan Academy of Social Sciences and Yunnan Foreign Affairs Office, thus taking the forum from civil society initiative to government level. Areas such as transportation and communication, tourism, trade and people to people exchanges were further discussed and every side made a statement about the present state of the transportation including ports and harbors adjoining BCIM countries, networks and possibilities. The Indian side proposed that the ports such as Chittagong and Yangon could be optimally used for furthering waterway transportation (Lu et.al. 2004). The forum expressed that while the BCIM region was rich in tourism resources, however, it was hindered by least cooperation in this sector, added by the difficulties such as rigid visa regimes, high travel and lodging costs as well as the lack of advertising tourism in respective countries (Lu et.al. 2004).

The **Sixth Forum** was held in New Delhi on March 30-31 in 2006. Besides, reiterating need for facilitation of 3Ts the forum also introduced other dimensions of the cooperation such as discourse on social and human development including issues such as HIV/AIDS and drug trafficking. A BCIM Car Rally was also proposed between Kunming in Yunnan (China) and Kolkata in West Bengal (India) and it finally took place during February-March 2013. The **Seventh Forum** was held in Dhaka between 31 March and 1 April 2007. The forum issued 'Dhaka statement 2007.' The forum expressed satisfaction while reviewing the progress made since 'Kunming Initiative' in 1999 and recognized that the BCIM initiative can now fructify at the official level and can evolve into formal sub-regional programs at government and non-governmental levels. It was agreed that at the Eighth BCIM Forum in Myanmar, an invitation may be extended to governments to send representatives. 'Critical importance of improved transport connectivity' in the BCIM region for rapid movement of goods, services and people was reiterated again (DS, 2007). Areas such as trade facilitation, transport connectivity, cooperation in tourism sector and scientific and cultural exchanges were identified for follow up actions (DS, 2007).

The **Eighths Forum** was held in Nay Pyi Taw, the new capital Myanmar during 23-24 July 2009. The take away from this forum could be setting up of the BCIM Business Council. The form also issued a statement called 'Nay Pyi Taw statement 2009.' Cooperation in three broad areas such as trade facilitation, transport connectivity, cooperation in tourism sector was reiterated. It was suggested that member states may take measures to strengthen border trade, the removal of trade barriers; and facilitate and simplify market access, the flow of people, goods and vehicles (SEASAS, 2013).

(iii) Third Round 2011-2013

The **Ninth Forum** was held on 18 January 2011 in Kunming China. Some of the highlights of this meeting were the signing of 'MoUs' on establishment of the BCIM Business Council, launching a joint newsletter, and the route survey for BCIM Car Rally. The forum felt that the mechanism has become a 'multi-track' platform for cooperation albeit now moving under the leadership of 'Track-I'. It was also decided in this forum that the 'Forum on Regional Economic Cooperation among BCIM' will be officially renamed as the 'Forum on BCIM Cooperation' in the next conference in India given the widening reach of BCIM cooperation in the areas such as trade, agriculture, tourism, culture, education, health, science and technology, poverty alleviation, climate change, rational water use and security, etc. (BCIMRF 2012)

The **Tenth Forum** was held in Kolkata on 18-19 February 2012. A Joint Statement was signed at the meeting that called for enhancing connectivity by road, rail, water and air. The Route Survey Team after completing the survey recommended that the BCIM Car Rally be undertaken from Kolkata to Kunming in 2013. This meeting also diversified BCIM cooperation in the areas of science and technology, public health, education, agriculture, climate, water resources and energy security. The **Eleventh Forum** was held on 23-24 February 2013 in Dhaka. Dhaka forum deliberated on cooperation in the areas of trade, investment and finance, multimodal connectivity, energy and institutional arrangements. A statement called as 'Dhaka Declaration' was also issued. Meanwhile, BCIM Car Rally named 'Building Bonds, Fostering Friendship' also started off from Kolkata, India on February 22 and reached Kunming, China on March 5, 2013.

The forum had for long time wished to convert the mechanism from 'Track II' to 'Track I', though the Chinese scholars has already pronounced it as 'track I.5' owing to the increased interest from Yunnan government in its proceedings. After these nearly 15 years of sustained work and following their the 11th Forum meeting, India and China formally penned it down in the joint statement during Premier Li Keqiang's India visit that BCIM would be taken up as an economic corridor (BCIM-EC).

Joint Study Group (JSG) Meetings

After the BCIM-EC was put in the joint statement during Li Keqiang's India visit in May 2013, it was again reiterated in the statement signed during Manmohan Singh's China visit in October 2013. A JSG was specially created to look into the conceptualization of BCIM-EC, areas of cooperation as well as the time frame and costs involved. It could be said that henceforth from the Indian side this track II forum was officially converted into track I albeit the members primarily have mostly remained the same as from the previous BCIM forums.

The first meeting of the JSG was held in Kunming on 18-19 December 2013. According to the minutes of the meeting (CGI, 2013; Krishnan 2013) it was agreed that the corridor "could run from Kunming (China) in the east to Kolkata (India) in the west, broadly spanning the region, including Mandalay (Myanmar), Dhaka and Chittagong (Bangladesh) and other major cities and ports as key nodes. With the linkages of transport, energy and telecommunication networks, the Corridor will form a thriving economic belt that will promote common development of areas along the Corridor." The areas identified for cooperation remains almost similar to those discussed in the earlier BCIM Regional Forums conducted between 1999 and 2013 albeit it was proposed that a joint study need to be conducted as regards to each of these specified areas. The final report would be submitted by December 2014 during the 3rd JSG meeting in Delhi; the second JSG was proposed to be held in June end in Bangladesh, but it was postponed for September.

Evaluating the BCIM Regional Cooperation

Many in India believe that owing to official India's reluctance towards BCIM and many other such regional and sub regional initiative, the progress achieved by these mechanisms would be limited. However, if we look back at where BCIM started in 1999, look at the nature of region where it seeks cooperation, regionalisation and even integration and take a stock of the things where it has travelled to in these last 15 years, we can say that the BCIM has been successful in many areas, albeit much more needs to be done.

(i) Air Connectivity

As discussed above, the highlight of the second BCIM meeting in Delhi in 2000 was the starting of business charter flights between Kunming and New Delhi. This is how India and China were to be joined again by flights after half a century. Two years later on 28 March 2002 Chinese Eastern Airlines took its maiden flight MU563 from

Beijing to New Delhi, thus initiating the saga of direct flights from China to India. India and China officially opened direct flights. The flight was later also started from Shanghai to New Delhi, as Air India operated between New Delhi and Shanghai. On 1 April 2002, Yunnan Airlines started flights between Kunming and Yangon, and Kunming to Mandalay, first international route for a regional flight from Yunnan. Also, through the good offices of Yunnan government, since 27 October 2002, China Eastern Airlines agreed to have a stopover at Kunming (Ren, 2004). There is now air connectivity between Kunming-Kolkata; Kunming – Kathmandu; Dhaka – Kunming; Dhaka –Kolkata; and Dhaka Yangon. There are also other possibilities that Kunming-Guwahati, and Chittagong – Yangon are connected with direct flights (Rahmatullah, 2010:75)

(ii) Overland and Water Ways

Here again we see China has been able to link its regional developmental plans with those of BCIM regional cooperation or vice versa. Ever since China initiated the western development strategy in 1999, Yunnan aggressively developed its linkages with regions adjoining Southeast Asia and South Asia, which is one of the integral goals of the western development strategy, other two being 'Green Economy' and 'National Culture' Province. According to Ren (2004), since 2004 annual outlays towards the construction of expressways have amounted to 10 billion yuan and above; by 2005 most of the places in every prefecture were connected to Kunming with expressways. Since 2004, Yunnan started the construction of 10 high grade roads with an annual investment of 16 billion yuan. Especially the Kunming-Ruili highway that connects Longchuan (*Zhang Feng*), Yingjiang, Pianma ports, could further be linked to roads entering Myanmar, Bangladesh and India. Myanmar has also intensified the investment in infrastructure; in 2001 with the assistance from India it built a 160 km highway connecting India. In April 2002, Thailand, Myanmar and India agreed to build a road connecting Morey (India)- Mae Sot (Myanmar) and Messo (Thailand). The three also agreed to open sea channels connecting Thailand to Dawei deepwater port in Myanmar and the Indian ports. In April 2004 Bangladesh and Myanmar signed an agreement to build 133 kilometer long Dhaka -Yangon expressway.

(iii) Trade and Commerce

In this front, Yunnan is aggressively promoting business cooperation with East Asian and South Asian countries on one hand and investment environment on the other. It has established various platforms such as Kunming trade fair, commodity exhibition for South Asian countries, South Asia Business Forum besides BCIM initiative. Yunnan's trade with India reached $842 million in 2011 from a meager $82.24 million in 2004, registering an annual increase of 23.8%. The trade volume accounted for nearly 80% of its total trade with South Asia. However, in 2013, Yunnan-India trade volume was only $546 million, the decrease owing to overall decline in the India-China trade. In South Asia, Bangladesh is Yunnan's second largest trading partner. Yunnan's trade with Myanmar reached $4.17 billion for (2013), making it their largest trading partner (Wang et. al. 2014).

With the economic and trade exchanges, people to people exchanges has also increased manifold. In 2013, Yunnan hosted around 30000 foreign students; of these more than 80% belonged to Southeast Asia and South Asia.

Infrastructure Connectivity and Challenges

Transportation connectivity has been the main theme of all 11 meetings of the BCIM cooperation. Even if there have been some steps to develop the infrastructure, the task is uphill and investment required is huge, and may take years before we could see the channels of communion opening and connecting the people of this region fully. Let's examine the present infrastructure scenario as regards to roads, railways, waterways, and air transport that will be the basis of taking BCIM-EC initiative moving forward.

(i) Roadways

As far as building of major roads networks from inside India is concerned Prof. Indiresan (2000) offers two alternatives. One, reconstruct, admittedly difficult but shortest route to China, a 403 kilometer long Stillwell Road from Ledo in Assam to Mytkina in Myanmar. Two, a better link to Southeast Asia by extending the road India is already building from Moreh in Manipur to Tamu to Kalewa on the Chindwin River. This will established a link with Mandalay, already on the railway system of Myanmar. The professor recommends that both are important and India must take on both the projects. In addition, Mizoram could be linked to Akyab (now called Shi twe) in Myanmar, and if Bangladesh agrees, Agartala in Tripura could be connected to Chittagong. That will open up the entire northeastern region of India, making it the commercial outlet for its eastern trade. According to Rehmanullah (2010) Imphal-Dauki-Tamabi (bordering Bangladesh) is hilly and not fit for cargo trucks; however, Karimgonj (India)-Austragram (Bangladesh) that runs through Imphal and Sylhet is shorter route and will reduce almost 400 kilometers between Tamu (Myanmar) and Sylhet (Bangladesh). Rehmanullah prefers this road and says that comparing to Imphal-Shilong route this is more stable.

In Bangladesh, Rehmanullah proposes to convert Dauki (India)-Tamabil (Bangladesh)-Sylhet (Bangladesh) road and later segments into grade II or III two lane roads. After crossing Bangabandhu Bridge on Jamuna, A1 route will pass Benepole and enter Kolkata; while A2 route will connect Kathmandu.

China is perhaps the only country so far to have upgraded its road network most efficiently and aggressively. The Yunnan-Myanmar Road that connects Chuxiong, Dali, Baoshan and Ruili is long completed. The road enters Myanmar at Muse. Muse-Mandalay is all season 451 kilometer long road, and connects Tamu (India) after traversing around 600 kilometers. The work that needs to be done is Chittagong-Yangon highway and Kunming Shi twe Highway.

(ii) Railways

Most of the countries are having good network of railways, but connectivity amongst these countries's rail networks remains an issue. China is building Kunming-Mandalay line that will approximately run along the existing express way. The work on Kunming-Dali has been completed, and the surveys for the next phase Dali-Baoshan-Ruili has been conducted and work is in progress. The Chinese line will connect Muse and Lashio in northeast Myanmar. Lashio connects Mandalay; in order to connect to India, Myanmar only needs to extend the line from Kalay to Tamu on India's borders (Rehmanullah 2010)).

The Indian scene is not too bad; the line that needs to be connected is between Tamu and Jiribum that connects Mahisasan in Bangladesh with a meter gauge line. The work on Kumarghat-Agartala line is in progress, once complete will connect Assam to Agartala. Inside Bangladesh, the work to make Parvatipur-Jamtoil line broad gauge is in progress and there are plans to extend it to Chittagong (Rehmanullah 2010). Further there is an urgent need to unify the gauge systems in BICM-EC.

(iii) Waterways

According to Rejmanullah (2010), waterways have to be between Yunnan-Myanmar and India-Bangladesh. As far as Yunnan-Myanmar waterways are concerned, both can contemplate building a harbor at Bhamo on Irawadi River. The carrying capacity of ships would be between 400 and 800 tonnage (Rehmanullah 2010). As far as building waterways between India and Bangladesh are concerned problems are many. The Indian side has been proposing that the ports such as Chittagong and Yangon could be optimally used for furthering waterway transportation.

Importance of BCIM-EC

BCIM-EC has 40% of the world population and almost $11trillion GDP. The corridor has huge reserves of natural wealth be it fauna and flora, oil and gas, minerals or hydro potentials. Moreover, world's most populous countries termed as twin engines of world economic growth are parts of this corridor. The BCIM–EC would mean deeper integration amongst these countries, and opening vistas of opportunities in many diversified areas. The advantages and potential areas of collaboration could be:

(i) Integrated Transportation Network

An integrated transport network would be a boon to all the participatory countries, especially the land-locked areas such as northeastern provinces in India, and southwest provinces in China, large areas in Bangladesh and Myanmar. Zhao (2000: 402) citing professor Wen Fude former Director of Institution of South Asian Studies of Sichuan University (Chengdu) posits that the overland route from China via Kunming, Myanmar to Kolkata would substantially reduce a journey of 4000 kilometers comparing the sea route from Guangzhou to Kolkata that had to take a detour via choke-point of the Malacca Straits. Bangladesh is poised to play a greater and critical role as far as integrated waterways are concerned, and benefit immensely in terms of trade and investment, so will other nations as transaction costs would be greatly reduced. It would also connect South Asia with East Asia directly; Chittagong in Bangladesh will rise to prominence and act as a trans-ocean bridge.

As rightly pointed out by Prof. Chen Jidong (2005:11), another former Director of Institute of South Asian Studies of Sichuan University (Chengdu) certain areas of BCIM region especially southwest Yunnan, Northeast India, and Northern Myanmar has been 'extreme ends' as far as connectivity is concerned, it comes to standstill and does not move any further. As a result, the areas have remained 'closed or semi closed' for a long time in history. The BCIM area, therefore, is economically most backward and extremely underdeveloped; the backwardness of northeast India is graphically detailed in *North East Vision 2020*, prepared by the North Eastern Council of the Ministry of Development of the North East Region and released in 2008 (Rana et. al 2012:21). Transport connectivity in the region will alleviate such areas of poverty and integrate them into the mainstream economic development of respective countries.

(ii) Linking of the Markets and Better Access

There have been intimate trade links in the BCIM-EC for centuries, once the transport in the area is integrated by better rail, road and navigation networks, it will give better market access to many of the interested companies, especially from India and China in respective markets. Leaving the so called security issue behind, if we look at the positive side of the 2007 Beijing-Lhasa train connectivity, goods from Nepal, northern India and Bhutan could easily be transported not only to Lhasa but also further east to Beijing. If a similar connectivity is established between northeast India, Bangladesh, Myanmar and China, the goods instead of going through sea will move overland bringing prosperity and opportunities for these remotely located communities. Some of the sectors that will benefit could be pharmaceutical, information technology, agro products, food processing, textiles, fertilizers and minerals. Also, the smaller partners like Bangladesh and Myanmar will benefit immensely by getting access to bigger markets for their commodities, besides expanding their present capacities and diversifying products. The FDI inflows would also translate into technology transfer, thus pushing the economic growth rates further. Furthermore, the Chinese products flooding the markets through illegal routes will also come to an end as that channel will become less attractive.

(iii) Energy Cooperation

The BCIM–EC has reserves of natural and mineral resources. For example, south western region of China and eastern India have unexploited wealth of oil and natural gas, coal, minerals and water resources. The BCIM-EC framework of cooperation will lead to joint investment in construction of relevant industries in the areas. There are huge potentials in generating hydroelectricity in the region that will complement the industrial activity in the area. Furthermore, since these issue will essentially touch upon the trans-border and river issues, better mechanisms could be evolved to manage and solve such issues, especially between India-Bangladesh and China.

(iv) Cooperation in Tourism Sector

Two of the BCIM-EC counties – China and India – are ancient civilizations and have many places of historical and cultural significance. All the countries in the corridor have beautiful landscapes and rich bio diversity. The integrated transportation will not only foster deeper trade relations but also strengthen tourism sector regionally as well internationally expanding people-to-people ties. The region could venture into eco, heritage, and spiritual as well as cultural tourism areas. This will also attract investment in the relevant areas and open employment opportunities for the local people.

(v) BCIM– EC will Build 'Mutual Political Trust'

At the outset we have to recognize that it is owing to existing security issues between BCIM countries that the region has been 'sealed' and prohibited for normal human interactions and activities including travel, trade and transportation. Therefore, the underdevelopment and backwardness of the region is self imposed. Looking back, did we resolve these issues including the border between India and China, and India and Bangladesh by inflicting isolation? We did not. On the contrary, we made the region highly instable and insurgency infested. Furthermore, we have also not been able to stop the smuggling of small arms, drugs and other trade items in the region. Therefore, it would be on the basis of cooperation, common security and by building transparency through CBMs that we would be able to find a solution to these issues and ultimately build political trust between the respective countries. The intimate trade ties would certainly push respective countries in this direction in long run.

(vi) Strategic Significance for Neighborhood Policy

In recent years, India's has been widely criticized for its policy paralysis, which has been reflected in the dwindling economic performance and all time low Rupee depreciation on the one hand and dysfunctional foreign policy on the other, especially when it comes to India's smaller neighbors. In July 2013, it halted the subsidized fuel supply to Bhutan just prior to Bhutan's general election. It became an election issue there and the then prime minister and chief of the Druk Phuensum Tshogpa, Jigme Thinley suffered a defeat. Secondly, the Indian Parliament scuttled the Land Boundary agreement between India and Bangladesh at India's own peril in early September 2013, for the passage of the legislation would have enabled the swapping of enclaves thus solving our boundary issue with Bangladesh, and also bring relief to the hapless people living in these enclaves without any basic amenities since last 65 years! Worse, it would weaken the hands of pro-India Bangladesh prime minister and Awami League leader Sheikh Hasina, and strengthen the hands of *Jehadi* and anti-India forces in Bangladesh. India's Nepal policy has also met stumbling blocks and there are hues and cries for revisiting the treaties we have signed with Nepal. For example, mega hydel power projects on Saptakoshi, Karnali-Chisapani and Pancheshwar have been languishing for past 30 years as Nepal has clearly tilted towards China making it further difficult for New Delhi. (Sood 2014)

New Indian leadership has sent strong signals to the neighbors that it attaches priority to its neighborhood as demonstrated by SAARC members being present in Prime Minister Modi's swearing in ceremony on May 26, and his Bhutan visit on June 15-16, the first visit abroad. Similarly, foreign ministers, Sushma Swaraj, has visiting Bangladesh and Nepal as her first foreign visits. Prime Minister Modi has talked about stronger economic ties between India and its neighbors. BCIM-EC offers such an opportunity to strengthen business and people to people relations between India and countries in our vicinity. As China has gone whole hog to open up southwest China to business and infrastructural connectivity, India too needs to make northeast India as an integral and important part of its 'Look East Policy' rather than making Kolkata as the centre of BCIM-EC initiative. An economically stronger India and economically stronger neighbors are beneficial in every aspect, be it regional integration, geopolitics, or neighborhood security.

Future Challenges

Ever since the floating of the idea of BCIM Regional Cooperation Forum in 1990, holding of 11 subsequent meetings of the forum in respective countries, and India and China taking lead in giving it a political platform by converting it into a concrete framework of BCIM-EC, there has been significant progress in the areas of flight connectivity and trade. However, there are numerous challenges in the areas of overland and river transport connectivity, trade barriers, security issues. Let's examine some of the following to better assess its feasibility:

(i) Regional Representation Missing

If we examine the representation from the leading players in the BCIM Regional Cooperation Forum all these years, it comes to fore that in China it has been Yunnan centric, primarily dominated by the scholars of Yunnan Academy of Social Sciences and the officials of Yunnan provincial government. There is no participation from Sichuan, Tibet, Guizhou and Guangxizhuang regions. However, after pushing it to the political level by declaring it BCIM-EC, this representation may change. As far as India is concerned, the Institute of Chinese Studies in New Delhi has been steering the track II so far in all the 11 meetings and one meeting that was held in Kunming this year after the Forum moved to Track 1 as BCIM-EC officially. Often there is not a single participant from the northeast India, even Kolkata is not represented. This has been noticed by the Chinese side, and they wondered whether such 'academic' forums would have any impact as far as influencing government decision making is concerned (Chen 2005: 14). In 2013 when 'sister cities' MoUs were signed between India and China, the dissatisfactory voices in the northeast could be heard loud and clear. Commenting on Kolkata-Kunming 'sister-city' MoU, Hussain (2013) who writes on issues pertaining to peace and security in northeast noted that "New Delhi should have, for a change, paired Guwahati with Kunming. Guwahati, after all, is the city in India closest to Kunming and if India is serious about making the North–east the fulcrum of its Look East Policy, then it would have done well to pair Guwahati with Kunming. Such a move would have lived up to the name of the city's airport, 'Lokapriya Gopinath Bardoloi International Airport'." In the same article Hussain also mentions how the act of bypassing northeast has been opposed by Assam's political class as well.

Even though BCIM–EC is an intergovernmental initiative but the region involved makes it clear that state governments in the respective region would be the main drivers of such initiative. Therefore, the concerned state organs need to be taken into confidence if such a mechanism has to succeed. Secondly, there are issues related to the scope of the area involved; Indian side has certain perennial doubts about opening northeast region to China. Conversely, they are of the view that entire southwest China be part of the BCIM-EC. Bangladesh and Myanmar are better positioned as they consider all the regions of their countries as parts of BCIM-EC.

(ii) Security Environment is one Major Negative Factor?

India, though have agreed in principle to cooperate with China and Myanmar to open new and old routes in Northeast India, however, it is apprehensive about the security concerns due to her being hypersensitive about its turmoil-ridden northeastern region. It is almost a case of 'once bitten twice shy' approach especially after the Himalayan blunder of 1962. One of the fall out of that conflict was China forging an entente with Pakistan and encouraging the Naga and Mizo insurgency in India's northeast between 1962 and 1979 (Wang 1998: 272). Brig (Retd) Vinod Anand (2013), Senior Fellow at Vivekananda International Foundation posits that the 'prevailing security situation thwarts the successful outcome of BCIM forum and works against building trust and mutual confidence.' He cites conflicts between the armed ethnic groups in the region, Sino-Indian border tensions, Rohingyas crossing over to Bangladesh from Myanmar etc creating a negative impact which is not conducive to investment and development.

It is precisely for these reasons that India's strategic community including the academics has been cautious and reluctant in the BCIM-EC approach. Reacting to 'Kunming Initiative' Prof. at IIT Madras and a columnist Indiresan (2000) while saying that owing to 'rebellious elements' as well as 'drug trafficking' in northeast India, it makes sense to 'maintain the status quo and keep the borders closed'. However, there are even stronger reasons for opening these borders for the wellbeing of the local population and overall prosperity in the region. Sociologists like Oberoi (2013: 14) who have been the part of BCIM Track II cooperation mechanism feels happy that at least the mechanism will see the light of 'Track I' though she also fears that 'soft' issues such as society, culture and environment that are directly relevant to the livelihoods and aspirations of peoples of the borderlands are being diluted as was the case at the 11th BCIM Forum in Dhaka.

(iii) Poor and Backward Transportation Connectivity

Even though there are attempts from respective countries to enhance the infrastructural connectivity but so far there is a huge gap between the conceived idea of BCIM-EC and the kind of transportation integration is required for such a grand idea. So called 'Southern Silk Route', the 'Ancient Tea Horse Road' and the 'Stilwell Road' of the modern times has been discussed on paper alone.

There are no concrete strategies and time frame to rebuild these arteries of communion. Even if there are traces of these routes and people move to and fro but there are restrictions as regards people, vehicles, and customs issues. There are no standard norms as far as development of roads, railways and shipping facilities are concerned. The trade mart at Nathula on India-China border could be a reference point where irrespective of official agreement between two nations, infrastructure is pathetic. Ren (2013:4) while participating in 11th BCIM Forum had suggested that since the survey team has spotted various missing sections on overland routes, these need to be urgently repaired. Secondly BCIM countries need to conduct joint research on how to utilize the potential and advantage of inland water. And finally, there should be uniformity and coordination while contemplating rail and road projects in the region.

(iv) Disequilibrium in Regional Economic Cooperation

Regional economic cooperation demands that there are preferential trade arrangement, free trade areas (FTA), uniform customs regulations, common market and economic union, and comprehensive economic integration features. And if we apply these norms to BCIM-EC, it is clear that the region will take several years before incorporating such norms and practices. For example, even though BCIM-EC countries are having good trade relations and there is an upward movement in the bilateral trade, , none of the countries have liberalized tariff practices. Rahman et. al. (2009: 5-6; 2007) of the Centre for Policy Dialogue (Dhaka), maintains that the trade structure between BCIM countries is highly prohibitory. According to them, 'in 2007, India faced a 19.6 per cent preferential tariff in Bangladesh, whereas Bangladesh faced a 16.5 per cent tariff in the Indian market.

China imposed 1.8 percent and 3.5 per cent tariffs on Bangladesh and Myanmar. India faced a 9.5 per cent tariff in the Chinese market while China faced a much higher tariff of 14 per cent in the Indian market. Myanmar's market was the most liberalized, with Bangladesh and India facing 3.9 per cent and 3.4 per cent average MFN applied tariffs, respectively.' Besides, non-tariff barriers (NTBs) also remain a major bone of contention for trade between these countries. The NTBs which are commonly mentioned include certification and standardization, lack of harmonization of customs procedures, restrictions on transit, visas difficulties, customs regulations, limited line of credit (L/C) facilities etc. Intra-BCIM flow of FDI, especially FDI from major players like India and China remains extremely low.

Conclusion

Notwithstanding other initiatives such BIMSTEC, SAFTA , APTA, Ganga-Mekong Initiative between India, Myanmar, Thailand, Cambodia, Laos and Vietnam, . and other regional and sub regional initiatives, the BCIM-EC is yet another initiative and a very promising one if it is taken forward with strong political will from all sides. The BCIM-EC has great potentials in the fields of trade, transport, tourism, and many other areas of traditional and non tradition security cooperation. Above all, some of the landlocked regions of the BCIM-EC could be turned into nodal points of connectivity, be it trade, transport or tourism. This would mitigate poverty and backwardness from the region and the region would act as a bridge between the Indian Ocean and Pacific Ocean.

As India's Look East Policy has been widening in scope, the BCIM-TC is another area where the policy could be integrated, especially when we are thinking of developing landlocked and underdeveloped northeast region of India. India certainly needs to take a leaf out of China's experience as to how it has developed and connected its southwestern and southern states to ASEAN. Is New Delhi ready to forgo its sensitivities in Northeast in turn of economic development of the region? Can the massive trade between China-ASEAN and India-ASEAN percolate to the northeast India and northwest China? The answer to all these questions is yes provided we start looking at boundaries as gateways and not as barriers or buffers.

In the wake of India and China both signing FTA with ASEAN, the vigorous development of infrastructure in this region is even more important. The World War II vintage Stilwell Road proved a "blood transfusion line" during the World War II; if reopened, it could prove an artery for economic development of the region in the 21st century. In the wake of China's economic success story, China has shown extreme interest in the development of this road; it is for India to cast away its apprehensions, exhibit confidence, and initiate a positive and detailed partnership with China and Myanmar so as living standards of the marginalized Northeast India is enhanced, and the region converted into a logistic hub for its trade with the ASEAN and China.

There are various challenges in terms of integrating transportation, trade and tourism and enhancing traditional as well as non traditional security in the region. But with the concerted efforts of respective countries, the challenges could be overcome and opportunities seized. In this context, the revival of the "the southern silk route" connecting India's northeast region with Myanmar and China's Yunnan is need of the hour. In the same vein spreading standard railway links, a network of waterways through river and deep water ports could be game changers as far as economic development and regional security is concerned. With the signing of BCIM-EC there are greater possibilities of the region seeing the light at the end of the tunnel?

References

BCIMRF [The Forum on Regional Cooperation Among Bangladesh, China, India and Myanmar] (2012) "The Ninth Meting" http://www.bcim-forum.com/article.aspx?aid=182 (accessed on August 3, 2014)

CGI [Consulate General of India] Guangzhou (2013) "Minutes of the First Meeting of the Joint Study Group of BCIM Economic Corridor" http://www.cgiguangzhou.gov.in/news/news_detail/

60

Chen, Jidong 陈继东 (2005) "中印缅孟区域经济合作的构想与地区范围问题" (The Idea of BCIM Regional Economic Cooperation and problem areas) 南亚研究季刊 (South Asian Studies Quarterly), No. 1, 2005

DS [Dhaka Statement] (2007) http://www.ibiblio.org/obl/docs4/BCIM_Dhaka_Statement_2007_final.pdf

Deepak, B R (2001) *India-China relationsduring first half of the 20th Century*, APH Publishers, New Delhi

Duan Yu 段 渝 (2010) "中国西南早期对外交通:先秦两汉的南方丝绸之路, 四川社会科学 在线 (Sichuan Social Science Online) http://www.sss.net.cn/ReadNews.asp?NewsID=26826&BigClassid=9&SmallClassID=24&SpecialID=0&belong=sky (accessed on June 10, 2014)

Hussain, Wasbir (2013) "Guwahati Initiative' needed to push NE–Kunming Corridor" The Sentinel, November 16, 2013 http://www.sentinelassam.com/mainnews/story.php?sec=1&subsec=0&id=175500&dtP=2013-11-16&ppr=1#.U6PsFLFzCcw

Indiresan, P. V (2000) "Kunming Initiative" *Frontline,* 17 (4) April 1-14, 2000 http://www.hindu.com/fline/fl1707/17070980.htm

ISAS [Institute of South Asian Studies Beijing University] (comp.) (1994), *zhongguo zaijizhong nanya shiliao huibian*, shang (*Collection of South Asian Historical Materials from Chinese sources*) Vol. I, Shanghai Guji Publishing House, Shanghai.

ISESA [Information on Southeast Asia and South Asia] "中印缅孟地区经济合作的条件与机遇" (Premises and opportunities of BCIM regional cooperation) ISESA, (17) 1999

Ji, Xianlin (2000) 季羡林等校注: (大唐西域记校注) 北京: 中华书局 2000年 (Ji Xianlin Annotated 'Journey to the West in Great Tang' Beijing, Zhonghua Shuju.

KI [Kunming Initiative] (1999) http://www.ibiblio.org/obl/reg.burma/archives/199908/msg00946.html

Krishnan, Anath (2013) "BCIM corridor gets push after first official-level talks in China" The Hindu, December 21, 2013

Lu, Xiaokun and Guo Huiyan 卢晓昆 郭穗彦 (2004) "孟中印缅地区经济合作论坛第五次会 议在昆明召开" (Fifth Meeting of the Forum on BCIM Regional Cooperation Convened in Kunming) YASS [Yunnan Academy of Social Sciences] website http://www.sky.yn.gov.cn/dtxx/ynskj/682312892983412927 3 (accessed on 12 June 2014)

MEA (Minister of External Affairs, India) Joint Statement on the State Visit of Chinese Premier Li Keqiang to India, May 20, 2013 http://www.mea.gov.in/bilateral-documents.htm?dtl/21723/Joint+Statement+on+the+State+Visit+of+Chinese++Li+Keqiang+to+India

Oberoi, Patricia (2013) "The BCIM Forum: Retrospect and Prospects" ICS Working Paper 2013/11/1 http://www.icsin.org/ICS/WorkingpaperPdf/1.pdf (accessed on 12 June 2014)

Rahman, Md. Tariqur and Amin, Muhammad Al (2009) "Prospects of economic cooperation in the Bangladesh, China, India and Myanmar region: A quantitative assessment" Asia-Pacific Research and Training Network on Trade Working Paper Series, No. 73, July 2009 http://artnet.unescap.org/pub/wp7309.pdf

Rahman, Mustafizur; Rahman, Habibur Shadat, Wasel Bin (2007) "BCIM Economic Cooperation: Prospects and Challenges" Centre for Policy Dialogue (CPD), Dhaka, Occasional Paper Series 64, http://www.researchgate.net/publication/5224239_BCIM_Economic_Cooperation_Prospects_and_Challenges

Rahmatullah, M (2010) "推进孟中印缅交通连接及对策建议:孟加拉国的思考" (facilitating BCIM transportation connectivity and policy measures: perspective from Bangladesh) (东南亚南亚研究) Southeast Asia and South Asian Studies, 2010 (3)

Rana, Kishan & Patricia Uberoi. 2012. *India's North East States, the BCIM Forum and Regional Integration.* Delhi: Institute of Chinese Studies, Monograph No 1. http://www.icsin.org/ICS/ICSMonographspdf/1.pdf

Ray, H. P. (2003). *Trade and Trade Routes Between India and China.* Progressive Publishers, Kolkata.

Ren, Jia (2013) "Some Thoughts on Strengthening Transport Connectivity and Communication in BCIM Region" paper presented at 11th BCIM Forum held on 23-24 February 2013 , Dhaka Bangladesh http://www.oilseedcrops.org/wp-content/uploads/2014/02/Bangladesh_China_India_Myanmar-BCIM-Connectivity-Overview1.pdf

Ren, Jia, Wang, Chongli and Chen Lijun 任佳王崇理陈利君 (2004) "孟中印缅地区经济合作的回顾与展望" Yunnan Ribao, 22 December 2004 http://news.sina.com.cn/c/2004-12-22/12354597561s.shtml

Ren, JiaûNsO (2000, a) "中印缅孟地区经济合作的基本思路" (Preliminary thoughts about BCIM regional Cooperation) 云南社会科学 (Yunnan Social Sciences) (2), 2000, Yunnan

Ren, JiaûNsO (2000, b) "中印缅孟地区经济合作的战略意义" (Strategic importance of BCIM regional economic Cooperation) 云南社会科学 (Yunnan Social Sciences) (2), 2000, Yunnan

SEASAS [东南亚南亚研究网 Southeast Asian South Asian Studies] (2013) "孟中印缅地区经济合作论坛第八次会议联合声明" (Joint Statement of the 8th meeting of the BCIM Regional Cooperation Forum) http://www.seasas.cn/article-804-1.html

SEASAS [东南亚南亚研究网 Southeast Asian South Asian Studies] (2014) "达卡声明" (Dhaka Statement) http://www.seasas.cn/article-1233-1.html (accessed on August 1, 2014)

Sood, Rakesh, "A new beginning with Nepal", *The Hindu* (New Delhi), 23 July 2014, p. 12.

Vinod Anand (2013) "BCIM Economic Corridor: Prospects and Issues" Vivekananda International Foundation http://www.vifindia.org/article/2014/june/02/bcim-economic-corridor-prospects-and-issues (accessed June 17, 2014)

Wang Hongwei (1998), 喜马拉雅山情节：中印关系研究 (*The Himalayas Sentiment: A Study of Sino Indian Relations*), China Tibetology Publication, Beijing.

Wang, Lin, Shi Guanglin and Zhao Yuning 王林史广林赵宇宁 (2014) "云南阔步"孟中印缅经济走廊" (Yunnan's stride in BCIM Economic Corridor) Zhongxinshe June 1, 2014 http://www.yn.chinanews.com/pub/2014/yunnan_0602/82157.html (accessed on June 13, 2014)

Zhao, Weiwen (2000), 印中关系风云录：1994-1999 年 *(Records of Turbulences in Sino-Indian Relations: 1949-1999)*, Current Affairs (shishi) Publishers, Beijing.

3

BCIM Economic Corridor: Building Future *from* Shared Past

Zhu Cuiping

The ancient 'Silk Road' had shaped an unprecedented economic and cultural exchanges between the East and the West. It had made different civilisations and various religions achieve harmonious coexistence in the multicultural Eurasia. The BCIM Economic Corridor is an important part of the 'Southern Silk Road'. After 15 years development from the 'Kunming Initiative', this idea had been floating in the air and has finally taken a shape that can be scrutinised. All member states have reached a consensus at the governmental level, which means this economic corridor has entered a substantive new stage. Although there exists a general trend that countries like to strengthen cooperation with China, and that regional cooperation promises to benefit to all parties, promoting cooperation still faces many challenges. Especially China and India still lack substantive motivation to promote this cooperation. The key to promote common development of BCIM framework is to reach a consensus to jointly and plan to co-construct it through discussing with various other stakeholders both at level of experts as also with government officials giving full play to the comparative advantages of the two countries and building a realistic foundation. This chapter focuses on discussing the following questions: (a) the significance of revitalizing the Southern Silk Road; (b) the main progress that BCIM economic corridor so far; (c) what kind of common interests both China and India can harvest from the construction of BCIM Economic Corridor; (d) the consensus between China and India in the BCIM economic corridor construction; (e) challenges for China and India in constructing BCIM Economic Corridor; and (f) suggestions on promoting the construction of BCIM Economic Corridor.

China has launched series of new diplomatic ideas and measures since 2013 which represent the new wave of innovation and transformation of China's diplomatic, economic, and security strategies under President Xi Jinping. The outstanding ones include the MoU on China-Pakistan Economic Corridor was signed during Premier Li Keqiang's visit to Pakistan in May 2013, and the two sides have made their commitment clear and begun the construction of China-Pakistan Economic Corridor as they try their best to promote two countries' shared development. At the same time, China and India have also together proposed to carry out the construction of BCIM Economic Corridor. Upon attending the 2013 G20 Summit in St Petersburg followed by visiting of the four Central Asian countries, President Xi Jinping delivered a speech at the Nazarbayev University in Alma-Ata, Kazakhstan where he had presented his strategic vision to use the innovative cooperation mode to co-construct the 'Silk Road Economic Belt'. Later, President Xi Jinping further illustrated this strategic conception at the Shanghai Cooperation Organization (SCO) Bishkek Summit. In October 2014, President Xi Jinping visited the Southeast Asia, and put forward a strategic conception of '21st Century Maritime Silk Road' in Indonesia, echoing with the initiative of 'Land Silk Road Economic Belt' proposed earlier in Kazakhstan. Further, in the "Decision of the Central Committee of the Communist Party of China on Some Major Issues Concerning Comprehensively Deepening the Reform" adopted at the Third Plenary Session of the 18th CPC Central Committee, the Central Committee clearly put forward the strategic argument to promote the Silk Road Economic Belt, as well as construct the Maritime Silk Road in order to shape the new pattern of all-round opening-up. Premier Li Keqiang also pointed out in 2014 Government Work Report that China would make efforts to co-construct the Silk Road Economic Belt and 21st Century Maritime Silk Road. Later at the APEC summit in Beijing during November 5-11 2014, China announced to contribute $40 billion to set up 'Silk Road Fund' to strengthen the Asian connectivity.

During Premier Minister Li Keqiang's first visit was to India during May 2013 and later during President Xi Jinping paid a three-day visit to India on September 17-19, 2014, the new leadership also together with India's leaders endorsed their joint commitment to the BCIM-Economic Corridor that China considers part of its Belt and Road Initiative as it attaches utmost importance to Sino-Indian ties. It is a new change in China's westward opening-up strategy from being cautious to becoming active in designing to construct the Asia-Europe-Africa regional connectivity, along with policy of regular communication, road connectivity, unimpeded trade, monetary circulation, and people to people connectivity as President Xi Jinping has repeatedly elaborated in the context of 'One Belt, One Road' initiative. The purpose here is to assimilate values of ancient civilizations into building bridges for their commodity trade so that all countries along the route can achieve sustainable economic growth through forming the regional economic belt.

Revitalizing the Southern Silk Road

The critical significance of 'Ancient Silk Road' lies not only in facilitating mutual trade and mutual prosperity, but more so in its great contribution to the Eastern and Western technological and cultural exchanges. As Mr. Ji Xianlin says, it is never enough to evaluate the Silk Road's tremendous contributions and immortal supplies in the history of the development of human civilization and the

Chinese civilization, even though with a little knowledge of history, one can try and understand this point.[1] It is from this perspective of history that we need to begin our examination of recent trajectories of regional cooperation and locate analysis BCIM-Economic Corridor in that broader framework of analysis.

(i) Historical Origin of the Silk Road network

The Ancient Silk Road network on the land is usually classified into the Northern Silk Road and the Southern Silk Road. The Northern Silk Road is dated back to 138 BC when Zhang Qian was dispatched by Emperor Wudi of Han dynasty to seek another nomadic tribe Darouzhi's support to jointly fight against the Huns (another ancient nationality in China). Although Zhang Qian failed to win the alliance with Darouzhi, he made two epic travels throughout this Asian landmass. This tour started from Chang'an, along the Hexi Corridor heading westwards across Wuwei, Zhangye, Jiuquan, arrived in Dunhuang where it was divided into two roads: one starting with Yang Guan, along the northern foot of Kunlun Mountains heading westward via Loulan (now Xinjiang Shanshan), past Tian (now Xinjiang Hotan), Shache, Puli (now Xinjiang Tash Kurghan), Yucongling, to Darouzhi, then heading southward, to Juandu (now India); and then heading westwards to Anxi and reaching the east coast of the Mediterranean, and was called the South Route. The other started from Yumen Pass along the south foot of Tianshan Mountains to the west via former Jushi (now Xinjiang Turpan), pass Qarasahr (now Xinjiang Qarasahr), Guhei (now Xinjiang Akesu), Sheher (now Xinjiang Kashi), the Pamirs, to Dawan, then heading northwestward, to Kangju and Alans; going forward from Southwest to Darouzhi and Ashkâniân, and this was called the North Route. This route was later extended to the Mediterranean to reach the Roman Empire.[2]

In this process, Zhang Qian was to 'dig out' the Western Region, open up a channel connecting Asia to Europe and Africa thereby connecting Eastern and Western civilisations and thus a prelude to future cultural exchanges between

Eastern and Western countries. This Road network of course also experienced the turbulence of Wei, Jin, Northern and Southern Dynasties, the spectacular vision of Sui and Tang Dynasties, and the prosperity of Yuan Dynasty. Until Ming Dynasty, this Road had been responsible for the ties between the mainland and Western Regions, between China and Asia, and the political, economic and cultural interactions with European countries. In history, Chinese silk was the most prestigious commodity in this East-West trade. According to the historical data, it was proved that around 300 BC, Chinese silk had not only reached ancient India, but also reached Europe. Although the majority of silk was produced in the far south, most maps regarded the ancient capital Chang'an (now Xi'an) as the starting point of the Ancient Silk Road, crossing Longshan mountains, passing through Hexi Corridor, through Yumen Pass and Yang Pass, then entering into Xinjiang, further going through Central Asia, West Asia and North Africa along the oasis and the Pamirs, finally arrived in Africa and Europe. The whole length was more than 7000 km.

Another ancient route was the Southern Silk Road which is today closely related to the BCIM Economic Corridor that is being revitalised and rebuilt together by Bangladesh, China, India and Myanmar (BCIM). As early as in 126 BC, after returning from the Western Region, famous Zhang Qian had told Emperor Wu that he had found the 'Shu cloth' and 'Qiong bamboo cane' in Bactria (now Afghanistan) and that it was also shipped through Juandu (now India). Emperor Wu of Han Dynasty sent envoys to go to 'Southwestern' regions for four times to seek out the landroad that further expanded the Southern Silk Road. The Southern Silk Road now had two main routes: one was the west route, also known as Lingguan Ancient-post-road. Starting from Chengdu, passing through Linqiong (now Qionglai), Tsing Yi (now Ya'an), Zedu (now Hanyuan), Qiongdu (now Xichang), Yeyu (now Dali), arrived in Yongchang (now Baoshan), trekking through the Lancang River and Nujiang River, climbing up Gaoligong Mountain, reaching in the ancient Tengyue (now Tengchong), directly going into

Myitkyina of Myanmar and India. The other one is the East Route, also known as the 'Five Feet Road' because of the five feet road width. Starting from Bodao (now Sichuan Yibin), pashing through Yanjin, Zhuti (now Zhaotong), Bijie, arrived at Hanwei county (now Qujing). Later generations gradually extended it to ancient Dianchi (now Kunming), ancient Yeyu (now Dali), joining together with the Lingguan Ancient-post-road in Pupengyi. Since the ancient times, the Southern Silk Road has been the bridge of enhancing communication and obtaining identity for the Asian-European-African countries especially for region that is today BCIM, and it was a major too for their seeking out their common beliefs and in building mutual trust. For thousands of years, the Eurasian people had always been cultivating China, India, Egypt, Babylon and Greece five major ancient civilizations, and East Asian Confucianism, Buddhism in South Asia, West Asian Islamic civilization and the western civilization with Greece as the representative.[3] Their ancient equations were however to be changed by modern era, especially colonialism.

(ii) BCIM Economic Corridor as Key Part of New Southern Silk Road

The 'Ancient Silk Road' had shaped unprecedented events in the economic and cultural interactions between the East and the West. It was to contribute to the making of these different civilizations and various religions becoming mutual harmonious and inclusiveness ensuring peaceful coexistence in their pluralistic societies of the larger Eurasia continent. At the same time, the mutual communications in the fields of science and technology between China and the western societies also promoted their development process from Central Asia to West Asia, South Asia and various European societies. In this intersection of various Eastern and Western civilizations, the Eurasian region displayed impressive progress of science and technology and the economic prosperity.

Silk Road Economic Belt which was initially proposed in Central Asia at Almaty is therefore not confined to Central

Asian region. After all, from its underlying perspectives, the ancient Silk Road includes Northern and Southern Silk Roads which are sought to be replicated in the new Silk Road on land with multiple routes crossing across modern nations. Therefore, to re-construct BCIM Economic Corridor jointly proposed by China and India is an important component of the Southern Silk Road. BCIM Economic Corridor therefore does not only connect the southwest China, Myanmar, Bangladesh and the Northeast region of India from the land, but also combines with China's 21st Century Maritime Silk Road' strategic conceptions that seek to achieve both land and sea connection. These will link up China with Southeast Asia, and South Asia and extended to Europe, eventually building unimpeded channels for trade across Eurasian. It is in this larger perspective that BCIM Economic Corridor need to be analysed.

(iii) Strategic Demands to Re-vitalise the Southern Silk Road

The basic strategic thinking of 'One Belt, One Road' is, to put Central Asia, Southeast Asia and South Asia as a priority for infrastructure connectivity, and then gradually extend it to the Middle East, Europe and East African countries. Meanwhile, taking the facilitation measures for trade and investments as well as other key cooperative projects. Relying on the historical accumulation of mutual goodwill and humanistic value of 'Silk Road on Land' and the 'Maritime Silk Road' it seeks to create better business atmosphere and establish new cooperation platforms, linking Asian and European two largest markets, to create a community of interests and to form a community of destiny.

Firstly, the idea to re-vitalise Southern Silk Road is driven by the need to boost the Eastern and Western cultural exchanges, trade and prosperity. The Ancient Silk Road had originated from trade and traffic with silk as major commodity. Today, more important than trade is the Silk Road culture that has been passing down through two thousand years and has successfully transferred the concept of 'equality and mutual benefit, harmony, peace and development' for these societies. It not only promotes the peace and prosperity between Eastern and Western countries with different races, religions and cultural backgrounds, but also harvests their benefit-sharing. Under the current situation, the main purpose of Chinese leaders to put forward the 'One Belt and One Road' strategy is to excavate the equal, harmonious, peaceful, and cooperative value and philosophy from the historical and humanistic perspective of ancient Silk Road to promote mutual trust and inclusiveness in cooperation and exchanges, and to further strive to form the benign interaction of economic cooperation and cultural exchanges. All above, not only can this contribute to closer economic ties and build more extensive cooperation space among the countries and regions along the route, it can also facilitate regional economic integration as well as maintain regional security through common development and mutual inclusiveness.

Secondly, it is the realistic need to further accelerate China's opening-up to the outside world. In the past three decades, China's higher economic growth rate, especially the huge trade volume, has greatly benefitted from China's policy of reform and opening up to the outside world. It promises also to contributes to the economic growth of the other participating countries, contributing to the rise of Asia as well as economic development of the whole world. After all, successful trade or investments are always reciprocal and bidirectional. As an important part of China's all-round opening, the Western Region's opening-up towards neighbouring countries can not only optimise China's industry structure and accelerate the development of inland open economy, but also benefit to stockholder's mutual development. Taking Eurasian market as an example, in 2012, China's total trade volume with Asian and European countries had already exceeded $2,700 billion, in which, the trade volume with Central Asian, West Asian and South Asian countries stands nearly $400 billion. By the end of 2012, China's direct investment stock in Central Asian, South Asian and West Asian countries had reached to $14.86 billion. In the next 5 years, China is expected to import about $8,000 billion goods from Asia and Europe, and the direct investment in Asia and Europe will exceed $450 billion. China and Central Asian, South Asian and West Asian countries have complementary and mutually beneficial conditions in their economies, and also have mutual needs to seek faster economic growth and upgrade and transform their industrial infrastructures. However, there also exists realistic dilemma where regional advantages and comparative advantages are difficult to change into economic advantages for all, and mutual demands are also difficult to change into cooperative behaviour. This is where building BCIM Economic Corridor along the 'Southern Silk Road' can facilitate construction of cooperative platform for China's Western Region opening up facing southwest in order to cultivate the newly opened-up economies with inland characteristics. This promises to enhance the level of advancing international economic cooperation of the Western Region.

Thirdly, it is an urgentneed to ensure regional safety-nets by strengthening bilateral and multilateral economic collaboration. When entering the 21st Century, each country has been confronted with unprecedented development opportunities. But they have also been involved in development plight brought by the continuously exacerbated strategic competition among major powers and the turbulent security situation. The surrounding environment has become more complex bringing the security issues to the forefront. From the perspective of geopolitics, South Asia, as the flank of the Middle East, as well as the flank of the world's oil centre, has played a decisive role in the global strategy of great powers. The South Asian sub-continent forms the junction of regions including Europe, the Middle East and East Asia, Australia. At the same time, the geopolitical value of Southeast Asia can not be ignored, which is the key strategic area to connect the Pacific and India Ocean Region. The construction of BCIM Economic Corridor can help change and improve China's political relations with the neighbouring countries through channels like cultural exchanges and economic cooperation. This can also ensure smooth flow of maritime transport channel, and to maximally increase the economic interests of each countries along the route, as well as to relieve the peripheral security dilemma which China and other countries face.

Fourthly, BCIM-Economic Corridor can also help advance the evolving new Indo-Pacific economic integration and achieve the rise of Asia-pacific. Currently, the economic growth of the world faces multiple challenges. On one hand, the revival of developed economy is slow and, on the other hand, although the growth rate of emerging economies are higher than the global average yet their growth momentum remains weak. In Asia, the intra-regional countries are often seen competing with each other in the fields of politics, economy and military etc. Great powers outside Asia also try to exert their influence on this region. They together with neighboring countries have also maintained a cautious approach, even a suspicious attitude, toward the rise of China. More or less, almost all countries have chosena balanced strategy for their foreign policy to strive for interests. This results in mutual distrust among neighbours thereby further exacerbating the instability and complexity of strategic environment of the larger region. In this background, there is an urgent need to strengthen sub-regional cooperation and cultivate new economic growth pole. Also, there are many existing Asian cooperative mechanisms with scattered and limited functions. China's timely taking of effective measures to implement the strategy of 'One Belt, One Road' through advocating to build the 'Asian Infrastructure Investment Bank', promises to contribute $40 billion to set up Silk Road fund. It goes without saying that these measures have offered new opportunities for Asian countries to speed up the construction of infrastructure. In line with these initiatives, the BCIM Economic Corridor forms and important sub-regional cooperation mechanism, which can greatly promote the common development of China and its neighboring countries. It can also contribute significantly to create an more spacious platform and better inclusive mechanism to achieve the evolving Indo-Pacific economic integration and facilitate the rise of Asia.

Constructing BCIM Economic Corridor

Well-known scholar Stavrianos depicts a picture of the world during Song and Yuan Dynasties in his *Global History by* saying that —

> Eurasian Continent in Song and Yuan Dynasties launched the unprecedented goods and technology exchange. Marine led to all directions, there appeared mutual communication and influence between technology and market, raw materials and goods, living customs and religious beliefs, thoughts and arts. From Northeast Asian Japan, Korea, to Southeast Asia and India coasts, and to Persian Gulf and all ports of East Africa, a "small globalized" active trade network had formed. Today, where China has become the biggest trade partners of more than 120 countries around the world, including South Korea, Japan, ASEAN, Brazil, Russia, South Africa and so on, and the biggest export market of more than 70 countries and regions. The proportion that China accounted for of global goods trade volume changed from less than 1% in 1978 to 12% in 2013; the number of China's trade partners changes from several dozen in 1978 to 231 countries and regions at present.[4]

As a very important part of Southern Silk Road, the construction of BCIM Economic Corridor can form a regional economic belt connecting China to neighbouring countries of South and Southeast Asia. Looking from the current function and scope, the directly related areas of BCIM includes Yunnan, Bangladesh, Myanmar, all states in India Northeast, covering an area of about 16,500 square kilometres, and a population of 440 million. The population of BCIM region accounts for about 6.7% of the world's total population, while the trade volume between the intra-regional countries accounts for about 2% of the world trade volume. Another reason can not be ignored is that this region is an underdeveloped region, which means backwardness but also huge development potential that co-exist simultaneously. Yunnan scholars had put forward the idea of constructing the BCIM sub-regional cooperation mechanism in 1999. In that year, four nations of BCIM held their first conference on economic cooperation in city of Kunming and signed the 'Kunming Initiative' document. From then on, four countries held 15 cooperation forums and 11 conferences, but the progress of economic cooperation was so limited. China's trade volume with India, Bangladesh and Myanmar rose from $4.453 billion in 2000 to $85.929 billion in 2013. Trade volume of China's Yunnan province alone with India, Bangladesh and Myanmar rose from $416 million in 2000 to $2.803 billion in 2012. In the fields of investment and project contracting, the mutual investment between these four countries has increased significantly starting from year 2000. In 2000, China's project contracting volume in India, Bangladesh and Myanmar was $408 million, while in 2012, the volume reached $10.353 billion. In 2003, China's direct investment in India, Bangladesh and Myanmar was $1.56 million, while in 2012 this amount reached to $408 million. Compared with the huge development potential of various countries, BCIM sub-regional cooperation is low in level, narrow in fields, and small in scale.

However, BCIM Economic Corridor can not only connect the immediate regions of the Ancient Northern Silk Road, but can also connect coastal port cities of key regions along 'Maritime Silk Road', which is convenient to promote economic and trade cooperation in the larger region using both land and marine connections. In May and October of 2013, Premier Li Keqiang and Prime Minister Manmohan Singh had paid each other a visit within same year and their Joint Declarations formally incorporated mention of the construction of BCIM Economic Corridor. In December of 2013, the BCIM Working Group met in Kunming city of China, where experts from four countries reached a certain degree of consensus on the development prospects, cooperative fields, as well as cooperation mechanisms of BCIM Economic Corridor. Nevertheless, this idea remains still floating in the air though this academic idea has reached to the national level, entering a takeoff stage compared to its previous preparation stage. Based on the Joint Initiative to form a consensus, the top priority is to put the jointly re-construction of Economic Corridor into the practice. In this it is indispensable to rely on Kunming, Mandalay, Dhaka, Calcutta and other nodal cities along route to substantially operationalise BCIM sub-regional cooperation mechanisms. This may further activate the vigor of the boarder provincial level cooperation that has been marginalised for a very long time.

As first direct benefit of BCIM Economic Corridor initiatives, the transportation costs of intra-regional road connectivity as well as trade and transaction costs will be greatly reduced by exerting the comparative advantages in various sectors of trade and investment in the border provinces of various countries. It can spread into Pakistan, Sri Lanka, Maldives and other South Asian countries along the Indian Ocean, and to the Middle East countries along the Indian Ocean including Iran, Saudi Arabia, Oman, Kuwait, Iraq and so on. To the east, it can extend up to the Southeast Asian countries along the Indian Ocean including Thailand, Malaysia, Singapore, Indonesia, East Timor and other countries, and further to the Western Pacific countries such as Japan and South Korea, and to the Oceania of Australia. All above can not only promote the linkage between the core BCIM countries, and also contribute to the process of Asian economic integration.

Common Interests of China and India

At present, the Sino-Indian bilateral ties have gradually reached a sound and interdependent momentum of development. If the two countries can try to carry out new measures in their extant fields of cooperation and accelerate their cross-border cooperation, it will be able to address their regional interests underlined by the decision to jointly reconstructing BCIM Economic Corridor. To begin with it promises to jointly benefit their underdeveloped peripheral provides by facilitating their opening-up to the outside world.

Building the BCIM Economic Corridor can provide the critical opportunities for geographically disadvantage China's Southwest and India's Northeast and also provide new opportunities for their major regional cities like Kunming and Kolkatta bringing them to their respective nation's edge zone into the forefront of national reforms and opening up in the future. This can greatly contribute to the balance development of their regional economic engagement. Currently China faces the challenges of enormous gap between its eastern and western regions but its underdeveloped regions also have enormous growth potential although as of now there is only a small proportion of the trade volume that emanates from China's western region. China's western region has been critical to its the new pattern for all round opening-up to the outside world and BCIM Economic Corridor will provide a kickstart to such earlier initiatives.

India as well has been facing similar situation and challenges in its northeast region. If India wants to break through the wall of the domestic economic underdevelopment, accelerate its reforms and open-up then BCIM-Economic Corridor must be its first consideration. Further, if India intends to open its northeast region, infrastructure and road connectivity are bound to the key point. Even the famous Stilwell Road, that during the Second World War, was the most critical connection between India's northeast region and China's southwest region can be rebuilt. As the old Chinese saying goes: 'to get rich, first to build road' hold true here. Simply by solving the road connectivity problems may create conditions for Indian cross-border trade with neighbouring countries and further alleviate the situation of poverty and unrest in India's northeast region. From the geopolitical point of view, directly opening India's northeast region to Southwest China, Bangladesh, Myanmar and so on, can also indirectly expanded its links to ASEAN, the West Pacific Ocean and even the whole Asian-Pacific region, which also conforms to India's Look East Policy.

Secondly, if infrastructure and traffic connectivity of

BCIM region can be gradually improved, logistics costs will be reduced, so the scale of trade and investment will expand. This will not only narrow each country's domestic regional development gaps but also strengthen Sino-Indian trade and investment cooperation. It is obvious that export competitiveness of Chinese and Indian products will be intensified, and more growth and development opportunities will be created for the neighboring countries. As we can see, China-India trade volume was only $7 billion a decade ago. In 2011, the China-India trade volume amounted to $73.9 billion. Affected by the global economic downturn from 2007, the trade volume of two countries has stayed around $65 to $70 billion in recent past. At the same time, according to figures released by the China's Ministry of Commerce, in 2011, China's investment in India was only $180 million and India's investment in China was only more than $40 million. By 2011, China's total investment in India was $575.7 million, India's total investment in China reached to $441.7 million. But China's promised investments in India have now moved up to $50 billion though these will take long time to materialise. As the world's two largest developing countries, China and India have the total population of more than 1.2 billion each. However, there is asymmetry between the huge demand potential of two markets and less than $70 billion trade volume of the two countries. In comparison, South Korea only has a population of 50 million, but the China-South Korea trade volume has exceeded $200 billion. Both China and India have strong desire for economic cooperation. So it is only expected that two sides will have to find ways to create a win-win situation in bilateral trade and investment and enhancing mutual trust and reducing suspicion based on constructing BCIM economic corridor.

Thirdly, from the point view of their comparative advantages in manufacturing sectors, all four countries of BCIM region are at different stages of development with different culture, different resource endowments and national circumstances, yet highly interdependent and economically complementary. So it is natural for these four countries to pursue broad manufacturing strategies to enhance their economic cooperation. In India, prime minister Modi's government has been paying close attention to infrastructure construction as well as advance manufacturing in order to achieve rapid economic growth. To reach this goal, India requires a large amount of capital and technology transfer as well as some good experience which China can offer. During the visit of Chinese President Xi Jinping to India in September 17-19 of 2014, he had promised investments worth $20 billion to India in the next five years. China will set up the industrial parks in both Gujarat and Maharashtra. The former mainly produces electric transmission and transformation equipment, the latter focus on producing auto parts. These investment and cooperative projects will help promote India's development of infrastructure and the capacity of manufacturing industry, which will benefit to Sino-Indian economic collaboration. It is part of the emerging trend among countries along the 'Silk Road' which have experienced increasing cooperation with China with benefits to all stockholders. But some countries are hesitating and have not taken any action thanks to misunderstanding or suspicions about China's strategy of 'One Belt, One Road' which Chinese government advocated since 2013. The key to solve this problem is to hold regular discussions at all levels to build consensus amongst countries along the 'Silk Road' first at the scholar level following by their governments, and promote the joint construction of projects like BCIM Economic Corridor.

Building Consensus on BCIM Economic Corridor

In fact, there is a strong desire for cooperation between China and India, but the key is how to put it into practice. Presently, if two countries can cooperate in the fields of manufacturing with their respective local advantages and help each other to strengthen their respective advantages in the competitive fields, lower the effect of political factors on economy, then the world has enough space to accommodate the common development of these two rising major Asian powers. Given their size and stature, this also means that building consensus between China and India also remains critical for the construction of BCIM Economic Corridor.

Firstly, the BCIM Economic Corridor has already been upgraded from the Track-II to Track-I level. This means that all the four countries have reached a consensus to build the economic corridor at their government level. The connectivity mainly includes the physical connectivity, which is the foundation of building the BCIM Economic Corridor. The institutional connectivity, which is the support base to build the Economic Corridor, the people-to-people connectivity, which is the guarantee that the Economic Corridor will bring effective and lasting benefits to stakeholders will have over period of time. As a golden mean, all the BCIM countries can basically agree to first focus on physical connectivity. The first route can be from China's Kunming, via Ruili, into Myanmar, passing through Lashio, Mandalay and other places into India, Bangladesh from Shura, passing through Dhaka, finally entering into Calcutta of India. The first BCIM Car Rally Championship were successfully held in February 2013 along this route, which means that connecting this route remains feasible. But its connectivity cost will be substantive. Also, the historical Stilwell Road can also illustrate feasibility of connectivity.

Secondly, both China and India also remain convinced that their economic interests can benefit from sub-regional cooperation. As the heavyweight countries with huge landmass and large populations, as part of the emerging economies of the G20, the two core states of the BRIC countries, it goes without saying that China and India can create economic miracle only if the two countries can ensure their joint efforts and collaborations. The high speed growth rates of two countries in recent years inevitably make people compare these two developing countries when thinking the evolving changes in the international system. An article titled "A New World Economy" in an American journal

Business Week author explains how the influence of China and India's rise simultaneously on the global economy in the future is comparable to the rise of the United States in 19th Century. As India's minister of Commerce and a well-known economist Jairam Ramesh had said in 2005 that if the advantage of 'world factory' with 'world office' can be combined, China and India will respectively contribute to the stability of a new world economic order. No doubt, China and India also face plenty of similar problems and challenges. Both challenges and comparative advantages which two countries are facing, to a certain extent have elevated the demand for their mutual cooperation. Based on basic premise of competition, their strategic competition has reinforced benefits of better distribution and these two countries definitely can be good cooperative partners in ensuring mutual benefit. The key to promote Sino-Indian ties is to push political trust through mutually beneficial economic and security cooperation making full use of the manufacturing sector's advantages of China and services sector advantages of India. BCIM Economic Corridor construction, as a breakthrough to strengthening their economic cooperation, need not be based on their 'relative gains' politically, but it must achieve the 'absolute gains' economically through win-win cooperation.

Thirdly, the construction of BCIM Economic Corridor is conducive to expanding the common space of development. The first BCIM Forum held in Kunming in August 1999, producing the "Kunming Initiative" was followed by several conferences held in New Delhi, Dhaka, Yangon and Kunming respectively. These series of conferences evaluated the role and the positive significance of the BCIM forums and did the ground work in evolving consensuses on critical issues like cooperative principles, cooperation framework, priority-developed fields, connectivity routes, cultural exchanges and so on. Moreover, this also produced consciousness regarding trade potential of BCIM countries which is now universally considered to be optimistic. Participants repeatedly underlined how their bilateral trade and multilateral trade as also their overall foreign trade could be substantially expanded by the BCIM trade facilitation. As a result, whether at experts level or government level, China and India have consistently agreed on the basic principle of how 'cooperation contributes to both countries while confrontation can only hurt each other', and this is consistent with the concept of 'no confrontation, no conflict, mutual cooperation, mutual benefit and win-win result' as President Xi Jinping has advocated. The BCIM region is also an important junction connecting this region to other sub-regions of Asia. To solve the connectivity issues in this region through building the BCIM Economic Corridor can not only increase the trade volume between China and India, but also can solve in a certain extent the trade deficit problems currently existing between China and India. On the one hand, China does not deliberately pursue the trade surplus, on the other hand, from the point of view of economics, the trade balance is not only based on the exchange rate, but also depends on a country's income level and the demand or demand elasticity of its consumers for another country's exports. China has more advanced technology in manufacturing, electric power and telecommunications equipment and project contracting, and it has strong and rich management experience in the field of infrastructure construction. This obviously can contribute to the development of Indian manufacturing industries and infrastructure improvement. India is relatively more developed in the information and communications industry, software outsourcing, pharmaceutical and cultural industries. Based on these competitive advantages, if both sides can create systemic arrangements of trade facilitation for their own products with comparative advantages and relative to the needs of the market, and increase the investments, this will not only help to narrow India's trade deficit to China, but also create more job opportunities, and thus improving the ability of sustainable development of both economies. The trade network of BCIM sub-regional cooperation can be formed to increase the regional trade to East Asia, South Asia, Southeast Asia and other regions.

It is a well known fact that, thanks to the demand of development, China will expand towards West and India will expand towards East for their development. This means the Southeast Asia will be the common region or market for two countries implementing their strategies of development. By combining China's 'westward development' with India's 'eastward policy', it can promote the connectivity of two of Asia's biggest markets. This will not only expand the cooperation between China and India, but also to cultivate a new economic growth pole and further form an open economic zone for rise of Asia.

Fourthly, Yunnan has played an irreplaceable role in promoting the conception and construction of BCIM cooperation mechanisms. As a gateway of China's reform and opening up toward West, Yunnan continues to be the frontier province in President Xi's strategy of 'One Belt, One Road' thanks to its unique geographical advantage. To the north, Yunnan can connect the Northern Silk Road through Chengdu and Xi'an; to the south, it can be connected to the 'Southern Silk Road' and 'Marine Silk road'. Especially, almost every channel from China to Southeast Asia, South Asia and the Indian Ocean passes through China's Yunnan province, so Yunnan's unique geographical advantage will be fully exerted in the strategy of 'One Belt, One Road' initiatives. This geographical advantage of Yunnan will be of great importance both in China's integrating towards the region and the regional economies integrating with China. In recent past, Yunnan has made great efforts in the construction of connectivity, including channel network, infrastructure construction of the ports and international logistics system etc. with the support of national policy. With the re-construction of ancient 'Southern Silk Road', Yunnan will play more and more roles in connecting China with Southeast Asia, South Asia and even European continent, which will further promote traffic connectivity and the economic and social development of neighbouring countries.

Challenges for China and India

BCIM Economic Corridor can be regarded as a completely new growth pole for Sino-Indian strategic partnership. However, there are still many risks and challenges to construct the 'Silk Road' of the new era. Firstly, barriers of terrain, road connectivity has been compounded by poor infrastructure in the BCIM region. As one of the sub-regional cooperation mechanisms, the construction of BCIM Economic Corridor is also related to their cross-border issues. As we all know, the connectivity has been one of the key topics of the BCIM Forum from very beginning. This was also regarded as one of the hardest issues to be resolved. Three main corridor routes were discussed in the BCIM Forum. The first option is the North Route namely, Kunming-Dali-Tengchong-Myitkyina-Ledo-Kolkatta in which the segment from of Kunming to Ledo was called the Stilwell Road constructed during the World War II. There is only 467 km from Baoshan-Tengchong-Myitkyina of Myanmar to Banshao. Starting from Kunming, there is only about 1,200 km highway mileage from Kunming through Baoshan, Tengchong, Myitkyina to Banshao, which covers more population, but it seems construction cost is the lowest of the three routes. Another option is the middle route, that is Kunming-Dali-Baoshan-Ruili (Myitkyina)–Mandalay-Demu-Imphal-Shillong-Dhaka-Kolkatta which is the route that was used by the BCIM Car Rally in February 2013, and this is also the most easily connected route. Another option is the South Route, that is Kunming-Dali-Baoshan–Ruili-Lashio-Mandalay-Magui-Mengdu-Teknaf-Cox's Bazar-Chittagong-Dhaka-Kolkatta. This is the most convenient and promising route for four countries to connect the deep-water harbours which is greatly related to construct Maritime Silk Road. What is more important to construct Maritime Silk Road is not only to improve the freight transport volumes between China and Indian Ocean economies, but to elevate the harbour capacity of each related countries and further represent the commercial value of ports through connecting these ports with inland industry of each country. The BCIM

Economic Corridor can not only closely connect two big markets of China and India, but also can connect with the Beibu Gulf in the Pacific Ocean through Kyaukpyu port, Sittwe port, Chittagong port, Kolkatta port and other ports in the India Ocean. The land and maritime connectivity will further promote the linkage of Asian-African-European markets, and form the huge international economic growth belt. But each route faces the dilemma of poor infrastructure. There are lots of difficulties to form the connectivity network, in particular, the funding gap is huge.

Secondly, what makes implementing some of these initiatives difficult is lack of mutual trust between China and India. It is no exaggeration to say that the vast majority of Indians have very strong wariness about China. In October-November 1962, massive failure in the Himalayan war still lingers in their memory. China's friendly supports for Pakistan for many years, as well as the growing military deployment by China make Indians far more alert. In addition, they remain uncomfortable about the cheap commodities imported from China that can make Indian companies bankruptcy at home and overseas. For instance, in the construction of BCIM Economic Corridor, choosing the North Route, that is to restore the historically famous Stilwell Road, India remains worried about its boundary problems. India worries that if the military conflict occurs, after the Northeast Area is opened and the connectivity with Myanmar, Bangladesh, Southwest China, India will be in a disadvantageous position, which will increase the political uncertainty. Between China and India, in addition to the divergence and contradiction derives from historical problems, there exists the strategic competition after the rise of two emerging powers, as well as the strategic conflicts result from China's westward development and India's Act East policy, which aggravates mutual distrust. Although prime minister Narendra Modi tries to stop the downward slide of economy through increasing the intensity of economic reforms which should provide some boost to Sino-Indian economic cooperation. But continuous trade deficit of India to China need to be solved through enlarging investment and cooperating in the field of infrastructure in the short run and raise bilateral trade volume based on the economic complementarity and comparative advantage of the two countries in the long run. For a long time, thanks to the low trust and ineffective communications, it has been difficult for both sides to reach a credible and a binding agreement. The economic relations between the two countries have therefore been non-cooperative, which means the momentum for changing the non-cooperation into cooperation remains insufficient. If India's official thinking and policy can be changed from passive to active, the relationship among BCIM countries will improve through physical connectivity, institutional connectivity and people to people connectivity. In order to achieve the goal of economic growth and increase the regional influence, the most important is to improve economic power, which is the base of political and military power. Surely, in the foreseeable future, both China and India's policy goal will focus on promoting economic development through solving the difficulties, and further enhance the international competitiveness and strive for more voice in the region and world.

Thirdly, thanks to the underdevelopment in BCIM region, they face lower efficiency in newer initiatives. Stability is the key to opening the door of the future. There is also general increase in the global competitiveness pushing the members in a unfavorable social position thus into abandoning their cooperative role. Yunnan, located in the southwest border of China, neighbours China's Guizhou Province, Guangxi Zhuang Autonomous Region in the East, connects with Sichuan Province in the north, borders on Myanmar in the West, and is adjacent to Laos and Vietnam in the south. Yunnan has been the land route connecting China to these Southeast Asian countries since ancient times. China's Yunnan province is not far from Thailand, Cambodia, Bangladesh, India and other countries of the region. As a frontier, ethnic, and mountainous province, Yunnan is the largest place where the ethnic minorities are concentrated in China,. With backwardness in education and ideas, and seriously lagging transportation and infrastructure, weak industrial base and the low level of urbanisation compared to the eastern region of China, China's southwest faces lots of poverty. People and the farmers in Yunnan province have much lower income levels. India's northeastern region is located in the important transport corridor among the Southwest Region of China, Indo-China Peninsula and the Indian subcontinent. This region includes Assam, Meghalaya, Sikkim, Manipur, Mizoram, Tripura, Nagaland, and other states. Its southwest and east areas respectively connect with Bangladesh and Myanmar, the northwest area neighbour Bhutan, and the northern area is adjacent to China. This northeastern region in general belongs to the underdeveloped area, mostly covered by mountains, with characteristic of poor infrastructure, large number of poor population, and low urbanisation. Both China's Southwest and India's Northeast have the unique geographical location and occupy a favorable position. But the two regions belong to resource rich mountains and valleys, though with poor infrastructure, which calls for large capital investments, and difficulties of re-construction. It is quite clear that, in the long-term, this region has large development potential but both adjoining regions of China and India inevitably face problems such as the unbalanced input and output and the low product efficiency in the short term, which inevitably discourages bilateral cooperative impetus.

Fourthly, complicated geopolitics of this region also carries historical baggage with implication for the construction of BCIM Economic Corridor. For a long time, both Southeast Asia and South Asia were sensitive to political dynamics of cole war. These were seen as hot spots that the great powers used to compete with China. In 2011 again, the United States pivoted to the Asian-Pacific region to balance the rising influence of China by strengthening the ties with China's neighbouring countries such as Myanmar and India. This has created a situation where several countries are now depending on China in economy and relying on the United States in security. China's neighboring countries have similarly chosena balanced foreign policy with both the United States and China in order to harvest more benefits. This virtually results in creating a negative impact for construction of the BCIM Economic Corridor. Moreover, the 'China threat' also remains a lingering shadow on India's psyche. In the past decades, both Chinese and Indian scholars have spent lots of time to study how to build BCIM cooperative mechanisms. Indian government expresses willingness to support joint construction of BCIM Economic Corridor, but it has not resulted in any explicit policy initiatives from India. This delay is caused by the 'China Threat' derived from the public debates and media. In fact, threat assessments depend on the strength of your opponent including soft power and hard power, they seldom stem from the clash of strategic intention. India is accelerating its Look Eastpolicy by collaborating with Southeast Asian countries in the fields of military, economic and security. At the same time, for the sake of economic interests and common development with neighbouring countries, China's strategy of 'Opening up to the West' aggravates Indian psychological uneasiness rather than encourage cooperative opportunity of two countries in Southeast Asia. After all, India has always regarded the subcontinent of South Asia and Indian Ocean as its 'sphere of influence'. It seems that the engagement of India's Look East policy and China's 'Opening up to the west' strategy has intensified the strategic competition between China and India. This makes the disputes and competition between China and India transformed from the fixed situation left over from the history into the dynamic trend by geopolitical competition, which to some extent increases the uncertainty and challenges on Sino-Indian relations, and further affects the construction of BCIM Economic Corridor.

Future of BCIM Economic Corridor

Both the central area of the Silk Road on land and the key points of Maritime Silk Road are the geopolitical bridge that has attracted big powers for various reason creating some barriers for constructing BCIM economic corridor. As part of their long-term sub-regional cooperation mechanism, the BCIM nations can not ignore these difficulties and challenges. BCIM has already achieved some early harvest in building this sub-region. Examples like the Greater Mekong Sub-regional (GMS) cooperation mechanism, China-ASEAN Free Trade Area (10 +1), India-ASEAN Free Trade Area (IAFTA) and the Regional Comprehensive Economic partnership (10+6), represent the backdrop of the construction of BCIM Economic Corridor. They also make it potentially plausible and practical. The role of culture can not be ignored. When we talk about strengthening economic cooperation it implies combining economic cooperation with cultural exchanges to provide a push the political trust-building. This can promote their common development and prosperity through the construction of BCIM Economic Corridor and other related initiatives.

Firstly, making great efforts to reach consensus of co-construction, benefit-sharing and win-win situation remains critical for constructing BCIM Economic Corridor. It has already had experience of 15 years since the BCIM sub-regional cooperation ideas were originally proposed in 1999 in Kunming. During this long period, several academic studies have triggered by the relevant countries though the reaction from government of Bangladesh, India and Myanmar has been complex. There are positive attitudes as well as negative or doubtful feedbacks from experts. If Bangladesh, India and Myanmar have no enthusiasm and they lack initiative, if China pushes it singularly, it is impossible to build the infrastructure and road connectivity, let alone shaping the structure of all-round regional opening-up. The conceptions of rebuilding the Southern Silk Road and Maritime Silk Road may give rise to some doubts and concerns of neighbouring countries and revive 'China Threat' fears. Especially, India has been cautious all the time to China's actions related to Indian Ocean also about its relations with littoral nations along Indian Ocean. Therefore, it is urgent for China to strengthen exchanges and communication with Bangladesh, India and Myanmar, and build cooperative consensus among these countries. BCIM has to build new sub-regional cooperation agreement from governmental, academic and people-to-people levels. Based on their cultural identities, forming the cooperative idea of co-construction, benefit-sharing and win-win situation through promoting policy coordination and the rule-making process call for great attention on this among all the four BCIM countries.

Secondly, BCIM will have to go beyond just Economic Corridor and construct a community of interests based on consensus to provide solid basis for this operative initiatives. To create a community of interests needs collaboration of all the stockholders from the fields of politics, economy and security. It is necessary to promote economic cooperation through excavating the cumulative historical and cultural values since days of the ancient Southern Silk Road. All four countries must secure cooperation in addressing critical challenges like piracy, terrorism and other non-traditional security threats. With the aid of various sub-regional cooperation mechanisms, the reform of financial systems should be a priority to push forward the facilitation of trade and investment and take cooperation projects such as jointly ventures in building industrial parks to push investment into enterprises of each other. Only under the governmental approval and support of all four countries, can we substantially accelerate the construction of BCIM Economic Corridor. It should be seen as part of promoting Asian economic integration and achieving the rise of Asia.

Thirdly, co-constructing of transport infrastructure should be top priority. BCIM Economic Corridor provides all four countries with a great opportunity to accelerate their road connectivity. BRICS development Bank, Asian Infrastructure Investment Bank, together with Silk Found can serve to create conditions by offering fund supports and attracting capital even from the outside world to make this region integral to the development of Asian countries. Four countries must seize this opportunity to co-construct their national infrastructure as well. As for the highway, it is necessary to accelerate the construction of the South Route, that is, the construction of big channel of Kunming-Ruili-Mandalay-Magui-Kyaukpyu link. At the same time, they must also support the construction of the Middle Route, namely, Kunming-Tengchong–Myitkyina–Banshao-Ledo Road, and the North Line, namely, Kunming-Ruili-Mandalay–Dhaka-Kolkatta. If the highway from Myitkyina of Myanmar to Ledo of India's northeast region gets connected, it will take only 10 hours for locomotives to move goods and people from Kunming through Tengchong to Ledo in India's northeastern region.

Fourthly, all four countries of the BCIM have to treat building this cooperative project of Economic Corridor in terms of shared development for the entire region. None can deny how commercial force can play an important role in promoting economic prosperity and regional stability. This cab be easily found in the history of ancient Silk Road network. From the rise and fall of great powers in the past, we can learn how profound influence the navigational trade had on common development of these societies and how commercial forces could promote the changes in the regional geopolitics and even change the world order. In the new historical period, to jointly construct the Economic Corridor based on Ancient Silk Road can especially deepen closer economic ties between China and the countries along the routes and further expand the broad space for common development. In particular, to develop long-term and stable friendly cooperative relations with India is an unswerving policy of the Chinese government. What calls for special attention for China is that, China is the first trade power of the world with nearly $ 4 trillion foreign exchange reserve at its disposal. The best way to invest this capital is to partly focus on non-resource cooperative projects and invest in people's basic needs like health and education, and not just resource in manufacturing industries for profit purposes. The former approach will help avoid causing misunderstanding amongst China's neighbouring countries and ensure its peaceful rise.

In the end, when the intense strategic competition happened between the great powers and the rising powers, it is pertinent to ask how to avoid breaking out of conflicts or war? Chinese leaders have repeatedly stressed that China must break the curse of historical conflict between the emerging powers and great powers through exploring paths for peace development. The strategy of 'One Belt, One Road' of which BCIM Economic Corridor is an integral part, has been advocated by the Chinese government as one such path for China and the neighbouring countries. All stakeholders need to work together jointly to cope with the changes in international environment and to defuse the risks in this critical period of reforms and development, thus creating a reasonable and institutionalised mechanisms to maintain the economic prosperity and regional stability and peace for a long period of time.

Endnotes

1. Ji Xianlin, *Research on the Trading History of Silk Road*, (Lanzhou: Gansu People's Publishing House, 1991), p. 3.
2. Shen Jishi, *Silk Road*, (Beijing: Zhonghua Book Company, Chinese Ancient Book Publishing House, 2010), p. 8.
3. Pang Changwei: "Energy Cooperation: the Breakthrough of the Silk Road Economic Belt", *Journal of Xinjiang Normal University* (Philosophy and Social Sciences Edition), April 2014, Vol. 35, p. 2.
4. Wang Jinbo, "Social Sciences in China", *Social Science Journal*, October 24, 2014, Issue 660, 2014, p. 9.

4

India and the BCIM-EC: Functional and Sub-Regional Approach

Binoda Kumar Mishra[1]

Starting from 1999, the Kunming Initiative (later known as the BCIM Forum) took a decade and half to find place in the Track-I agenda of the four member states. While from the beginning China, the initiator of the idea, had been pushing for sub-regional economic integration of South-west China, Myanmar, Bangladesh and Northeast region of India, the other major player in the arrangement, i.e. India had been seen as a reluctant player. After operating at the Track-II level for fifteen years and holding 12 Forum meetings, the BCIM could find its place in the joint declarations of May and again in October 2013 between India and China at the summit levels. Now there are expectations that the BCIM Economic Corridor (BCIM-EC) will emerge as a multilateral integrated economic zone offering greater economic opportunities to all four member states and even beyond. The economic corridor idea figured during the meetings of the BCIM Forum meeting primarily as a suggestion from the Chinese side. It is hard to trace the exact source of the Economic Corridor idea but according to Joint Secretary (East Asia) of India's Ministry of External Affairs, the idea was first articulated by a Chinese economist

Professor Dr. Ms. Ren Jia, then Vice President of China's Yunnan Academy of Social Sciences during one of the regular deliberations at the BCIM Forum.[2]

This chapter seeks to explore the reasons for the slow movement of these initiatives and examine India's approach to these arrangements. The central argument of the chapter is that India, though responsive to the economic needs of its eastern and north-eastern provinces, has been apprehensive of opening this region for interaction with its immediate neighbors, especially China. Security concerns pertaining the northeast of India coupled with fears of relative loss to rising China's economic leverages has forced India to respond but reluctantly to the BCIM arrangements. However, there is a growing realization in India that allowing India's north-east provinces to interact directly with China can offers better growth opportunities to them but there are also concerns regarding region's security situation and the non-existing economic infrastructure. It is feared that if the region is allowed to be part of any economic arrangement involving China then the region may end up turning into a periphery in the Chinese sphere of influence. This explains continued cautious pro-activeness in India's approach to the BCIM-EC.[3] Finally, this chapter contends that there are signs of India beginning to engage in the BCIM-EC on a functional (sectoral) basis and at the sub-regional (provincial) levels which makes if a promising case for coming years.

The Background

In pursuance with the proposal of the Chinese Premier, Li Keqiang, on 23 October 2013, in a Joint Statement both, the Prime Minister of India and the Premier of China, had declared their intent to explore possibilities of establishing an economic corridor comprising South-western part (Yunnan Province) of China, Myanmar, Bangladesh and North-eastern and Eastern parts of India.[4] As their first concrete step forward, their Joint Statement proposed to constitute a Joint Study Group (JSG) for the purpose of undertaking an exploratory study on this subject. The JSG has met once in Kunming in December 2013 and was expected to produce a roadmap by December 2014. Though these are seemingly positive developments, there remain serious doubts over the idea finally materialising in the near term future. Most doubts emerge from India being sensitive about its North East Region (NER) particularly when it comes to linking NER to China. There is a security prism through which China is viewed in India and one cannot be very hopeful about any sudden change in that perception in India. The pertinent question is why such doubts continue to persist at the highest political level between these two most important trade partners? To find an answer the main aspects that need interrogation are: how was BCIM proposed in first place; why was it proposed by China; who is expected to benefit and how much; who is most reluctant partner and why?

The Bangladesh, China, India and Myanmar (BCIM) was launched as Kunming Initiative in 1999. It was a Track-II sub-regional initiative to promote sub-regional economic integration. The basic premise was to economically re-integrate these parts that were already integrated culturally for several centuries, if not more. This Initiative intended to address the deep-routed structural impediments to the development of the region that flowed from disputed borders and impoverished populations in their border regions. In the long run, it aimed at making borders irrelevant, increase connectivity, and facilitate economic development on the principle of mutual economic complementarities. The broad rationale of the Initiative was to create conditions for the overall development of the region by providing the region access to sea – especially applicable to landlocked Southwest China and for Northeast India as also to provide economic opportunities to Bangladesh and Myanmar to gain from their engagement with bigger economies like India and China. Their economic logic was sound and there was an equally sound reason for China to initiate this arrangement. From mid-1990s, China had implemented a deliberate strategy of opening up its border provinces (selectively) for transnational economic interaction.[5] Yunnan had since been one such case province that was allowed to lead China's interactions with economies of Southeast and South Asia. In the Chinese policy terms Yunnan is called as China's "Bridgehead" to South and Southeast Asia.[6]

Yunnan has been rather successful in building bridges with several ASEAN countries and is fast emerging as a regional trade hub between China and the ASEAN economies. The success of this policy for Yunnan's economy can be measures from the fact that it has been growing at 12.1 per cent annually (Brian Eyler, 2013). It remains unclear though as to what specific benefits China wishes to draw from BCIM-EC arrangement for its Yunnan province? The general logic given by most scholars is that China seeks to obtain Yunnan access to Indian and Pacific Ocean. Yunnan's present engagement with ASEAN, particularly its strongest engagement with Myanmar, does promise to provide it sea access given Yunnan's stronger engagement with ASEAN as also its slow momentum in BCIM this remains perhaps only one of the many and even a weak motivation for building BCIM arrangement. The second reason advanced is the access to Indian market. This can also be a plausible explanation. But considering that the original BCIM idea takes only Northeast India into consideration which is not an improved market the logic of accessing Indian market within the BCIM framework also does not appear to be that strong. It can make sense only if the whole of India is taken as a part of the BCIM arrangement. It can certainly be argued that even the Chinese strategy does include the whole of India and the whole of China even as the scope of BCIM increases in future. The Chinese declared objectives in BCIM arrangement is to promote development in its peripheral regions to facilitate Chinese strategy of "peaceful rise" and "friendly neighbourhood" that must go together (Li Jun, 2014).[7]

The BCIM idea has not yet been officially elevated to the Track-I level as the Chinese tend to believe it. However, because the term "BCIM" figured in the joint declaration of both the Premiers during their meeting in October 2013 have made China discontinue Track-II to re-enforce its elevation. No doubt, Chinese have lent full government support to the arrangement from its very beginning, the Indian side continues to be the one most reluctant. Myanmar and Bangladesh, the other two players to the arrangement, have also begun to welcome the BCIM idea at Track-1 as well. The idea has become acceptable to everyone in principle even when there is little progress on the ground. But as both China and India are now planning to put the idea into action serious deliberations have begun in all the four countries and more particularly in India as it has been the most reluctant player in these arrangements. Conversely, China has been the most active protagonist which also need to be examined.

The PRC after it began liberalizing its economy since early 1980s had experienced rapid economic growth to the extent that it has since 2005 replaced Japan from the position of being the largest economy of Asia. But this unprecedented economic growth in China have not been uniform and there have emerged severe disparities among its provinces. Broadly, coastal provinces of China have experienced rapid industrialization in comparison to the western and south-western hinterland provinces. These provinces such as Yunnan, Tibet and Xinjiang have lagged considerably behind the developed coastal eastern provinces in terms of economic progress that China experienced. This has necessitated introspection on the part of the Chinese leadership to find reasons for the relative underdevelopment of these provinces as also to explore ways and means to improve the economic scenario in these underdeveloped provinces.

Among the reasons that are accounted for the relative underdevelopment of these western provinces, prominent include their landlocked character, poor resource base and lack of access to immediate markets. In order to overcome these shortcomings and to put these provinces on the path of rapid growth trajectories to catch up with the rest of China, the Chinese government realized the need for granting some amount of autonomy to these provinces to interact with the immediate neighbors who would either obtain them access to the high sea, increase their access to resources and to markets for their products. Emerging Southeast Asia since 1970s was seen as great opportunity so also the geographically contiguous South Asia which has also been growing from early 1990s. Yunnan was granted relative autonomy as compared to other provinces to engage itself with its geographically contiguous neighbors. Yunnan quickly took advantage of its geographical location and turned itself into a gateway for China to the ASEAN. The ASEAN engagement has provided Yunnan with growth opportunities which have resulted in a growth rate of 11 per cent compared to the national growth rate of 7.4 per cent (Keith Bradsher, 2014).[8]

Encouraged by such growth and realizing the need for sustenance of such growth Yunnan has been trying to expand the scope of its regional engagement beyond its current level of engagement with the ASEAN. Emerging India has since come to be seen as potentially attractive partner for long-term economic prosperity for China's south western region. If one looks at the initial articulation of the BCIM idea it was about inclusion of the north-eastern part of India and not whole of India. This recent indications of expansion to entire India alludes to Yunnan rationalizing their economic engagement with this part of India on geo-economic similarity. The rationale often provided for this focus on increasing economic integration of the proposed region is to increase the scales of economy for this relatively underdeveloped region through mutual cooperation. It makes a sound argument for sub-regional cooperation among these four nations that experience partial underdevelopment due to lack of either resources or market; or technology and finance; or connectivity within the region as also to the outside through the seas. But the next question is who would gain the most from such facilitation. In international relations economic gains are not always calculated in absolute terms. This means that relative gains could also convince stakeholders to initiate and expand cooperation.

More often than not gains are calculated by states in relative terms and particularly so when it involves partners, the dominant ones specifically, are pitted in a rather competitive mode than a cooperative mode. In International Relations theory, there are good amount of literature discussing the conditions under which States are more likely to be sensitive to relative gains. In general it is argued that, in an anarchic international system, States are more likely to prefer relative gains to absolute gains. Robert Keohane suggests that States' preferences to relative gains is not universal; rather it is conditional and only "when there are only two major players, and one side's gains may decisively change power relationships, relative gains loom large" (Keohane 2004: 31). Joseph M. Grieco argues that "fundamental goal" of states "in any relationship is not to attain highest possible individual gain or pay off; instead it is to prevent others from achieving advances in their relative capabilities" (Grieco 1990:39; of Liberman 1996; 150-51). In this case, India and China are not the countries that would calculate their pay offs from any arrangement in absolute terms given their juxtaposition in the emerging international order, the baggage of history and the almost irresolvable border dispute. There being a constant perception of mutual hostility both (at least India) remain(s) sensitive to the possibility of the gains from economic cooperation being translated into military advantage (for China). As Grieco further suggests that sensitivity to relative gains "depends on the probability that they will be converted to military threats" (Liberman 1996:151), it can be concluded that given the vulnerability of India's NER to possible Chinese economic or military aggression, India would prefer relative gains to absolute gains vis-à-vis China in any arrangement involving its NER.

Who Gains?: The Relative Gain Calculations

India has substantial economic incentives to interact with her eastern neighbours and a compulsion as well. India's NER is economically stagnated, and needs to be opened to the external world to improve the economic situation. In the present era of globalisation and trend of regionalism, to obtain benefits from regional economic arrangements, India certainly can think of regional arrangements to benefit its NER particularly when all other domestic endeavors have failed to achieve economic development in the NER. Coming to think of economic development of NER through economic engagement, the idea has been the driver of India's successful Look East Policy (LEP), even though as an afterthought of India's initial engagement with original ASEAN-5. It is an afterthought because the chronology of LEP does not lend support to the argument that NER was central to India's enunciation of its LEP in early 1990s. The LEP was initiated in 1992 when India's NER did not have the benefit of sharing borders and geographical contiguity with ASEAN. It was only with Myanmar joining ASEAN in 1997 that the geographical contiguity was finally the reality. Only in post-1997 arguments one can see NER being projected as a prime factor in India's LEP. Even now, though there are lot of rhetoric regarding NER benefiting from the LEP nothing has actually materialized. Arguably this is because of the continued clash of arguments that project security first or development first making it difficult to reach decisive decision and make clearer policies on BCIM-EC.

In any credible analysis it comes to the fore that NER can never benefit from LEP unless China is taken to be part of India's calculation. India's LEP was conceived to engage primarily the major ASEAN economies. It is to be remembered that Myanmar was not part of ASEAN till 1997 and therefore ASEAN was never contiguous land neighbor of India or its NER. It was only with Myanmar joining the ASEAN in 1997 that ASEAN became a land contiguous neighbour sharing land borders to India's NER. Desperate articulations of NER being part of India's LEP are often made with the hope that this may change the fortune of the people of India's NER. But in reality it has also been seen as a hindrance to India's LEP. The example of India failing to obtain the gas from Myanmar coast to India suffices to highlight the gap between reality and rhetoric. Similarly, when Bangladesh refused transit to India for the Myanmar gas to reach Kolkata, attempts were made to route it through India's NER. Both for the cost of the transport and for security reasons the project was abandoned resulting in China obtaining the same gas.[9]

The second reason that NER has not benefited much from India's LEP is because the developed economies of major ASEAN economies like Singapore, Thailand, Malaysia, are connected to India through the seas and there is no rationale for them travelling all the way through the NER to reach rest of India. Therefore, NER gaining from BCIM-EC engagement and from ASEAN through LEP seems misplaced. The question is are we serious about developing the NER or is it that political rhetoric of development alone is good enough to serve New Delhi's interests? If there is a serious political will to develop NER then it must be connected to an economy that has multi-sectoral opportunities, larger scales. In this case China's Yunnan seems to fit the bill better.

While India is trying to figure out how to make LEP work for its NER, the Chinese economy which is much developed than the Indian economy and growing faster than India offers an opportunity for economic engagement not as act of benevolence but due to her own pressing requirement. The South-western parts of China (Yunnan province in particular) are relatively much less developed than the mainland Chinese economy and the Chinese have understood the importance of Yunnan's need for economic engagement with its immediate neighbors. India faces the predicament of how to tap the economic potential of a China for its NER? Adding to the predicament is not just the baggage of history but also the future which clearly is going to remain competitive owing to the fact both these billion plus populations will increasingly require enormous resources to sustain their increasing consumption levels. This is bound to position them more often competitively than cooperatively. Any cooperation experienced till date or in future are likely to be guided by expediency dictated by their own existential or developmental needs. For example, the cooperation at the Climate Change Conferences is aimed to sustain their economic developments driven by their rapid industrialization.

But change remains the only permanent reality in human universe. Engagement of NER with China may have been an oxymoron two decades ago but in the changed environment of globalization, without notice, India and China have expanded their economic partnership moving from trade to investments. It can be argued that in spite of heavy trading to the extent of China emerging as India's largest trading partner, the level of political trust between the two countries is yet to reach a level where India and China can engage each other on pure economic rationale. For example, while both the countries are trading in excess of $60 billion per year their mutual investment have remains negligible. China's investments in India have not reached one billion dollar though, in their 2014 New Delhi summit, China agreed to invest $20 billion in coming five years. Chinese cumulative investment in India from 2000 to March 2014 stands at $ 402.31 million (Ministry of Commerce and Industry, GoI 2014) and Indian investment in China is much lesser in percentage terms though it is slightly higher in absolute value.[10] There are either lot of restrictions on mutual investment plus there is lack of trust in each other. The latter is not a standalone impediment as both India and China are the largest growing economies of the world fairing much better than developed economies. While China prevents Indian investment into certain geographical regions on the pretext of sensitive regions, India blocks investment in some sectors on the pretext of sensitive sectors.

Economists from BCIM countries and outside have tried to drive home the complementary nature of Indian and Chinese economies and have inferred that such complementarities also exist within the BCIM region in terms of markets and resources – natural, financial, technical. Especially technological complementarities make the case for cooperation within BCIM very strong (Ravi Bhoothalingam, 2013; Debapriya. Bhattacharya, 2013; Chen Jidong, 2013; Prabir De, 2013, Nimmi Kurian, 2005; Rajen Singh Laishram, 2006; Kisan Rana and Patricia Oberoi 2012; Rahman, M., H. Rahman and W. Bin Shadat, 2007; De, P. and B. N. Bhattacharyay, 2007; Md. Tariqur Rahman and Muhammad Al Amin, 2009). Given NER's compulsion for engaging rising China, BCIM should look as an attractive proposition for India. But, the fact that China's initiatives in the arrangement are viewed as proactive and India is alleged to be the spoilsport in the entire process creates complications. Such diagnosis is based on the Neo-liberal Institutional understanding of regional cooperative arrangements that there is a convergence of interest of BCIM countries in making the sub-region economically integrated. Such an analysis is based on the understanding that the states active in a particular issue-area must share common interests that can be attained only through functional cooperation.

One cannot say that Indian policy makers are unaware of the potential of functional cooperation turning this area into economically prosperous region. But still India chooses to go slow and remain cautious given its persistent security concerns. The address of the India's former Secretary (East) in Ministry of External Affairs, Mr. Rajiv Sikri, encapsulates India's approach (Sikri, 2006).[11] He clearly spelt out that the Indian government is against structuralizing BCIM. At the same time he calls upon the Forum to come up with economically viable specific projects for the region which will allow mutual confidence to grow step by step. In his own words, he proudly discussed the achievement of India engaging the other nations through various other Forums.

Why then is India against any structural arrangement of BCIM?

A reading between the lines of Mr. Sikri's address clearly reveals the official mindset. These apprehensions are directly related to non-economic issues that bother India vis-à-vis China. Some worries on the economic front were visible in his address. His stress on economic viability of the specific projects is indicative of the fact that India does not wish to lose control of the economic situation in the region.

The fear is of a loss in relative terms to China at least during the initial years of engagement. China is certainly going to gain more from the BCIM arrangement by dint of its stable political situation, expertise in infrastructure building, construction and manufacturing, larger scale of economy and a controlled wage structure. Given the fragile peaceful relationship India has managed to have with China, the intermittent flare-ups on contentious border issues, and China's claims over Arunachal, it is natural that India apprehends trouble its policy makers. What is shown as the economic threat is actually not the real threat perceived by the Indian policy makers. It is believed that in the event of economic integration, the goods from China would flood the markets of India's NER. This, at best, is a symptomatic expression of the real fear.

There is no study available to calculate the relative payoffs of China and India from economic arrangements under BCIM-EC, but the present advantages of China over India in terms of preparedness for availing of economic opportunities is jittery enough for India to apprehend that in the event of economic integration of the region, the total control of the regional economy would be at the Chinese hands. At present, Southwest China is already not as poor as India's Northeast and has more industries, and once the region opens up in terms of connectivity to the sea and to larger markets through Myanmar, India and Bangladesh, this region of China will experience rapid industrialization. But the same cannot be said about India's NER. Given the advantages mentioned above, Southwest China may offer itself as the best destination for establishing industries. These industries are to be built on the resources of the region, i.e. Myanmar, Bangladesh and India's NER. The NER is feared to become a perpetual periphery to China (Yunnan) production centers. India feels to be gaining less in comparison to China from the region's economic integration. Moreover, if this happens, the only rationale for India to be part of BCIM, i.e. developing NER, will probably be lost forever. Such risks for the future of NER must be avoided and caution must be taken to ensure that NER must not be allowed to engage with China from such vulnerable position.

Such a possibility, under present circumstances, is disincentive enough for India to become unconditionally interested in BCIM-EC arrangements. On an earlier occasion, Mr. Rajiv Sikri had expressed the hope of travelling from Kolkata or Guwahati to Bangkok through Dhaka or Yangon. Interesting to find out that China or her Southwest provinces did not figure in Mr. Sikri's scheme of things. Such exclusion seemed intentional, and points to the fact that India is not comfortable with the idea of directly engaging China within any multilateral arrangement. It is the notion of space that forces India to keep away China from regional arrangements wherein India feels it may be proved to be a lesser player vis-à-vis China. Second important economic worry for India is the possibility of Northeast India developing a patron-client relationship with Southwest China. This apprehension of relative loss becomes alarming in its possible political spin-offs. Considering the fact that both India and China are going to remain juxtaposed as a competing pair, there may be chances of the unresolved issues flaring up and escalating time and again. In those times a dependent India may not be in a position to negotiate or deal with China from a position of strength. One can now connect with why India has been reluctant to operationalise the BCIM.

What are the Disincentives?

Apart from the relative gain calculations with China and the fear of losing a position of strength in any future eventuality with China, there also exist some practical worries in Indian minds that count heavily when India considers its option of opening up NER to the neighbours. The other, rather contiguous neighbour is Myanmar. Myanmar itself is going through an unpredictable phase of transition to democratic reforms and, in any case, the writ of the central government of Myanmar seems to be limited to some parts of Myanmar leaving large parts of the border provinces in the hands of the ethnic minorities. It is only to India's concerns that some of these ethnic minorities are in collusion with Indian insurgents and provide them shelter inside Myanmar and within their stronghold areas. One cannot be sure whether freer interaction among people from both the sides will further strengthen the insurgency movements or reduce them. The concerns turn anxious when Myanmar seems struggling to find a rapprochement among the ethnic communities; some of whom are heavily armed. Continuous seizure of arms with Chinese markings indicates towards the existence of a well-oiled network of underground (non-state) actors in the region. The story of smuggled arms reaching NER is not new. Developments like the Wa (called the Speed Tribe) State Army actively manufacturing and circulating legitimate or illegitimate Chinese guns along with lethal methamphetamines cause shiver in the spine thinking of the consequences. For instance, as one of the first manifestations of the consequences of the speedy effects of Methamphetamines is the threat of extinction to the traditional opium consuming Shangpo tribe of India's Arunachal Pradesh.

Even economically dealing with Myanmar has emerged more as a concern than an opportunity. The border trade agreement between India and Myanmar was signed in January 1994 and came into force in April 1995. With the opening of a cross border trade point between Moreh

(Manipur, India) and Tamu (Sagaing Division, Myanmar) the volume of trade through this pass had looked encouraging initially but it slowly went down (*See Figure 1*). In 1996-97, the volume of border trade amounted to Rupees 31 crore of Indian exports of and 15 crore of imports. This figure declined to the level of Rupees 5 crore in export and import by the year 2004-5 (Kuppuswami, 2006). The available data (for 2010-11) on border trade at Moreh puts the volume of both way trade at Rupees 4.06 crore.[12] This is in contrast to the overall increase in bilateral trade between the two countries. The possible reasons for such decline in the official volume of border trade can be presence of insurgents in both sides of the border and more importantly the insurgents taking over the trading activities and running a parallel trade in both legal and illegal items. Whatever may be the reason, the net result is that the border trade is not helping the local community in NER for whom it was primarily initiated. Rather it is contributing to the strength of the insurgent groups as evident from the increasing insurgency activities in NER during this period. There has been a constant rise in the insurgency related incidents in the state of Manipur during the period corresponding border trade. It has been argued that with development of the local economy, there would be enough in the mainstream to lure the underworld (insurgents) to abjure their current occupation. But at this point in time the risks appear to be far bigger than the prospects.

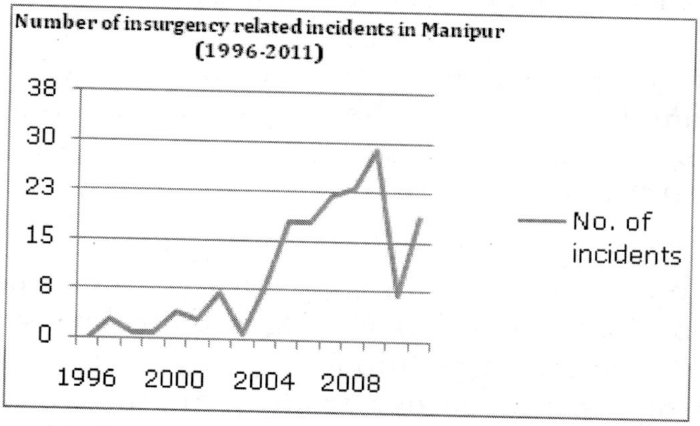

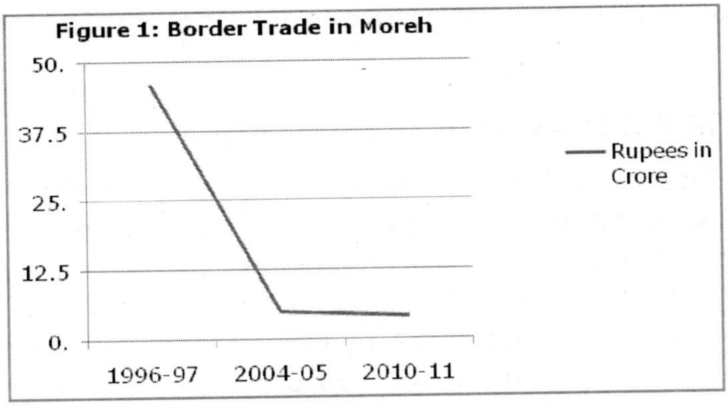

Source: Institute of Conflict Management (http://www.satp.org/satporgtp/countries/india/states/manipur/data_sheets/majorincidents.htm)

Similarly the worries of NER vis-à-vis Bangladesh have also been far more than the expected benefits. The illegal migration of Bangladeshi population into India has been a thorny issue in Indo-Bangladesh relations. The fundamentalist forces inside Bangladesh coupled with issue of illegal migration has made India so cautious that it often contemplates withdrawing some of the lenient provisions of the existing Indo-Bangladesh visa arrangement.[13] States in NER like Assam are scared about the possibility of change in the demographic features of the NER due to the influx of people from Bangladesh. Apprehensions about this trend have been increasing with liberal interactions. In the case of illegal migration, Myanmar and Bangladesh have been posing a combined threat. The Rohingya issue has taken crisis proportion in Myanmar and has a chain effect on India. India now wakes up to the possibility of around half a million displaced Rohingyas from Myanmar and Bangladesh heading towards India.[14] While there is great sympathy for homeless people everywhere, one cannot be oblivious to the possibility of these stateless population bearing no allegiance to any nation-state can, or can be used to, cause an additional internal stir in India. Looking at the bleak future of a harmonious ethnic arrangement in Myanmar wherein Rohingyas will be accommodated; and the unwillingness on the part of Bangladesh to entertain them does not promise anything better either for the Rohingyas or for India.

Is BCIM-EC Desirable at this Time?

If there are still so many disincentives with regards to the BCIM, should India go for such BCIM-EC arrangement? On close scrutiny, it would reveal that it may look all pessimistic about BCIM-EC but there is also a requirement for encouraging such arrangements if India's NER is to develop. The paradigmatic approach that Government of India has adopted towards NER has failed the bring about development in the region. In this context of economic compulsion, one needs to think what BCIM-EC offers for India. It is true that the potential of BCIM-EC for NER's development cannot be ignored. Engagement with the rising Chinese economy promises to provide India's NER much larger scales and markets whereas engagement with Bangladesh and Myanmar are likely to add complementary resources as also an opening to the seas, lack of which is always considered a hindrance to the NER's development. But the predicament remains as to how to deal with rising China that might benefit much more than India considering the advantages China enjoys in terms of economic preparedness. A model that was prescribed to reduce tensions between the former superpowers in their nuclear faceoff during early years of the Cold War can be improvised and presented to both – and to India in particular – to deal with this predicament of mistrust and to ensure positive results and to minimise both strategic and economic risks.

Charles Osgood had proposed a model called Graduated Reciprocation in Tension-reduction (GRIT) where mutually suspicious nuclear rivals were advised to initiate a chain of luring cooperative unilateral measures towards reduction of nuclear arsenals (Osgood, 1962). These carefully calibrated unilateral measures were expected to reduce trust-deficit and build confidence about the benign nature of the offers being made by the adversary. With each initiative in the chain having some advantages to offer to the other party, one can expect the other party to realize the benefits of cooperation and would reciprocate to initiatives with initiatives that would lead towards reduction of tension between the parties without risking own security. This can be modified to be applicable to the economic engagement between India and China. Since India is the reluctant party to the BCIM-EC arrangement, the other important party to the arrangement, i.e. China must initiate a chain of lucrative initiatives inviting India to respond. In practice China must demonstrate the intension of seriously engaging India by inviting investments in sectors where India is stronger, such as pharmaceuticals, IT and the IT related service sectors. As the other initiative in the chain, China can provide easy (preferential) market access to Indian goods. Since India's NER is resource rich but infrastructure deficient, no economic arrangement should be proposed that would look extractive to the NER population.

BCIM-EC and NER

While these are some the initiatives China can take, India should also formulate her own initiatives from her position of strength that are luring enough to China. In practical terms cooperation primarily with China and the other BCIM-EC countries must be incremental in nature. India must assess the present potential of Eastern India's (including NER) economy. It is true that NER is industrially not developed at all but still there are some sectors that can unleash the potential of NER economy if opportunities provided by the Chinese economy are tapped. Therefore, engagement of India's NER with China must begin in a graduated manner - incrementally and sector-wise. The NER must also be seen as part of the larger India-China economic engagement maximizing on NER's strengths, confidence and requirements. The economy of NER is much weaker than the economy of Yunnan but there are certain sectors where the NER states can negotiate from a position of strength.

One way that India can ignite an economic dynamism in NER is by providing it with real opportunities of encashing on its relative advantages in tourism, handicraft, horticulture, non-timber forest produce, etc. Of late, without any government intervention, healthcare services in parts of NER are proving to be a success. The talent of NER youth in IT sector is well acknowledged. Based on these advantages that India's NER has vis-à-vis China's Yunnan, India can initiate the process of limited economic engagements with China and subsequently expand the scope to include the other economies in the arrangement. For example during the 9th meeting of the Kolkata to Kunming (K2K) Forum[15] held in November 2013 in Kolkata, the state of Tripura expressed that if Tripura can get Chinese technology in the bamboo sector and market access for bamboo products from India that can contribute tremendously to the economy of Tripura. Similar optimism exudes from other NER states about the prospects of engaging with China. Based on such advantages, if NER is gradually welcomed to get involved in the India-China bilateral first and subsequently BCIM-EC level interactions, the dormant economy of NER is likely to gain fresh momentum. If this dynamism initiates an economic stream like a rivulet, tributaries and distributaries of economic activities can be generated to expand the rivulet and further economic development can be effected with Indian economic intervention and other initiatives like BIMST-EC. An economic rationale can emerge in matters of time, not so distant in future, to invest further in the infrastructure and to improve connectivity within NER and expand it within the region.

China may not be much concerned about economic vulnerabilities vis-à-vis India's NER economy or the economies of Bangladesh and Myanmar but others in the BCIM-EC arrangement, viz. Bangladesh, Myanmar and particularly NER have vulnerabilities that run the risk of being exploited to the advantage of China. Therefore, beginning with the limited engagements has the advantage of not risking the vulnerabilities that exist in the economy of NER. The anxiety of losing out to China in a relative gain calculation can be moderated by the fact that the initial engagements will be from India's position of strength and will ensure higher relative gains to India than to China. NER states have certain advantages in several specific sectors.

To be specific, for instance, Arunachal Pradesh has a strong potential in the field of agro-products. Rice, wheat, maize, millet and pulses are grown under food crop, besides, black pepper, large cardamom, oil seeds, potato, zinger, turmeric, chillies, sugarcane, tea, fresh vegetables and other horticulture product like pine apple, citrus fruits, apple, walnut, passion fruits, also grown as commercial crop products. These items have a ready-made large market in China. Other potential areas of Arunachal Pradesh are cane and bamboo. Similarly the agro climatic condition of Assam is ideal for the cultivation of spices, mushrooms, broccoli, bamboo shoots and other vegetables. More than 8 per cent of India's total spices is produced in Assam alone and about 60 per cent of India's ginger is produced in Assam. Another potential area is orchids. Out of 925 verities available in India, as many as over 600 verities are grown in Assam because of favourable climatic conditions. About 200 verities of orchids produced in the state are unique and ornamental in nature. These products can easily make their way into the Yunnan market that is fast developing an appetite for such items. Rare herbs of Assam are the other important products of Assam. Horticulture items like ginger, turmeric, orange, pineapple and banana are grown in large quantities in Meghalaya. In fact some of those products are produced over and above local demand. Surplus quantities are exported to other Indian states or to Bangladesh. For example 80 per cent turmeric produce in Meghalaya is marketable surplus and need right market destinations. The turmeric produce in Lakadong village of Meghalaya is the best turmeric in the world. But due to non-use of technology in processing and preserving these products the full potential of these products in contributing to the economy remains sub-optimal.

Along with horticulture and floriculture in which Mizoram has similar potentials as the other NER states, it has handlooms and handicrafts. A good volume of handloom products and woolen products are produced in Mizoram states, but the production is not very well organized. As a result, the producers don't get proper price. Linking these products to a growing market like China can turn this into a major sector contributing to Mizoram's and thus NER's economy. Tripura is the second largest producer of natural rubber in the country after Kerala and produces almost 37,200 MT per annum. About 57000 small growers are engaged in the production of natural rubber covering an area of 62,000 hectors. The production level of natural rubber is expected to double by 2020. The natural rubber is a raw material for more than 50,000 products and therefore there exist good opportunity to develop rubber based industries in Tripura. Along with Assam, Tripura is a major tea growing states and the black tea of India is slowly catching up to the Chinese tea in China itself. Thus, tea is a potential tradable item for Tripura along with cane and bamboo products. Tripura produces large quantities of quality cane and bamboo. Handicrafts on these raw materials certainly have high market potential in China and subsequently in the whole BCIM-EC region. This list of items is in no way exhaustive and there are huge reserve of natural resources upon which environment friendly industrial ventures can be built to cater to the nearby Chinese market and in a later stage to the BCIM-EC.

China of course will gain in absolute terms from its engagement with NER in these specific sectors. Keeping in mind the ultimate goal of achieving an, at par, developed economic neighbourhood, China can allow such incremental process to continue till the sector specific limited engagements spills over to cover all sectors that are complementary between Southwest China and India's NER to begin with. Only later they can cover the entire BCIM-EC region involving all four member states in total. Only with a vibrant economy in India's NER will emerges any full implementation of the idea of BCIM-EC. The other advantage of this incremental and select sectoral process is its graduated nature that allows slowly deepening and expanding their engagement; building on the success of the limited engagements while retaining the flexibility of arresting any negative spin-off that might emerge during the initial limited engagement.

Conclusion

In the present global, regional and bilateral set ups it is difficult to imagine that India and China will soon embrace each other and would agree to open and unregulated economic engagement. Thus, the establishment of the BCIM-EC is an ambitious long-term objective and both the countries – and India in particular – show enough political will to at least start limited and graduated economic engagement. The compulsion of developing India's NER provides New Delhi with the rationale of engaging China's Yunnan to begin with and only later expanding it to Myanmar and Bangladesh. The concerns related to insurgency in NER are yet to reduce. The dilemma of security first or development first is yet to be resolved. Added to the Indian dilemma, there are uncertainties regarding the political developments within Myanmar. The ceasefire agreements, between the former military rulers and the various ethnic groups, on which the domestic peace of Myanmar hinge, remain very fragile. An acceptable arrangement for harmonious cohabitation of all ethnic groups in Myanmar still remains elusive. In one of the likely events of Myanmar's political transition not managing a harmonious ethnic accommodation, the spin offs of the trouble will definitely have an adverse impact on the economy and society of India's NER. The political situation in Bangladesh is also far from stable and it can relapse into a political chaos at any point putting any regional arrangement into risk.

The proposed idea of a BCIM-EC may not prove to be a panacea of all the problems of the region; but in any analysis not having economic engagements will not help either. Mutual distrust that is perceived to be there will only deepen in the absence of mutual interactions. In any informed calculation of the pay offs for India from BCIM-EC, incrementally, the economic gains would gradually outweigh the strategic fears around BCIM-EC. Finally, there are even economic compulsions and political will on both sides have to appreciate that part. BCIM-EC arrangements have to face the hurdle of the old but persisting non-economic issues between India and China. For example The Idea BCIM-EC will soon run into the issue of boundary and territory. The status of Arunachal will be a contention in any engagement involving China's Yunnan and India's NER. India cannot have a conception of NER excluding Arunachal Pradesh. Can, and will India agree to engage China within BCIM-EC arrangement keeping Arunachal outside the arrangement? Probably there is no easy solution to such long-standing questions at this moment but prudence would demand both China and India to lead interacts respecting the geopolitical status quo of the region till we develop enough mutual trust to settle the persisting differences on border.

References

Brian Eyler, "A Quick Glance at Yunnan's 2013 GDP," http://www.eastbysoutheast.com/quick-glance-at-yunnans-2013-gdp/

C. S. Kuppuswami, "Indo-Myanmar Relations – A Review," Paper No. 2043, South Asia Analysis Group, November 30, 2006, p.3.

Charles E. Osgood, An Alternative To War Or Surrender, Urbana: University of Illinois Press, 1962.

Keith Bradsher, "Growth Rose 7.4% in First Quarter, China Reports," The New York Times, April 15, 2014.

Ministry of Commerce and Industry, GoI, http://dipp.nic.in , 2014

Rajiv Sikri, Secretary (East), at the 6th Bangladesh-China-India-Myanmar Forum, New Delhi, March 30, 2006, http://www.mea.gov.in/press-releases.htm?dtl/2157/Address+by+Mr+Rajiv+Sikri+Secretary+East+at+the+6th+Bangladesh ChinaIndiaMyanmar+Forum+New+Delhi

TUSIAD report, 2012, http://www.tusiad.org/__rsc/shared/file/India-investment-in-China.pdf

Li Jun, China for peaceful, prosperous and open Asia, Address to BIISS, Dhaka, 23 April 2014, http://bdnews24.com/economy/2014/04/23/china-for-peaceful-prosperous-and-open-asia-li-jun

Marie Lall, "Indo-Myanmar Relations in the Era of Pipeline Diplomacy," Contemporary Southeast Asia, Vol. 28, No. 3 (2006), pp. 424–46.

Rahman, M., H. Rahman and W. Bin Shadat, "BCIM economic cooperation: Prospects and challenges", CPD Occasional Paper No. 64. Centre for Policy Dialogue, Dhaka, 2007.

De, P. and B. N. Bhattacharyay, "Deepening India-Bangladesh economic cooperation: Challenges and opportunities", RIS-DP#130. Research and Information System for Developing Countries, New Delhi, 2007.

Md. Tariqur Rahman and Muhammad Al Amin, Prospects of economic cooperation in the Bangladesh, China, India and Myanmar region: A quantitative assessment, Asia-Pacific Research and Training Network on Trade Working Paper Series, No. 73, July 2009, http://artnet.unescap.org/pub/wp7309.pdf

Bhattacharya, Debapriya. Reflections on Institutional Arrangement for Effective Cooperation among BCIM Countries.' Paper presented at the Eleventh International Conference on Regional Cooperation among Bangladesh, China, India and Myanmar (BCIM), http://www.cpd.org.bd/11_BCIM/Papers/Session%20IV_Institutional%20Arrangements%20for20Effective%20Cooperation/Debapriya%20Bhattacharya.pdf, 2013.

Bhoothalingam, Ravi, China and its Peripheries: Beijing and the BCIM. Institute of Peace and Conflict Studies (IPCS), New Delhi, Issue BriefNo. 216 (May 2013): IB216-Bhoothalingam-ChinaPeriphery-BCIM.pdf, 2013.

Chen Jidong, The BCIM Trade Corridor and its Development. In Tan Chung, Zhang Minqiu, & Ravni Thakur (eds), Across the Himalayan Gap: A Chinese Quest for Understanding India, pp. 321-331. New Delhi: India International Centre & Konark Publications, 2013.

De Prabir, Cooperation in the Areas of Trade, Investment and Finance: Challenges, Prospects and the Next Agenda.Paper presented at the Eleventh International Conference on Regional Economic Cooperation among Bangladesh, China, India and Myanmar (BCIM), http://www.cpd.org.bd/11_BCIM/Papers/Session%20I_Cooperation%20in%20the%20Areas%20of%20Trade,%20Investment%20and%20Finance/Prabir%20De.pdf, Dhaka, 23-24 February, 2013.

Kurian, Nimmi. 2005. Prospects for Sino-Indian Trans-border Economic Linkages, International Studies, vol. 42, nos. 3&4, pp. 295-306.

Laishram, Rajen Singh, The Kunming Initiative: Prospects for Sub-regional Cooperation, The Asian Scholar (Bangkok), No. 3, http://www.asianscholarship.org/asf/ejourn/articles/rajen_sl.pdf , 2006.

Rana Kisan & Patricia Uberoi. India's North East States, the BCIM Forum and Regional Integration. Delhi: Institute of Chinese Studies, Monograph No 1, 2012.

Robert O. Keohane, Power and Governance in a Partially Globalized World, London and New York: Routledge, 2004.

Peter Liberman, "Trading with the Enemy: Security and Relative Economic Gains, International Security, vol. 21, no. 1, Summer 1996, pp. 147-75.

Joseph M. Grieco, Cooperation among Nations: America and Non-tariff Barriers to Trade, Ithaca, New York: Cornell University Press, 1990.

Endnotes

1. Author is Director, Center for Studies in International Relations and Development (CSIRD), Kolkata, West Bengal, India. Email: bkmishra27@gmail.com
2. During an interaction with this author on 13 August 2013, Mr. Gautam Bambawale, the then Joint Secretary (East Asia) of ministry of External Affairs made this point that the idea of BCIM-EC was conceptualized by Prof. Ren Jia of the Yunnan Academy of Social Sciences.
3. Though the BCIM idea originated in 1999, India did not show enough enthusiasm as evident from the fact that the BCIM Forum was always attended by government representatives from China, Bangladesh and Myanmar whereas India did not send any government representatives to the Forum. It was only in the year 2012 that Indian Government representatives actively facilitated the organization of the Forum in Kolkata.
4. Joint Statement: "A vision for future development of India-China strategic and cooperative partnership" (accessed on 24th September 2014) available at http://mea.gov.in/bilateral-documents.htm?dtl/22379/Joint+Statement+A+vision+for+future+development+of+IndiaChina+strategic+and+cooperative+partnership
5. Though allowing border provinces of the Chinese hinterland is a preferred strategy to encourage development in the border

provinces it is not uniformly applied to all the border provinces. For example, the autonomy granted to Yunnan province to interact with the neighbouring countries is not granted to Tibet or to Xinjiang.

6. In July 2009, during President Hu Jintao's visit to Yunnan, he articulated the idea of making Yunnan the 'Bridgehead' towards southwest opening up. http://www.blekinge-yunnan.org/ENGLISH/124.html

7. The idea that BCIM is part of China's objective of promoting peaceful neighbourhood which has been pronounced from time to time at various levels of Chinese policy makers. The most recent was remark of the Chinese Ambassador to Bangladesh who during his address to Bangladesh Institute of International and Strategic Studies (BIISS) on 23 April 2014. http://bdnews24.com/economy/2014/04/23/china-for-peaceful-prosperous-and-open-asia-li-jun

8. This year he Chinese economy is growing at 7.4 per cent as reported for the first quarter of 2014. See, Keith Bradsher, "Growth Rose 7.4% in First Quarter, China Reports," The New York Times, April 15, 2014. The current growth rate of Yunnan is claimed to be 11 per cent as claimed by the Governor of Yunnan during an interaction with this author on March 28, 2014 at Raj Bhawan, West Bengal, India.

9. After Bangladesh refused transit, India explored the feasibility of transporting the gas through NER but "the pipeline bypassing Bangladesh would have to be 40 per cent longer and cost around US$3 billion." (Marie Lall 2006).

10. The current figure for Indian investment in China is not available but according to the TUSIAD report of 2012 Indian investment in China was $240.81 Million. http://www.tusiad.org/__rsc/shared/file/India-investment-in-China.pdf

11. Address by Mr. Rajiv Sikri, Secretary (East), at the 6th Bangladesh-China-India-Myanmar Forum, New Delhi, March 30, 2006, (accessed on 25 September 2014) at http://www.mea.gov.in/press-releases.htm?dtl/2157/Address+by+Mr+Rajiv+Sikri+Secretary+East+at+the+6th+Bangladesh ChinaIndiaMyanmar+Forum+New+Delhi

12. Central Board of Excise & Customs, Department of Revenue, Govt. of India, http://mdoner.gov.in/content/border-trade#b

13. There were plenty of media speculation before the visit of Indian External Affairs Minister Smt. Sushma Swaraj's visit to Bangladesh that India would impose visa restriction. The

speculations were based on the new Indian Government's electoral commitment to curb illegal migration of Bangladeshis into India. Though no restrictions were imposed during the visit there were resentments from bordering state Assam for not toughening the visa regime vis-à-vis Bangladesh. See, "Assam rejects revised visa-relief proposal", http://timesofindia.indiatimes.com/city/guwahati/Assam-rejects-revised-visa-relief-proposal/articleshow/36996357.cms

14. There are around 5,00,000 Rohingyas in Myanmar and Bangladesh. Given the persecution they suffer in Myanmar and they being not acceptable in Bangladesh, their migration to India is constantly rising.

15. The K2K Forum (Kolkata to Kunming) originating in 2002, is the only civilian initiative between India and China at the provincial level. The Forum facilitates economic, cultural and academic engagements between Southwest of China and Eastern provinces of India.

5

Institutionalising BCIM Sub-Regional Cooperation

Liu Peng

In year 2013, BCIM forum made a significant progress: it was lifted from track two to track one level with all four countries — Bangladesh, China, India, Myanmar — not just coming on board but also agreeing to set up an Economic Corridor as their top priority. From the perspective of institutionalism or institutionalisation of the BCIM sub-regional cooperation it was seen as a major breakthrough yet nothing much has changed after this upgrading. The BCIM cooperation remains still mainly a platform for dialogue and the only change is that of the participants of its dialogues have changed from think tanks and academics to government officials and agencies. BCIM was been lifted from track two to track one cooperation after long drawn efforts of nearly 15 years to promote the institutionalisation of BCIM sub-regional cooperation. But as of not it seems more like a pipe dream without any consensus on what should be the next step of BCIM ensure continuity and acceleration in BCIM initiatives.

It is not that BCIM countries have had no experience in either sub-regional cooperation or in institution building as all of these have been important members of various regional and global organisation and regimes. These international regimes are not only the achievements and main manifestation pattern of the regional and sub-regional cooperation, but also provide an important impetus to promote the regional and sub-regional cooperation. International regimes, created cooperatively by sovereign states, are subject to all these sovereign states, thought relatively independent. So the international regimes have an important role in guaranteeing the continuity and stability of regional cooperation. This paper seeks to examine the evolving contours of the current institutions in BCIM Cooperation to figure out its strength and weakness as also to explore what needs to be done to achieve further institutionalisation of the BCIM cooperation. This paper will also analyse respective perceptions of the four BCIM countries with regards to the process of institutionalisation of BCIM and examine the validity of various roadmap for institutionalisation have been suggested from various perspectives.

Sub-Regional Cooperation Redefined

To begin with, the BCIM-Economic Corridor has been conceptualised as a mechanism resulting from a blending combination of both geography and economy. According to the definition of the Asian Development Bank, Economic Corridor seeks to connect the economic bodies within a certain region; it can also connect the economic centres from different regions. After the concept of Economic Corridor was formulated, it has been widely used not only in the domestic economic development discourse, such as the Yangtze Economic Corridor, or Xiang River Economic Corridor, but also in international economic cooperation processes like the East-West Economic Corridor (EWEC) proposed under the framework of GMS cooperation. Economic Corridor is an attempt to realise the economic connections among several geographically-connected areas and important economic nodes, to realise the regional economic development through building of economic integration. Similarly, to define sub-regional cooperation, especially in case of BCIM, it first appeared as the regional economic cooperation. Sub-regional cooperation means the cooperation pushed through agreements by those governments between adjacent geographical regions from adjacent three or more than three countries. It involves comprehensive cooperation in economic, political, environmental, health, safety and other fields.[1]

From the analysis it seems that Economic Corridor and Sub-regional Cooperation are two concepts with certain intersection but referring to the different ranges as their core spheres. The scope covered by the Sub-regional Cooperation is far more widespread, and if Economic Corridor is implemented within the Sub-regional range, then the Economic Corridor will become one of the ways to promote Sub-regional Cooperation paradigm. This line of argument is especially apt for the BCIM-Economic Corridor which is one of the mechanisms for building BCIM sub-regional cooperation. Therefore, any examination of BCIM Economic Corridor must begin with a proper study of the Sub-regional Cooperation paradigm.

International regimes or international institutions refer to a series of clear arrangements reached by international actors through negotiations to stipulate, prohibit or authorise themselves with regard to certain defined initiatives.[2] International organisations, therefore, flow from international agreements that constitute the main core defining the nature, scope, structures and functions of international regimes. The intertwining nature of the relationship between international cooperation and international regimes therefore has remains central to the study of international relations. Robert Keohane points out in his *After Hegemony: Cooperation and Discord in the World Political Economy* that the international regimes play an important role in reducing transaction costs, shaping behaviour expectation, reducing the cooperation betrayal, etc. which is also the key factor for the continuous international cooperation in the absence of hegemonic power in the international environment. Therefore, not only do we need to discuss the institutionalisation of BCIM Economic Corridor, but also the institutionalisation of BCIM sub-regional cooperation. The institutionalisation of BCIM sub-regional cooperation remain therefore a prerequisite of great significance to enhance the level of this regional cooperation, and to ensure its efficacy and sustainability.

Literature Review on International Regimes

Another well-known scholar in the field of International Regime building, John Ruggie introduced international regimes into the domain of international relations for the first time in 1975. International regimes have since become one of the most often used concepts in understanding cooperation and conflict in international relations. But apart from these western experts, Chinese scholars have also elucidated their understanding of international regimes. Almost all Chinese scholars Qin Yaqing, Su Changhe, Wang Yizhou, Men Honghua etc. have published various papers and books on this theme. In the beginning, various Chinese scholars mainly translated the related works of foreign scholars. In 1999, however, Liu Jian published his book Order *Reconstruction: the International Regimes of the Era of Economic Globalization*. He was followed in 2000, by Su Changhe publishing a monograph *Global Public Issues and International Cooperation: an Analysis of System*. Their works showed that China's home-grown scholars had started changing frcm introducing the international regimes theory into laying equal stress on the introduction and independent innovation into regime building. At present the main object of China's indigenous scholarship on international regimes theory is largely driven by neo-liberalism in international regimes theory, which is used to analyse East Asian regional cooperation, China's foreign policy and China's international organisational diplomacy etc, and the research studies in these areas has also gained a large amount of traction in the field.

Most experts of the international regimes theory consider the founding of regimes as the starting point for international cooperation. This discourse is mainly divided into two schools namely, Normative Institutionalism and

Rational Choice Institutionalism. The former attaches importance to the normative role, and believes that institution is a result of social construction, especially during the cohering and forming process of social consensus. The consensus of the international community constitutes a reason for the generation of international regimes. The Rational Choice Institutionalism, on the other hand, takes example by the theories of economics, considering that regimes are generated to reduce transaction costs and promote the realisation of their own interests in the international society in the absence of government. The see generation of international regimes as the result of rational choice of state actors. These two major schools essentially underline two core issues of international regimes, namely the effectiveness and validity of international regimes. The issue about the effectiveness is the impact of international regimes in the international community, particularly in promoting the international cooperation; the issue about the validity is their legitimacy. In fact, the effectiveness and legitimacy of international regimes constitutes a measure standard for international regimes.

In current study that seeks to place BCIM-Economic Corridor in the genre of building international regimes, it seeks to underline how academia has basically reached a consensus about the first step of agreeing on the universal importance of international regimes. However, the current studies of international regimes theory are also undergoing a paradigm shift and thus moving from only studying the importance of international regimes to studying how to construct a reasonable and effective international regime. This is also the core issue that this chapter seeks to address, that is, how to evolve the institutionalisation of BCIM sub-regional cooperation and how to build a more effective and higher institutionalised sub-regional mechanisms like the Economic Corridor to make BCIM effective.

Existing System of BCIM Sub-regional Cooperation

(i) The Development Course

The BCIM cooperation mechanism is a dialogue platform that was initially launched by Chinese and Indian think tanks. In August 1999, Yunnan Academy of Social Sciences and Economic and Technological Research Centre of Yunnan Province had sponsored the "BCIM Regional Economic Cooperation and Development Conference" that was held in Kunming. The conference had issued the *Kunming Initiative* document. This conference is therefore seem to mark the beginning of the journey of the BCIM cooperation. This was the mechanism basically to sustain a dialogue by holding a conference every year. In 2000, the second "BCIM Regional Economic Cooperation and Development Conference" was held in Delhi. In 2002, the third conference held in Dhaka where these ad hoc conferring activity was formally named the "BCIM Regional Economic Cooperation Forum", and participants also issued the *Dhaka Declaration*, appealing to all governments to support this mechanism, and asking them to raise the current cooperation mechanism from the "track two" to "track one" level amongst governmental agencies. Then the subsequent forums were hosted in turn by the Bangladesh, China, India and Myanmar, and had issued *Statement of the 4th Conference (Yangon)* (2003), *Kunming Cooperation Statement (2004), Delhi Declaration* (2006), *Dhaka Declaration* (2007), *Naypyidaw Declaration* (2009), and *Joint Statement on Promoting BCIM Regional cooperation* (2011) and so on. Since this 9th conference in 2011, *BCIM Regional Economic Cooperation Forum* was again renamed as *BCIM Regional Cooperation Forum.* In 2012, the 10th conference was held in Kolkatta (India) and it issued the *Joint Statement (Calcutta).* In 2013, the 11th conference of BCIM Regional Cooperation Forum was held in Dhaka Bangladesh, and issued the *Joint Statement of the 11th Conference of BCIM Regional Cooperation Forum.* All this shows the continuity that was maintained by BCIM stakeholders to sustain their efforts that finally made all governments formally recognise this initiative.

(ii) Main Achievements

(a) Shift from Track-2 to Track-1

The most significant achievement of Kunming Initiative and its follow-up conference was it formal cooption by all four governments. Sine the BCIM cooperation mechanism was proposed first in a conference in New Delhi in 1998 and the first conference was held in 1999 in Kunming, the idea had stayed at Track-2 level. It was mainly promoted and led by think tanks and semi-official organisations. Among these four countries participating in the BCIM cooperation mechanism, China put the most efforts into the operation to sustain and develop this mechanism, which was promoted and led mainly by the local government of Yunnan province which was to become the Secretariat of BCIM. From all those participating in the conferences of cooperation mechanism, Myanmar was the first State to bring on board its official representatives who were authorised to participate in this conferences. It was Ministry of Foreign Affairs of the federal government of Myanmar that had formally participated in all these aforementioned conferences. The Center for Policy Dialogue represented Bangladesh and brought on board several formal officials into the leave of its participants into this mechanism. This ensured participation of high-level official representatives from Bangladesh that participating all 11 conferences of the BCIM. From India, those who attended these annual deliberations for building cooperation mechanisms were mainly two think tanks Institute for Chinese Studies and the Centre for Policy Research. Later there were still some other think tanks joined, such as Azad Institute of Asian Studies (Kolkatta); and there were few occasions when Indian side had officials attending these conferences. But on the whole, India's participants in this mechanism was mainly from Indian think-tank.

Since the 3rd conference of BCIM Regional Economic Cooperation Forum in 2002, all parties had begin to appeal to their respective governments to raise this platform from Track-2 to Track-1activity. Actually, these deliberation had gradually become a "quasi track one" cooperation mechanism in the later period except for India that remains reluctant for long time. When Mr. Li Keqiang visited India in May 2013, he formally proposed the construction of BCIM-Economic Corridor, and again expressed his commitment towards building it during the follow-up visit to China by Prime Minister Manmohan Singh. China also established the BCIM economic corridor Working Group led by China's National Development and Reform Commission, and India also set up a corresponding working group. The 1st conference of BCIM-Economic Corridor Intergovernmental Working Group was held in Kunming in December 2013. It can be said that through 14 years efforts, in 2013, the BCIM cooperation mechanism had achieved the upgrade from the dialogue platform among think tanks to the cooperation mechanism among governments, competing the transition from track two to track one.

As a regional dialogue platform led by think-tanks of these four countries, the idea of creating a BCIM cooperation mechanism was put forward in 1998, the first conference was held in 1999, and this dialogue mechanism remained uninterrupted for 14 years, which is one of the greatest achievements of this forum. This uninterrupted running of dialogue platform cannot be separated from efforts the Yunnan Government. For China, the BCIM cooperation mechanism has been promoted and led by Yunnan Province from the date of its conception and founding. The relationship between the central and the local government in China's unitary regime and the competition between local governments make Yunnan Province have power to promote this mechanism which makes it to continue to play a greater role in this process. After the BCIM cooperation mechanism was upgraded to the BCIM Economic Corridor mechanism, the Yunnan Province still remains China's main force to lead the construction of this Economic Corridor project.

(b) Car Rally Was Held Successfully

Building connectivity amongst existing infrastructures of the four BCIM countries has been a major aim to achieve a break through in establishing BCIM cooperation mechanisms. Economic Corridor here is the basic framework of BCIM cooperation. From the beginning of the 3rd conference of BCIM Economic Cooperation Forum in 2002, its discussion always included focus on building connectivity. In their decade long deliberations, transportation infrastructure of Yunnan Province has been greatly improved. It basically formed today a model for all four countries' opening up of their existing infrastructure to the BCIM Economic Corridor thereby connecting Kunming to Ruili to Kyaukpyu; from Kunming to Hekou to Hanoi, and from Kunming to Tengchong to Myitkyina. Their highways, railways and other infrastructures have been gradually put in place and need to be connected. However, other than China, other three countries have not made great progress in infrastructure construction and regional connectivity. Also at present, all parties have different views in the orientation and the construction priority of BCIM connecting their existing highways.

Realising their existing domestic and bilateral difficulties in connecting their existing highways, the BCIM Economic Cooperation Forum has been actively encouraging some experimental work. One of these experiments was to carry out the BCIM car rally whose essence was to showcase a practical investigation of existing lines of BCIM road connectivity. After the initiative was proposed, and through five years preparation, in March 2013, the first BCIM car rally was finally organised. This was one of a few substantive projects in the BCIM cooperation mechanism that was formally put in place demonstrating both the possibility as also potential of connectivity in this region.

(c) Business Council Was Established

The 8th conference of BCIM Economic Cooperation Forum held in 2009 had recommended for the establishment of the BCIM Business Council. The 9th conference held in 2011 formally established the BCIM Business Council. The establishment of the Business Council was further expanded and enlarged the contents of BCIM cooperation mechanisms from the pure think-tanks dialogue platform to the pragmatic cooperation in economy and trade. This was first step to take BCIM deliberation beyond think-tanks and academics to business world and this is expected to greatly facilitated the process of materialising the BCIM cooperation mechanism. The setting up of this Council was surely a step forward in encouraging all four governments to also come forward to uplift this forum from Track-2 to Track-1 and is likely to continue to ensure further expansion and consolidation of BCIM cooperation mechanisms.

(iii) Existing Regimes of BCIM Cooperation

As mentioned above, the forms of international regimes are often bound around international organisations and international agreements. In addition to this, some more tangible or intangible principles, standards, rules etc.[3] are also included. According to this definition, although BCIM sub-regional cooperation exist in form of some international regimes in a certain sense yet, these regimes remain very weak. First of all, this regional cooperation doesn't have any international organisation or international organisation prototype to back it and ensure regularly in its institutionalisation. Also, it is not clear whether these four countries have any willingness to establish an international organisation for this region. Secondly, this region also does not have clear international agreement signed amongst these four countries' governments that defines both the objectives and process of building BCIM cooperation mechanisms. If BCIM sub-region has certain international regime, the pattern of this international regime is mainly the existence of a certain form of rules, that is, some broad consensuses on strengthening BCIM cooperation. The international regimes of BCIM sub-regional cooperation though are expected to be far more detailed, subtle and complex to design and develop various visible and invisible, informal rules into international agreements and international organisations.

From the perspective of participants, the existing regime of BCIM sub-regional cooperation can be divided into two categories. One is the think tanks of these four in the regional cooperation forum that have become its stakeholders since 1999; the other is these four intergovernmental work group conference that was started in 2013. Though the central governments of these four countries has expressed supportive attitude towards the Regional Cooperation Forum since its inception, this attitude in some countries is more substantive than others, and in some countries it is only symbolic. From the perspective of forum's positioning and the four-country organisations participating in the forum over one-and-half decade of deliberations, this forum remains essentially a Track-2 activity; informal, loose international regime. From the angle of international regimes, the biggest achievement of this Regional Cooperation Forum is that the BCIM Forum has not just met uninterruptedly but also created some elementary rules in its declarations adopted at each of its meetings and other statements issued after conferences that have emphasised shared understandings on principles. In spite of its limitations, these four have also allowed differing interpretation about the detailed contents of achieving common development through cooperation and it can also be said that this forum advocates an international cooperation principles for this region.

The Intergovernmental Work Group Conference of four countries is an apex forum in building BCIM regimes. The Intergovernmental Working Group Conference as the dialogue platform at the level of BCIM central governments. If these four countries can give this platform continuous support, this platform have the potential to reach an international agreement or develop into an international organisation. But at present, this dialogue platform just began, and the parties still have different opinions on whether or not to use the Working Group Conference. Their Talk have continued to be held in New Delhi, Kunming and Dhaka. The support and authorisation that the parties give their Talks is still facing uncertainty. Overall, the level of institutionalisation of the BCIM sub-regional cooperation still remains relatively low, without formal international organisation and international regime. The existing principles and rules are mainly reached by non-government level. It is still uncertain whether they can become the officially approved principles and rules.

Advantages and Challenges of BCIM

(i) Advantages of Current BCIM Mechanisms

(a) Flexibility

The current regime of BCIM sub-regional cooperation is composed of a semi-official forum and a fledgling Working Group Conference. The essential characteristic of this combination is informality. Being informal and semi-official just make this regime have great flexibility, which can guarantee that it is difficult to be influenced by fluctuating political relationships amongst these four countries, and give a large elasticity to this evolving regime. With regard of BCIM cooperation mechanisms, there exists a territorial dispute between China and India, and contradiction in trans-boundary rivers and territory between India and Bangladesh. With regard of present BCIM sub-regional cooperation, the advance of cooperation must rely on supports and authorisation by all four governments. The regime itself does not have any independence; especially the government-level cooperation dialogue is more susceptible to changing official equations. If the existing BCIM sub-regional cooperation mechanisms are entirely government-level dialogue platform or working group talk, once events like China-India 'tent confrontation' of April 2013 or other such unexpected event between India and Bangladesh occur, these governments may stop or quit from the government-level BCIM dialogue and talks, which will make the regime face the possibility of collapse.

In comparison to the Intergovernmental Working Group, BCIM Cooperation Forum of think-tanks has far great autonomy and flexibility. This is because Forum is a Track-2 level dialogue platform, the influence of changes of bilateral or multilateral relations on the forum is therefore limited. Even if bilateral relations become deteriorated, the Track-

2 level dialogue mechanism can still continue. Indeed, Track-2 is actually meant to ensure there is dialogue even when their governments stop talking and this is what makes the Forum mechanism have greater elasticity. Such a Forum therefore is very important for building cooperation between countries having significant differences. The regime can exist for a long time due to its semi-official properties. Under good bilateral or multilateral relations, countries can officially give greater support and authority to think tank dialogue platform, thus achieving the purpose of promoting cooperation. Conversely, under poor bilateral or multilateral relations, countries can officially reduce authorisation, but think tank dialogue platform won't stagnate because of this, thus ensuring the long lasting efficacy of such a regime.

(b) Openness

The BCIM sub-regional cooperation mechanism is the only multilateral cooperation mechanism for these four countries currently. Although the main topic of the mechanism at the beginning of the founding was the economic cooperation, currently the Economic Corridor that parties strive to promote is not just an economic issue. There is no denying that problems that this region face are not just economic, and economic cooperation can not solve all their problems. This regional cooperation mechanism must eventually include other issues in addition to economic issues. At present the BCIM regional cooperation forum, therefore, as an open forum. It has the possibility of incorporating other issues. In fact, in recent years the forum has not only covered economic issues, but also several non-traditional security, education, culture related issues have also been included in its deliberations. This openness and inclusiveness of mechanism provides a possibility that the international regime of BCIM cooperation can develop into a comprehensive one.

(ii) Challenges of the Existing BCIM Cooperation

(a) Prospect of BCIM Economic Corridor

The BCIM cooperation mechanism has undergone four names: 'China-India Myanmar-Bangladesh Regional Economic Cooperation and Development Conference', 'BCIM Regional Economic Cooperation Forum', 'BCIM Regional Cooperation Forum', 'BCIM Economic Corridor'. The transformation in nomenclature reflects the fact that the cooperation mechanism is not mature enough and is uncertain. After the BCIM cooperation mechanism transforms from an open forum and dialogue platform led by think tanks into BCIM Economic Corridor led by governments, all parties must answer a question: what is economic corridor or what is the vision of economic corridor? This will help in building consensus on what are the goals of this Economic Corridor, and what kind of economic cooperation mode is to be established. The goal of BCIM Economic Corridor should be to establish a Free Trade Area or quasi Free Trade Area or a regional international organisation. If the mode of wading across the stream by feeling the way serves as a progressive cooperation model in regions with strong cooperation willingness and good cooperative foundation, the applicability of this way will be poor in the BCIM region with poor cooperative foundations. The BCIM Economic Corridor therefore must begin by defining the goals and its corresponding paths at the beginning of its construction, so as to cohere consensus of all parties and promote the development of the Economic Corridor.

(b) Policy Uncertainty

The BCIM cooperation mechanism at present is in its initial and run-in stage after being upgraded into Track-1 Economic Corridor. At present, central and local governments of China are making efforts to promote the building of Economic Corridor. China's policy is to maintain stability. The attitude of India toward the BCIM cooperation mechanism has always had great uncertainty. Although Indian side had agreed to carry out the preliminary research of BCIM Economic Corridor during the visit of Premier Li

Keqiang to India in May 2013 and also during the October 2013 visit of Prime Minister Singh to China, the support of Indian government to the building of this Economic Corridor still faces great uncertainty. On the one hand, 2014 Indian election brought to power a new government of Bhartiya Janata Party (BJP), which after taking office is still not clear whether it wishes to continue to support this mechanism, On the other hand, even if the BJP government continues to support the building of BCIM Economic Corridor, the inefficiency of India government, and disputes between central government and each of the relevant provinces will make it difficult for Indian government to provide substantive support measures in the short term. Bangladesh has always had a positive attitude toward the BCIM cooperation mechanism. Considering their existing differences on many issues between Bangladesh and India, for Bangladesh, the Bangladesh-China-Myanmar Economic Corridor excluding India is an acceptable option. Before the democratic reform in Myanmar, Myanmar holds a more positive attitude toward the BCIM Economic Cooperation mechanism. However, after reform, it is not clear how Myanmar will treat this mechanism and whether the new government is going to be influenced by New Delhi.

(c) 'Myanmar Problem' in BCIM

For China, the node of BCIM cooperation mechanism is not India, but Myanmar. The BCIM cooperation mechanism, in addition to being a platform strengthening the cooperation between China and its southwest neighbouring countries, plays a more important role in realising China's opening to Indian Ocean rim, and to connect China's relatively closed southwest region with Indian Ocean. This makes China change from being 'one ocean country' to becoming a 'two oceans country'. Therefore, for China, especially for its Yunnan province, Myanmar is the key to the BCIM cooperation mechanism. For Yunnan province, without Myanmar participation, the BCIM mechanism basically has nothing to offer. Therefore, for China, the foremost concern in BCIM cooperation mechanism is Myanmar, and therefore

Myanmar's attitude is the key to determining the success or failure of the BCIM cooperation mechanisms.

(d) Difficulties of Connectivity

Connectivity does not only represent the fundamental basis of the BCIM economic cooperation, it also is the main attraction for Beijing. China holds a positive attitude towards building BCIM connectivity. China has basically completed the domestic construction of relevant sections of the highway and railway, and funded to construct part sections abroad, but the huge investment and risks in the infrastructure of interconnected overseas sections aren't what China could and should bear. India has done plenty of plans and constructions for the whole road network construction of its northeast region, but the construction process is slow. In addition, the whole road network construction in the northeast of India is 'internally-oriented', that is, at present India is mainly committed to realising the connection among the internal provinces of the northeastern India and among this region's main cities. India's considerations about the connectivity of BCIM region mainly focus on the domestic security. At present therefore India mainly holds a reluctant attitude. Bangladesh holds a positive attitude towards the realisation of connectivity, especially hopes to realise the connection between China, Myanmar and Bangladesh. Bangladesh, therefore, has made the preliminary planning, and has a certain foundation, but due to economic development and the attitude of Myanmar, the current progress has not been very impressive. Myanmar, again, remains the key junction for realising this BCIM connectivity, no matter whether it is the proposed south line, the middle line or the north line. Each of these three must pass through Myanmar. But Myanmar's relatively backward infrastructure, its increasing doubts about China and the promotion of democracy make Myanmar face uncertainty.

(e) Domestic Difficulties

The BCIM sub-regional cooperation mechanisms are not only facing problems of cooperation among countries.

This efforts are also facing problems with the process of domestic integration difficulties of each of these four countries. The geographical range of the BCIM sub-regional cooperation covers China's Yunnan, India's northeast region and West Bengal, the north regions of Myanmar and Bangladesh and all of these have been facing political uncertainties. All countries of this mechanism however can surpass these political and geographical limitations provided they arable to calibrate their complementaries.

Especially Yunnan, which is the major province of China participating in efforts for building BCIM sub-regional cooperation. China expects Yunnan to become the gateway of China's southwest region opening it to the outside world by participating in the BCIM cooperation mechanisms. However, other provinces in China's southwest have their own international positioning and all hopes to become the central actor in the opening up to the outside world in this region. Chongqing has been engaged in constructing 'One river Two railways Three oceans'[4] as its international trade channel, hoping to be the central player in opening to the outside world in China's southwest region. Similarly, Sichuan province sees itself positioned as an 'important intersection and traffic corridor connecting Central Asia, South Asia and Southeast Asia'. Guizhou province has positioned itself as national important base, traffic junction of southwest, demonstration area, innovation zone, etc. Guizhou has also put itself forward striving to build itself into 'globally famous and domestic first-class tourist destination, leisure resort, and important cultural communication platform'. So all of China's five southwest provinces want to become the window opening to the outside world in the southwest region, and have made the corresponding preparations. Therefore, if Yunnan wants to be the gateway opening to the outside world in the southwest region, it is also going to face fierce competition at home.

India is divided into Northern, Southern, Eastern, Midwest and Northeast regions as well. West Bengal in the Indian official definition belongs to the eastern region. The states of India's northeast region occupy a total area of 178.4 thousand square kilometres, accounting for 6% of the territory of India. This region has a population of about 44.21 million, accounting for 3.65% of the total population of India. The states in northeastern region, except Assam, cover a small area and are mainly mountainous terrains. There exists an obvious gap in economic and social development levels between the northeast of India and other regions of India. In 2009 the GDP per capita of northeast region was 21 thousand rupees, approximately accounting for a half of national average level of 41.968 thousand rupees. In addition, there exist obvious internal differences among the states in northeast region. Besides, India also has a rather complex relationship between the central government and the local governments. In addition, the ruling party of each state is not the same, and the ruling party of each state could possibly be different from the ruling party of India's central government. There also exists large differences between states on various other indices. Therefore, letting all states be involved in the BCIM mechanism has faced the problem of internal integration. The integration of Indian and Chinese domestic actors in the BCIM cooperation mechanism therefore remains a difficult challenge. Indeed, the integration of Myanmar's all domestic actors in BCIM cooperation mechanism is more difficult than in other BCIM countries. The BCIM mechanism, no matter what plan or traffic route are selected, cannot bypass the local ethnic armies of northern Myanmar. The complexity and persistence of Myanmar's local ethnic armed forces makes this problem far more difficult for the central government of Myanmar that seeks to integrate the local ethnic armed groups in Northern Myanmar that must be reconciled and involved to ensure that BCIM cooperation mechanism can develop smoothly.

Review Standards for BCIM Cooperation Mechanisms

This paper seeks to examine how to design and improve the international regimes in BCIM sub-regional cooperation.

One way to evaluate such a proposition is to first know about the standards of international regimes, that is, whether the mere existence of international mechanism is enough to guide higher levels of institutionalisation of the BCIM sub-regional cooperation mechanism. Similarly, any examination of whether or not international regimes of BCIM sub-regional cooperation are successful must be based on two aspects for evaluation: effectiveness and legitimacy. The argument about the effectiveness of the international regime flows from the rational choice theory, that is, the existence of any international regime is meant to solve the specific problems in a certain field, and thus whether the corresponding system is designed to effectively solve the problems in this field is one of the major indexes to measure whether the international regime is successful. The legitimacy of international regime, on the other hand, is evaluated from the angle of sociology, that is, the production and role of international regime has in building a series of norms. In order to let the international regime be accepted by all parties and have a binding authority, it must conform to the corresponding norms, that is, pursue the legitimacy as an international regime. From a normative perspective, if a system is said to be legitimate, that means admitting that it has ruling rights, that is, the ruler can issue rules and punish those who do not obey or benefit those who obey to obtain their compliance.

Therefore, by using the effectiveness and legitimacy index to determine the level of institutionalisation of international regime in this region presents a more objective method for evaluating it. From a qualitative point of view, the international regime with stronger effectiveness and legitimacy should be legally binding while the international regime with weaker effectiveness and legitimacy has only a political or moral binding force. From the quantitative point of view, the effectiveness and the legitimacy of international regime can be distinguished from that whether it or to what extent it has government authorisation, collective decision, independent review and compulsory execution.[5] From the practice of international relations, the institutionalisation level of the vast majority of international regimes are relatively low, generally staying in the forum-like moral appealing, while the legally binding international regime are relatively few.

In evaluating BCIM sub-regional cooperation mechanisms in terms of their being an international regime based on the judging standards mentioned above, its institutionalisation level still remains in the lower levels. Judging from the current practices of BCIM sub-regional cooperation, there are two parallel 'regimes' in this region namely, the BCIM regional cooperation forum led by think tanks and the intergovernmental work group talks on BCIM economic corridor led by the governments of these four countries. The BCIM regional cooperation forum obtains a limited government authorisation, and does not have the ability of collective decision and compulsory execution. Its effectiveness is mainly reflected in the selection of issues, which means these four countries discuss what kind of problems can be incorporated into the discussion range through this forum. In terms of the legitimacy, the dialogue between think tanks to a certain extent can understand differences, and often manages to build consensuses. The process of organising the Forum, therefore, reflects the uncertainty of this regime. Since it was established in 1999, the BCIM Regional Forum theoretically should have held 15 conferences, which are sponsored by these four countries in turns. The fact is that the forum was not held in 2001, 2005, 2008, 2010 and 2014 due to various reasons. Myanmar should have hosted the 2014 forum, but Myanmar claimed they cannot host the forum because they needed to undertake the task of rotating presidency of ASEAN. From the effectiveness perspective, although the Forum has already drawn a series of issues under discussion from 1999 till now but has not yet formed a clear consensus on its agreed priority issue areas. In addition to holding its annual conferences the Forum has not produced any other effective initiatives.

Similarly, the Intergovernmental Work Group talks on BCIM Economic Corridor was launched in 2013. If the Work Group talks itself can sustain, it is a kind of international regime of this region as it also obtains a certain government authorisation yet, it is the results of Work Group talks that are expected to create and establish more effective international regime. The Group, however, is easily affected by the fluctuating relations between BCIM countries, and the support of each country to the Work Group talks can be withdrew at any time before the Intergovernmental talk result in creating any formal intergovernmental mechanisms. From the above analysis, therefore, it can be seen that the institutionalisation levels of the BCIM regional cooperation mechanisms still remains in lower levels. Deliberations at the Forum amongst think tanks have evolved some amount of legitimacy, but faced with their poor effectiveness and potentially withdrawal by any government's authorisation could undermine it. The Intergovernmental Work Group talks are still in the initial stage and whether they can form a regime remains yet to be seen.

Attitude of BCIM Countries toward Institutionalisation

An attempt to evaluate BCIM sub-regional cooperation mechanisms using the international regime model, first unavoidable problem to address remains the attitude of each of the four BCIM countries in terms of their commitment towards building an international regime for this region. If all four countries hold a positive attitude toward the construction and promotion of the international regime in this region, the prospect of this regime are far more optimistic than how it has been perceived by most experts. In order to better understand this problem, lets first review the attitude with which these four countries have been participating in building an international regime for the BCIM region.

(i) Attitudes towards Participation in Regime building

As mentioned above, the international regime includes international organisations, international agreements, international conventions, etc. To understand the situations of four countries participating in the international regime for BCIM sub-region, we need to know the situations of four countries participating in other international organisations, international agreements and international conventions respectively. Because the international agreements and international conventions include informal conventions, principles, etc., it is very difficult to carry out a comprehensive statistics on it. International organisations have a relatively fixed form and clear membership system. The situations of all countries participating in the international organisations are clear. Therefore, it is still feasible to consider the situations of all countries participating in the international organisations as index to evaluate all countries participating in the international regime although it is not comprehensive.

According to the statistics in the *Yearbook of International Organizations (2014)* issued by the Union of International Association, as of 2012, India participated in 3,471 international organisations of various types, including 191 international inter-governmental organisations, and 3,280 international non-governmental organisations. Among all above international organisations, there were 2,272 international organisations that only accepted countries as members. The number of international organisations that India participated in ranked twenty-sixth in the world, ranked second in Asia, next only to Japan. At the same time, India was the place where 68 international organisations headquartered. By the end of 2012, China participated in 2,840 international organisations, including 184 international inter-governmental organisations, and 2,565 international non-governmental organisations. Among 2,840 organisations, there were 1,956 international organisations that only accepted countries as members. The number of international organisations that China participated in ranked thirty-third in the world, and ranked fourth in Asia. China was a place where 52 international organisations headquartered. By the end of 2012, Bangladesh participated in a total of 1,347 international organisations, including 136 international inter-governmental organisations, and 1,211 international non-governmental organisations. Among 1,347 organisations, there were 816 international organisations that only accepted countries as members. The number of international organisations that Bangladesh participated in ranked seventy-seventh in the world, and ranked nineteenth in Asia. Bangladesh was the place where 6 international organisations headquartered. By the end of 2012, Myanmar participated in a total of 496 international organisations, including 75 international inter-governmental organisations, and 421 international non-governmental organisations. Among 496 organisations, there were 302 international organisations that only accepted countries as members. The number of international organisations that Myanmar participated in ranked 155th in the world, and ranked thirty-sixth in Asia. (See table below)

Participation Situations of BCIM Four Countries in the International Organizations in 2012-2013

Items	*Bangladesh*	*China*	*India*	*Myanmar*
The total number of international organizations to participate	1347	2840	3471	496
The number of international inter-governmental organizations to participate	136	184	191	75
The number of international non-governmental organizations to participate	1211	2565	3280	421
The number of international organizations to participate that only accepted countries as members	816	1956	2272	302
Global ranking	77	33	26	155
Asian ranking	19	4	2	36
The headquarter number of international organizations in this country	6	52	68	0

Data sources: collected and concluded from *Yearbook of International Organizations (2014)*, Union of International Association.

Note: The ranking was according to the number of international organizations to participate that only accepted countries as members.

From the above analysis, it sees that, except Myanmar, India, China and Bangladesh have frequently participated in the international organisations. Among over 50 countries in Asia, the number of international organisations that India and China participated in ranked second and fourth, and Bangladesh ranked nineteenth. The number of international organisations that Myanmar participated in was relatively small, mainly because the western sanctions limited its qualification to participate in international organisations for many years. After the reform and opening up, China's attitude towards the international regimes and the international organisations changed a lot. According to the statistics, China was one of countries with the highest degree of internationalisation and opening. India had the tradition and experience of participating in the international organisations, and was the most active country in developing countries on participation in international organisations. India also displays a strong political will to play a leading role in the international organisations.[6] Bangladesh, as the 'middle power' sandwiched between two major powers, has supported the international regime, and realised its own development through the international regime, which is its consistent tradition. After the democratic reform of Myanmar, the climax of joining in the new international regimes would come up.

The attitudes of all the four BCIM countries to participation in international organisations, therefore, appears more positive, and the number of international organisations they participated in has been relatively high. The above data, however, only shows the general attitudes of these four countries toward the international organisations and international regime. If there is no special consideration, we may assume that these four countries shall hold a positive attitude towards establishing the international regimes and international organisations in the BCIM region as well. But the attitudes of four countries towards the promotion of institutionalisation levels in the BCIM region requires still further deeper analysis.

(ii) Attitudes towards Promoting BCIM Regimes

Ever since the BCIM regional cooperation mechanism of Economic Corridor was proposed, China has been the main driving force for building infrastructure for this mechanism. In fact, it is because of China's insistent promotion for years that this mechanism has survived. China has provided a large amount of manpower, resources support for BCIM regional cooperation mechanism. The car rally, *The Newsletter of BCIM Forum*, and other proposed initiatives have had strong support from China. With this support from the central government, Yunnan local government has also played the role of promoters in building BCIM Economic Corridor. This BCIM regional cooperation mechanism has already evolved from Track-2 to Track-1 Economic Corridor, which was also out of China's initiative. In addition, China's thirty-year reform and opening up experience has been one of opening to the outside world and participating in the international regimes. Therefore, China is willing to further promote the institutionalisation of international cooperation regimes in this BCIM region as well.

India has had a rich experience in participating in international regimes, as mentioned above. India's passion for participating in the international regimes has been very high. But the attitude of India towards the BCIM regional cooperation mechanism has not been clear, indeed it has been ambiguous. This kind of attitude is visible at all levels of India society. India's official attitude toward the BCIM cooperation mechanism has been fuzzy. During the visit of Premier Li Keqiang to India in May 2013, and the visit of India Prime Minister Singh to China in October 2013, although the joint statement issued by both leaders mentions the BCIM Economic Corridor construction, the subsequently signed agreement between the two countries didn't have any contents about this Economic Corridor. In the BCIM Work Group talks in Kunming in December 2013, India had different opinions on whether to use the proposal of Work Group talks. In an interview with the China Radio International, India's Prime Minister Singh stated that the

BCIM Economic Corridor was proposed by Premier Li Keqiang upon a visit to India in May 2013, and India supported it 'in principle', because the BCIM Economic Corridor had the 'potential' for promoting and strengthening bilateral economic ties. India's media and the public didn't pay enough attention to the BCIM Economic Corridor. On India's main think tank websites including India Institute for Defence and Analysis, Institute for Peace and Conflicts Studies, Institute of Chinese Studies, or throughout India's mainstream media *The Times of India, Hindustan Times, Economic Times* and India's TV channels, it was difficult to find relevant reports and comments on the BCIM Economic Corridor. In addition, there appeared differences amongst various government departments. The Ministry of External Affairs was indifferent first and then supportive, and considered that the construction of Economic Corridor conformed to the common interests of these four countries; even senior diplomats put forward advice that the common development planning of four countries should be so formulated as to put the concept of regional cooperation into specific implementation. Ministry of Home Affairs, however, still considers the BCIM economic corridor as difficult to form if the border problems, and the potential dangers in northeast region, are not solved. The Department of Economic Affairs was not clear what kind of specific interests of BCIM Economic Corridor can bring to India. Firstly, these aspects showed that the domestic of India is not highly aware of the BCIM Economic Corridor. Secondly, it also showed that as long as the BCIM Economic Corridor produced practical improvement to the economy of India's northeastern region, India's Department of Economic Affairs is not likely to participate in cooperation.

Bangladesh has always been active in the BCIM mechanisms. After China and India put the BCIM Economic Corridor construction into their joint statement, Bangladeshi foreign minister Fsarul Amin and Chinese Foreign Minister Wang Yi held a bilateral talks on October 13, 2013. The foreign minister of Bangladesh said that Bangladesh supported the BCIM Economic Corridor construction, and agreed to negotiate the action plan with the other countries and strengthen the BCIM regional economic, trade and personnel exchanges. Myanmar's attitude toward the BCIM mechanism has experienced some changes after change of government in 2016. Before the democratic reforms began, it had been holding a positive attitude. After the democratic reforms, its attitude was not very clear. Myanmar's attitude toward this Economic Corridor depends mainly on two factors: One factor is the development of Sino-Myanmar relations; and the other factor is the solution of the ethnic and local armed problems in northern Myanmar. Before those ethnic armed forces in northern Myanmar are reconciled, Myanmar's attitude to carry out international cooperation in northern Myanmar would continue to face high levels of uncertainty.

Policy Options to Improve Institutionalisation of BCIM

The effectiveness and legitimacy have been the two critical indicators applied in this chapter to measure the institutionalisation level of the BCIM regional cooperation. It is commonplace that the main forms of current international regimes are international organisations, international agreements, international norms and principles. However, these three forms or stages of building international regimes do have remarkable difference in their respective effectiveness and legitimacy. Their effectiveness and legitimacy often depends on the specific situations and locations. For example, the international agreement on the diplomat protection as determined in the *Vienna International Convention* is not necessarily an inferior international organisation in its effectiveness and legitimacy. Yet, in practice their efficacy and legacy varies on episode to episode bases. Similarly, there exist a number of different options for BCIM regional cooperation and there remain areas to improve the institutionalisation level of BCIM sub-regional mechanisms.

For the difficulties mentioned above the prospective model of Economic Corridor has to be so evolved as to address these problems. In addition, the road map for institutionalisation of BCIM sub-regional cooperation has to cater to varying developments levels and directions of all four member states as well. Such a clear prospect makes not only all countries have a clearer expectation for the regime, but also all countries prepare the corresponding policies as soon as possible to guarantee the sustainable development of the regime in this BCIM region. At present, however, the development models of BCIM sub-regional cooperation mechanism roughly are of three types: the first model is to institutionalise the BCIM Economic Cooperation mechanism and build an Economic Corridor as a sub-regional cooperation organisation, that is, BCIM Sub-regional Economic Cooperation Organisation; the second model is to construct the BCIM economic corridor into BCIM Free Trade Zone; and the third model is to stick to the mode of 'wading across the stream by feeling the pebbles' (i.e. the pragmatic way), not set to specific targets, but seeking gradual progress.

(i) BCIM Sub-regional Economic Cooperation Organisation

Yunnan and Guangxi provinces, on behalf of China, have been participating in Great Mekong Sub-region Cooperation (GMS) mechanism. After 20 years of development, GMS has become a relatively mature sub-regional cooperation organisation. GMS's experience is a strong reference for the development of BCIM Economic Cooperation based on existing cooperation mechanism and developing these into sub-regional economic cooperation organisation. Great Mekong Sub-regional (GMS) Cooperation mechanism was established under the promotion of Asian Development Bank (ADB), and its main function is to promote the six countries in Lantsang-Mekong river basin to eliminate poverty, and promote economic and social development. Since it was founded in 1992, Great Mekong Sub-regional (GMS) Cooperation mechanism, under the financial support of ADB and western countries, has carried out a lot of work in transportation, electricity, communication, agriculture, environment, tourism, human resource development, trade and investment, drug control and substitute plantation, law enforcement and security cooperation, technical assistance and other fields. Currently, the social and economic situations of these four countries that BCIM economic cooperation mechanism has evolved several similarities within these six countries (China, Laos, Vietnam, Cambodia, Myanmar, and Thailand) in Mekong River basin. Yunnan province on behalf of China is one of the main participating parties in GMS cooperation mechanism. Myanmar is another member of this regime. So both these already have experience of working together in such a project of regime building. Bangladesh and the northeast region of India belong to the areas in which economic and social development is relatively backward, and that are faced with tasks of eliminating poverty and promoting development.

If considering GMS as the example and model, then BCIM Economic Corridor can develop in the direction of BCIM Organisation for Economic Cooperation and realise the change from Economic Corridor to the institutionalised sub-regional economic cooperation organisation. So in regarding the sub-regional economic cooperation organisation as a vision, the following three issues will need to be addressed:

The *first* issue is the willingness of all parties. At this stage, BCIM cooperation mechanism and its upgraded BCIM Economic Corridor only stay in the initial stage. Some countries actively promote, while some countries passively participate in. Its transition into sub-regional cooperation organisation is involved in more complex problems, including sovereignty transfer in a certain degree of participating parties, dominance, setting of the permanent organisation, organisation structure, etc. What need to participate in this process are not only administrative agencies of all parties, but also the authorisation of legislative bodies and the approval of relevant agreements.

The *second* issues is the perennial need to ensure sources of funds. The sub-regional cooperation organisation with the aim of eliminating poverty and promoting social and economic development always faces the challenge of how to get the required funds and technology for development projects especially when each country is underdeveloped. The funds and technology of GMS mechanism mainly come from Asian Development Bank (ADB), U.N. Economic and Social Commission for Asia and the Pacific (ESCAP), and some developed countries such as Australia, New Zealand, Japan, the European Union and other countries. In addition to China, the other five countries in GMS are small and medium-sized countries, and Laos, Cambodia and Myanmar are one of the least developed countries in the world. So it is understandable for developed countries to provide financial and technical assistance for this sub-regional cooperation organisation.

BCIM cooperation mechanism, on the other hand, includes the world's largest developing country - China and India; where both are amongst the fastest growing economies and China is the second largest economy of the world. Even though some international organisations may provide a certain financial assistance and project support for this BCIM Economic Corridor mechanism, it can be predicted that these funds would not be sufficient. Therefore the funds needed for the BCIM cooperation mechanism will mainly depend on BCIM members themselves, which seems like a formidable problem. In these four countries, China has the strength and it has the desire to provide some funds, but the matching of rights and obligations in decision-making on how to use these funds could also become an issue once funds are provided. Because it is still uncertain whether other countries will accept that the decision-making power a country possesses must be consistent with her provided funds, it remains yet to be discussed on what bases China will provide corresponding share or larger share of funds for BCIM Economic Corridor.

The *third* issues is relationship of BCIM Economic Corridor with various overlapping other international organisations with stakes in this sub-region. BCIM cooperation mechanism has many overlaps with the existing cooperation mechanisms and regional organisation in this region. China and Myanmar are participants of GMS cooperation mechanism, and are also the member states of China-ASEAN, that is 10+1 cooperation mechanism. Myanmar, Bangladesh and India are members of Bay of Bengal Economic Cooperation Organisation; Bangladesh and India are SAARC members; India and Myanmar are also the member states of Mekong-Ganga Cooperation Initiative of India. The main purposes of these organisations are to strengthen regional cooperation, and promote the economic development. It can be said that the number of sub-regional organisations in this region is large, and there is overlap between their respective goals. Therefore, after BCIM Economic Corridor is upgraded into BCIM Economic Cooperation Organisation, the key to test its vitality is how this organisation realises the niche areas of non-overlapping development with these other sub-regional cooperation organisations, and better achieves the goal of regional economic development.

(ii) Free Trade Zone Model

At present, the goal of the primary stage of regional and sub-regional economic cooperation will be to build a Free Trade Zone. At present, China has 18 Free Trade Zone under construction, involving 31 countries and regions. Among them, there are 12-signed Free Trade Agreements (FTA), involving 20 countries and regions; Free Trade Areas (FTAs) under negotiation are 6, involving 22 countries. India now has signed FTAs with Nepal, Sri Lanka, ASEAN and other countries, and is negotiating the Free Trade Zones with Australia, New Zealand and other countries. It should be said that the intra-regional countries China and India have a certain experience in negotiating and establishing Free Trade Zones and Free Trade Areas.

In addition, China-ASEAN Free Trade Zone has not only been built but has also made good progress. China and Myanmar belong to part of this China-ASEAN Free Trade Zone. Likewise, India–ASEAN Free Trade Agreement came into force in 2010, and India and Myanmar are a part of the India-ASEAN Free Trade Area. China, India and Bangladesh are members of the Asia-Pacific Countries Trade Agreement (APTA)[7], and they have the tariff concession agreement and experience. India and Bangladesh are also members of the South Asian Free Trade Area, which was officially launched in 2006. China, India and Myanmar are also members of the World Trade Organisation (WTO). It can be said that there exists an indirect Free Trade network between these four BCIM counties: China-ASEAN (Myanmar)–India, India-SAARC-Bangladesh and so on. Therefore, if all parties are willing to establish a Free Trade Area for BCIM, then these four counties of BCIM can use this experience to construct their proposed Economic Corridor which can be the basis of launching multilateral their negotiations for a Free Trade Area.

The biggest difficulty of establishing BCIM Free Trade Zone, however, lies in the trade relationship between China and India. China and India are the members of WTO and also members of the Asia-Pacific Trade Agreement. It has been difficult for them to establish a Sino-Indian Free Trade Area which has implications for constructing BICM Free Trade Zone. This is because there exists a large trade deficit between China and India. The two governments had once determined to expand the bilateral trade volume up to $100 billion as early as 2010 but this target remains unachieved in 2016. The bilateral trade volume between China and India has not risen but actually fallen in few recent years. India was the country among the member states of WTO that has repeatedly proposed anti-dumping investigations against China. India always holds a cautious attitude towards the opening its market for China. Coupled with its large amount of trade deficits against China, most Indians do not expect to establish a multilateral Free Trade Area with China; they also do not see absence of an Sino-India FTA having any big impact for India's domestic industries. Therefore, if the trade problem between China and India cannot be solved, it is extremely difficult to implement BCIM Free Trade Area.

(iii) Wading across the Stream by Feeling the Way (Pragmatic model)

Although the prospect of taking forward the BCIM Economic Corridor into building a Free Trade Area or the Sub-regional Economic Cooperation Organisation is tempting yet in view of problems mentioned above the BCIM economic cooperation mechanisms are very likely to continue along the current mode of "wading across the stream by feeling the way" which seems the most pragmatic model for their cooperation. Under this model, China's policy could focus on two core issues to promote Economic Corridor construction. The first core issues is Sino-Myanmar cooperation. Under the progressive model it will be wise to implement the BCIM cooperation mechanism step by step: Sino-Myanmar '! Sino-Myanmar-Bangladesh'! Sino-Myanmar-Bangladesh-India. The second core issue is the China-Pakistan Economic Corridor (CPEC) construction. The promotion of Sino-Pakistan Economic Corridor construction can have both positive as also negative implications for the construction of the BCIM Economic Corridor.

The body of existing BCIM sub-regional cooperation mechanism are Track-1 Intergovernmental Work Group talks and Track-2 BCIM Regional Cooperation Forum. Learning from the experience of GMS cooperation, the intergovernmental cooperation under BCIM Economic Corridor model must start from low politics, and from less-sensitive fields. According to the theory of functionalism, the cooperation effects of these fields will eventually spillover into other more difficult fields, thus promoting the cooperation in those other fields in this sub-region. Project-oriented cooperation and mechanism construction is an effective way. For conducting institutional design, they should promote one of the projects firstly as the breakthrough point, and then exert its demonstration effect. This may prove to be the most feasible method. In addition, Track-2 BCIM Regional Cooperation Forum should achieve further institutionalisation, from impractical discussion to the prospective studies and providing policy recommendations for the transformation of think tank forum. The

Regional Cooperation Forum should set up four country think tank network, and understand each think tank policy influence and its advantageous sectors for making value addition. On the basis of maintaining the core think tank of the existing regional cooperation forum, the corresponding think tanks of other countries should be invited to participate in the discussion according to the issues and priorities, forming a work group on a certain issue or set up special teams to conduct the longer term research on a particular issue. The special team in a neutral position should provide policy recommendations for cooperation in certain well defined fields, and continuously build consensus through successive negotiations.

Under this model of "wading across the stream by feeling the way", the BCIM Track-1 intergovernmental dialogue should focus on issues of system designing and look for making a breakthrough, while the Track-2 Regional Cooperation Forum should further improve the institutionalisation process, expand the participation of think tanks and their professionalism, to provide effective policy options. There has already been a big step forward for BCIM as it's economic cooperation mechanism has already moved up from Forum to Corridor, but given sub-region's challenge this seems only a small step for the whole BCIM economic cooperation. Whether it is Forum or Corridor, its eventual execution will be a long and tortuous process. If we can make these four countries reach consensus on economic cooperation model, it will be a good beginning for the regional economic cooperation.

(iv) Roadmap for Improving the Institutionalisation

The prototype of the BCIM sub-regional cooperation mechanism is the BCIM Regional Cooperation Forum. In 2013, driven by China, this Track-2 cooperation Forum was upgraded to Track-1 BCIM Economic Corridor, and then these four countries began the Intergovernmental Working Group talk on how to construct the BCIM Economic Corridor. Regional cooperation mechanism upgrading from Track-2 to Track-1 was an upgrade of the institutionalisation level for the international regime. This involved authorisation that this sub-regional cooperation regime which it obtained from all four countries. This was sufficient to begin with and its legitimacy basis were firmer. Now that we have the Track-1 Intergovernmental Working Group of Economic Corridor, whether the original Track-2 Regional Cooperation Forum should remain is also a point for discussion that this regime construction should consider. The original regional cooperation forum shall be kept, which will be useful for improving the institutionalisation of BCIM sub-regional cooperation.

(a) Membership Qualification

The membership qualification of the international regime for the BCIM sub-regional cooperation is the first question to enhance the institutionalisation level of BCIM cooperation system. This implies that all four states should become participants of all BCIM mechanisms. This would entail commitment to undertake responsibilities and it involves two aspects:

Firstly, the membership in the international regime of BCIM sub-regional cooperation means what countries should become full founding members of the BCIM international regime. Judging from the regime name, Bangladesh, China, India and Myanmar should be its original members. An Indian scholar has put forward that Thailand could also become one of the members of the regime. The core issue is the relationship between the number of member states and the effectiveness of international regime. In order to let the international regime better promote cooperation, limiting the membership can remove the countries with betrayal motivation from the international regime. In addition, raising the threshold of member states joining the international system can better understand the intentions of other countries, so as to increase the predictability of actions for each other. Therefore limiting the number of members joining the international regime is useful to enhance the execution efficiency of international regime, and better promote cooperation. For the international regime of BCIM sub-regional cooperation, the cooperation between these four countries have been faced with many problems. And, based on this experience, if the number of member states increases, this will make each party increase the cost of understanding the other's intentions and the process of building trust become difficult, which is not conducive to the development of the international regime and the realisation of international cooperation. Starting from improving the execution effectiveness of the international regime, it is possible to keep it to the four-country international regime, an issue-cantered core, and thus improving the effectiveness and enforceability of cooperation.

Secondly, the members of non-governmental cooperation in BCIM sub-regional cooperation may be allowed to increase some more. The consideration should be given to add new observers or formal members in the non-governmental regional cooperation forum, when the Intergovernmental Work Group talks keep a small scale and do not add new member states for now. If four countries agree, Thailand's think-tank organisation can be invited to participate in the Regional Cooperation Forum and serves as an observer at the beginning. A number of think-tank organisations of Bangladesh, India and Myanmar can be invited to participate in the forum at the same time. For China, the participation of Chinese think tanks also maintains the pattern of one dominating and others supporting. Increasing the number of participants in the Track-2 cooperation forum can add the representativeness of think tanks and enhance the legitimacy of the cooperation forum. It can also help them expand the range of issues covered, enhance the contact between each issue areas and its concerned actors.

(b) Issues to be Covered

The BCIM sub-regional cooperation mechanism was born from the regional economic cooperation forum and at present has been upgraded to the Economic Corridor. From the name itself, one can see that the main focus of the regime is on economic issues. Although the regional cooperation forum involved education, tourism, and cultural exchange issues sometimes, these issues are not the mainstream. Concerning the current BCIM economic cooperation, from which these four countries are possible to gain revenues, without integration basis, all parties are more concerned with the relative benefits of their own and not the absolute benefits. Each party would worry about the other party will change the surpassed relative gains into military strength to threaten it, therefore all parties are more concerned with the relative benefits not the absolute benefits in this sub-regional cooperation. The distribution of cooperation benefits from international regime is the key to continue of cooperation of all stakeholders. In terms of BCIM cooperation mechanism, all parties haven't fully recognised the benefits that the Economic Corridor and economic cooperation may bring to them. India worries that China will transfer the relative gains into the military advantage against India and Bangladesh worries of India doing the same to her. There is therefore need to expand the range of issues for deliberations; connect the fields that countries are concerned about with other fields, contributing to achieving the balance of overall national interests. This would especially be useful in reducing the concerns of some countries about the relative gains of specific fields, and thus promote their commitment to cooperation.

Economic cooperation and opening to the outside world has been one of key factors for China success, and China has a high degree of confidence about this method. India, Myanmar and Bangladesh have no similar experiences like China. What they worry is that China will gain more from constructing the Economic Corridor. If the issues of the sub-regional cooperation are only limited in the economic field, it will be unable to alleviate the concerns of other countries on the relative revenues, and the cooperation will also be difficult to promote. Therefore, the international regime of BCIM regional cooperation must incorporate economic, ecological, tourism, culture, education, science and technology, non-traditional security and other issues into the scope of discussion, so what needs to build is not only an Economic Corridor, but also ecological corridor, humanities corridor and so on.

(c) Centralisation of the International Regime

The centralisation of the international regime refers to the international regime becoming relatively strong independent and developing a personality of its own. It mean becoming more than the total-sum of members; to have powers of making decision, reviewing and implementing them. Some of these functions are generated due to some sovereign states transferring their sovereignty, and some are endowed by the development of international norms. The enhanced centralisation will have strong binding on all countries. At the beginning of cooperation, the behaviour of each country is not clear to the other, so the international regime is established to collect information, and increase the transparency of behaviour. In addition, to enhance the centralisation, the international regime can adopt multilateral negotiations to replace a series of bilateral negotiations, and thus reducing the cost of negotiation, and forming the scale of effect. The increase of centralisation of the international regime can lead to member-states willingness for sharing risks. For some challenges that one country wants to address it may face greater uncertainty and higher investment for reluctance of other members. This country can use the stronger international regime to realise risk sharing and promote cooperation.

In addition, enhancing the centralisation of the international regime is also beneficial to improve the enforceability of the cooperation. For the vast majority of international regimes, execution issues involve multiple difficulties. Although the international regime of BCIM sub-regional cooperation has not yet been finalised yet viewed from practices since 1999, the severity of the execution problem has been reduced and better highlighted. The BCIM Car Rally, for example, a kind of small-scale activity took 5 years from proposal to the end yet it finally succeeded.

The enhancing of centralisation of the international regime of BCIM cooperation can be said to be a key step for the increase of institutionalisation of the BCIM cooperation. After the institutionalisation increases, its decisions become binding on all parties and it enhances its efficacy, and its promoting effect on regional cooperation also becomes more obvious.

(d) Flexibility of the International Regime

The elements of flexibility and the centralisation increasing are not contradictory to each other. The World Trade Organisation is a highly centralised international regime. It contains a lot of exception clauses and can better adjust the economic and trade relations between member countries. In terms of the international regime for BCIM cooperation, its flexibility is a prerequisite to ensure that countries can participate in and continue to support this regime. If stressing the centralisation of this BCIM regime may lead to some of the BCIM countries withdrawing their participation and support at the beginning, it may cause this regime disappear. Here, the flexibility will make the international regime provide special care for countries with specific circumstances, and thus making each country progressively agreeable to participating in it.

In addition, the flexibility of BCIM cooperation mechanism can be shown by synchronously carrying out the intergovernmental cooperation mechanism and non-governmental cooperation mechanism. Maintaining the strong rigidness of intergovernmental cooperation mechanism while the flexibility can be achieved through Track-2 non-governmental cooperation mechanism. Therefore during the institutionalised process of BCIM regional cooperation, it is required to achieve the rigidness of inter-governmental cooperation mechanism and the flexibility of non-governmental cooperation mechanism. Thus BCIM Regional Cooperation Forum and BCIM Economic Corridor remain complimentary and mutually supportive of ensuring strong BCIM cooperation regime.

Conclusions

It the last 15 years since BCIM sub-regional cooperation formed in 1999, its updation from a Track-2 Regional Cooperation Forum to Track-1 Economic Corridor remains its most undisputed achievement as it continue to make progress towards building a strong cooperation regime. However, after so many years of gradual development, the institutionalisation level of BCIM cooperation mechanism needs a more accelerated pace for enhancing its regime building. This chapter evaluates the advantages and disadvantages of existing BCIM international regime. The advantage of existing international regime is openness and flexibility; at the same time, it also faces problems, namely, prospect model, policy uncertainty, Myanmar problem, connectivity problem, and domestic integration difficulties. It is also important to determine the measure standards of institutionalisation level of BCIM cooperation regime. According to the development of the international regime theory, it is much proper to select elements of effectiveness and legitimacy as measures for evaluating the institutionalisation process. In order to achieve the promotion in its institutionalisation level, it is required to learn about the attitudes of all the four BCIM countries towards the international regime paradigm. Although these four countries have held a positive attitude to participate in the international regime, the attitude of these four countries towards BCIM cooperation mechanism has varied widely. Attitude of China and Bangladesh has been positive, but that of India and Myanmar not so clear. After analysing the background information of above BCIM mechanisms, the first problem that BCIM sub-regional cooperation has faced is to build clear consensus on goals for BCIM sub-regional cooperation. The available options for consideration include building a sub-regional international organisation, Free Trade Area model, and maintaining the current model of both governmental and non-governmental talks. In addition, BCIM cooperation need to gradually acquire and ingrain elements of the international regime. These elements include evolving shared understanding of member states on issues of membership, priority themes, centralisation of regime, flexibility as also legitimacy of this evolving international regime. After these elements are clearly defined and agreed upon, the practice of international regime building can begin.

Endnotes

1. Wu Shish, Research on the Sub-regional Economic Cooperation between China and Southeast Asia, Ph.D. thesis of Central China Normal University, 2011, p. 7.
2. Barbara Koremenos, Charles Lipson and Duncan Snidal, "The Rational Design of International Institutions", International Organization, Vol.55, No.4, 2001, p.762.
3. Principles refer to beliefs about the facts, causality and honesty; standards refer to the behavior standards established in the form of rights and obligations; rules refer to the specialized provisions and prohibition on the actions. The detailed explanation of these concepts please see: Robert Keohane's, After Hegemony: Cooperation and Discord in the World Political Economy, Su Changhe et al. translated, Shanghai: Shanghai Century Publishing Group, 2006, pp. 57-61.
4. "One river Two railways Three oceans" international trade channel implies that Chongqing connects with the Pacific ocean through Yangtze River. Along the Chongqing-Lanzhou railway, that connects the Xinjiang Alataw Pass, across Kazakhstan–Russia – Belarus – Poland – Germany – Rotterdam to connect with the Atlantic ocean. And, along Chongqing-Guizhou railway, exiting along Guiyang – Kunming – Dali – Ruili, across Mandalay in the central region of Myanmar – Sittwe port connects to the Indian Ocean rim.
5. This judgment proposed in this paper is inspired by Tian Ye's distinction between formal and informal international regimes. For a detailed explanation please refer to Tian Ye, The Choice of System in International Relations, Shanghai, Shanghai People's Publishing House, 2006.
6. Zhang Guihong: "India's International Organizational Diplomacy", International Watch, No.2, 2010, p. 50.
7. "Asia-Pacific Countries Trade Agreement" is formerly known as 'Bangkok Agreement'. Bangkok Agreement was signed in 1975, under the host of Economic and Social Commission for Asia and the Pacific (ESCAP). It had reached its preferential

trade arrangement between developing countries. Its current member states are China, Bangladesh, India, Laos, South Korea and Sri Lanka. On November 2, 2005, the first ministerial council of Bangkok Agreement was held in Beijing, and each representatives passed new agreement text, decided to change Bangkok Agreement into Asia-Pacific Countries Trade Agreement, and implement the negotiation results of the third round of tariff concession after each member states finished the approval procedures in domestic laws.

6

Locating India's North East 'Region' in BCIM-EC

Satyabrat Sinha

The Treaty of Westphalia in 1648 is dated as the time of the rise of the modern nation states system. Accordingly, the contemporary International System traces its origins to that moment in European History. The period of European colonization beginning in the early 17th century and lasting till the late 20th century largely sought to reorganize most of the world within the pattern of European development of national and international system. As a result, Europe remained the center of the world till the early 20th century and by the time of the World War I, the United States was beginning to be drawn into that 'concert' of European powers that had so far been the subject matter of all International Relations discourses. The decolonization process at the end of the World War II was accompanied by a cold war between the two Superpowers. It was with the end of cold war that various regions of the world gained autonomy and consequently the discipline of International Relations responded to the freeing of the regions and focused on various regional and sub-regional formations with now BCIM being one such entity.

For the purpose of this paper, it suffices to mention that as soon as the various regions of the world were coming into their own after a long drawn process of colonization, they were pushed once again into the new global competition of the cold war; the bipolar world. The cold war saw the two super powers reaching across the globe in their struggle for influence. While the behavior of various regions was dramatically altered from how it was during the colonial era, the cold war still circumscribed their independence, making several of them subservient to the great powers and their ambitions. In effect, the cold war delayed the rise of 'regions' as independent centers and loci of power in international relations. It, in many ways, sought to re-enforce the colonial linkages of patron-client relationship between these former colonies and their metropole power in Europe making big countries like China and India stay apart with little interaction or interdependence. Developing a sense of a sub-region like India's North East Region or the sub-region of India's Northeast plus China's Southwest and Bangladesh and Myanmar was surely an uphill task given the strong and persistent grip of conventional thinking.

Essentially, a region is a spatial concept, defined by geographical proximity, the intensity of interactions, shared cultural identities and institutional frameworks. But regions are also dynamic entities, not so much measurable building blocks of the international order as spatially defined cultural, economic, and political constructions, whose nature and functions are transformed over time (Griffiths and O'Callaghan 2004: 274). The 'region', therefore, can and has been studied from multiple perspectives; each of these perspectives entails their limitations and their functionalism. The focus on regions also received an impetus from the growth of regionalism, in the 1980's, in the tripolar economy encompassing, North America, North East Asia and Europe that accounted for almost 85 per cent of the world trade and was moving towards some sort of institutional framework. Also contingent here is that the growth of 'regions' and the processes of 'regionalism' and 'regionalization' have been different for different parts. This also appears to be in seen happening this short to medium term and in a linear developmental vision which foresees that regions would come to represent the structure of the current European Union (EU) model in some form or the other. Others have though challenged this linear development of all regions and regional structures argument[1]. For, while some or the other forms of a regional community is well neigh possible in the various regions of the world, they are more likely to take different trajectories and exhibit myriad differences. This debate into the nature of future regionalism has its pessimists who believe that this phase of globalization is like any other and not in any manner irreversible considering the immediate past of the early 20th century (Zedillo 2001). This debate has clear implications for the future trajectories of the BCIM-EC which presents a unique experiment at regionalization of disparate sub-regions involving large number of peripheral minorities of four former colonies.

Chasing Regional Imaginations

Reflective of contemporary times is the phenomenon that multiple Regional groupings are part and parcel of the present global economic order driving it. Regional trade agreements (RTAs), called a 'spaghetti bowl' due to their numbers and overlapping nature, are accepted as the 'second best' of free trade, or multilateralism (Raipuria 2002: 3581). There are few RTAs of consequence and concern to the major economies of the world. These would include the North American Free Trade Agreement (NAFTA); and the Association of South East Asian Nations (ASEAN), and Southern Common Market (Mercosur). Despite this, RTA's models hold the advantage of negotiating with a small number of countries easier and more expedient and more over harnessing the dynamism of the countries coming together.

As regards the Bangladesh-China-India-Myanmar Forum for Regional Cooperation (BCIM) that was founded in 1999, also known as the Kunming Initiative, it is a regional plan to harness the economic buoyancy of China and India as also resources f this region to achieve development for establishing peace and stability. Geographically, centered at the conjunction of South and South East Asia and South West China, the BCIM Forum is an organization that brings together the three sub-regions of Asia to maximize benefits from their complementarities. As Sanjib Baruah (2003) writes,

> The idea that South Asia is a discrete geographical region separated from Southeast Asia is a fiction. There are no "natural" geographical boundaries separating South and Southeast Asia along the Indo-Myanmarese border...Northeast India's ties – historical, cultural, social and economic – do not stop at these international boundaries.

The concept of sub-regional cooperation, the idea of having a sub grouping within a grouping has been in existence for many years and in most cases has been quite successful. It has contributed to the broader idea of thc regional cooperation within the framework of other such groups. In Asia, the idea came about when a group triangle comprising Singapore, Malaysia and Indonesia was put forward in 1988 and they formed this group triangle in spite of the fact that all the three countries are also members of the ASEAN (Rahim 1997: 25).

In tying the provinces of Yunnan in the South Western region of China, Myanmar, the North Eastern Region (NER) of India and Bangladesh, the BCIM Forum brings together what can be described as a natural economic region segregated by these post-colonial nation-state formations. Especially for both India and China, their North Eastern region and the South Western region respectively, is landlocked, lacking opportunities to avail their national export led growth model of development. The BCIM is a national level initiative and, from the Indian perspective, seeks to harness pre-colonial and post-colonial linkages of the North Eastern sub region of India with the dynamism of China, Myanmar (and also part of the ASEAN) and Bangladesh. The importance of the BCIM is also drawn from the fact that it is a Forum in which India engages China on a regional context which is helpful given their trust deficit (Uberoi 2013: 2). This sub-regional approach can maximize advantages of faster growth rates in China and India without being affected by their historical and political problems as also benefit these turmoil ridden peripheral regions of all four participating countries.

The focus of this paper is on highlighting the co-existence of both harmony and dissonance in the 'national' and the 'sub-national' constructions of Regional Trading Arrangements and especially with regard to the North East Region (NER) of India. It was in a lecture in Singapore in 1994, that the then Prime Minister Shri P.V. Narasimha Rao's first broadly articulated India's desire and rationale for connecting with its eastern neighbours which is now known as the Look East Policy (Ghoshal 2013: 21). Since that first exposition, the North East region lays at the centre of every regional foray[2] that India has made to the east be it BCIM or BIMSTEC, Look East Policy (LEP) or any other formulation (Bhattacharya and De 2006). The origins of the much celebrated LEP have been variously traced to many factors as also to their combinations starting from early 1990s. These include the end of Cold War, Balance of Payments Crisis facing India, situation in Myanmar after the military assumed power in 1988 and the expanding influence of China and Pakistan, deteriorating security situation in North East India, Indian prime minister Rajiv Gandhi's visit to China in 1988 and also that the initiative of opening up to the east was essentially strategically driven. But it would be important to point out that the operational side of India's Look East Policy was mainly driven by its economic component.

The BCIM-EC fits in closely with India's Look-East Policy (LEP) and also with the long-term demand of India's North Eastern Region (NER) for the opening of trade, connectivity and people-to-people contacts with the neighbouring countries that constitute some 98 per cent of the region's borders (Uberoi 2013:2). Expansion of ASEAN to include Myanmar and Indo-China has clearly re-enforced this centrality of India's NER to India's LEP as also increasingly to the China-India relations making BCIM-EC a major hope for resolving persistent lack of development and peace in this region. This in turn is expected to further strengthen India's engagement with both China and ASEAN.

NER as a Sub-Region of BCIM

Before proceeding further, we need to understand NER better. For many scholars, NER as an entity has been 'shaped, reinforced by certain features, issues and agendas' (Ngaihte 2013). In arguing for a pan-North Eastern entity, Ngaihte states that the term North East comes into vogue with the creation of the North Eastern Frontier Area (NEFA) in 1951 and that subsequent developments, specifically, the naming of a number of organizations and institutions[3] with the prefix North East that strengthened the idea of North East India as an entity (2013). But NER also remains full of diversity, variety and contradictions which also need to be underlined to put things in perspective.

In sharp contrast to Ngaihte, Haokip (2012: 84) calls these efforts to call North East India, a region, 'generalised presumptions, [that] time and again, overlook[s] the diversity of the region' and clubbing them together as lazy analysis by mainland India experts. Further, Haokip (2012: 84) cites Wasbir Hussain to reiterate that "...such clubbing together of the region, in an attempt to look at it as a single entity, has led to stereotyping of the problems that plague the area...", and in citing historian Manorama Sharma who observed that, "The north-eastern states of India may be looked upon as a political unit for purposes of administrative convenience by the Government of India today, but historically at no point of time has it ever been a political unit, either culturally, economically or politically". The academia has also been instrumental in reinforcing NER as a distinct political, ethnical, cultural and geographic entity as we have a number of centres of North East Studies in various Universities in India as well as it being a subject of numerous seminars and conferences.

The institutionalization of NER as a distinct region incorporates in it not merely the strategic geographical location, connected to *mainstream* India by a narrow land corridor called the *Chicken Neck,* but also the Indians of mongoloid racial features. The region though also includes large number of non-mongoloid populations, especially immigrants from mainland India. The region during the colonial period served as the 'frontier', a peripheral space inhabited by distinct cultural and ethnic tribal communities that were loosely administered or unadministered, with close affinities with the people of South East Asia. The decision makers in independent India continued to perceive the region in colonial terms considering the challenges that emanate from the region to the postcolonial Indian state in the early years and the little contribution of the region in the Indian economy. The lack of policy initiatives, and worst, the poor implementation of these in the region led to grievances of 'neglect' and allegations of continuation of the colonial legacy (Ngaihte 2013).

The gamut of foreign economic policies that we refer to as the Look East Policy (LEP) also inadvertently promote the understanding of NER as a self-contained region of its own which is often urged to break out of its isolation. As Prabhakar (2004) in a commentary titled, "Is North-East India Landlocked?" in *Economic and Political Weekly* (EPW) points out that the concept of a landlocked state and the underlying assumption of a 'closed border' as an impediment to growth ought to be questioned. The argument Prabhakar makes is that the landlocked status of the NER as a whole has received a lot of attention but a related feature of the region, that the states of the region 'are internally locked- ... unable to connect with each other physically in terms of poor transport links' are ignored (2004: 4608).

Professor Sanjib Baruah, in making a case for cross border region building, alludes to a historical context for the developmental challenges that the NER faces. The first and the most debilitating was the loss of connectivity and market access as a result of the partition of India and later creation of Bangladesh. But an even older and fundamentally a deeper structural change had been the advent of the colonial age and with the discovery of sea routes that put the overland trade from Asia to Europe out of business (Baruah 2003: 7-8). NER was one of the Southern trails of the Silk Route and it was pushed out of focus due to the global forces of colonialism and post colonial geo-politics. For, as Baruah elaborates, the British conquest of the region led to the drawing of lines between the hills and plains, put new barriers on trade with Myanmar which became a new strategic frontier of British India thereby cutting off NER from rest of the South and South East Asia. However, the most enduring legacy of the colonial empire was to put in place a new transportation infrastructure to take tea and other resources out of Assam, thereby disrupting older trade routes connecting this BCIM sub-region (2003: 7-8).

There have been various reasons put forward for the persistent armed insurgencies in NER. These include economic issues of discrimination and underdevelopment but also include upfront issues of political violence and the general state of affairs in NER. They are often explained as a result of the region's underdevelopment and lack of its integration to the Indian 'mainstream' nation (Baruah 2003: 10). It is important to underline that the British colonial government never had any direct administration in these regions and with the change in state strategy, from autonomy to integration, after India's independence resulted in a volatile neighbourhood that lay beyond this newly integrated region. Moreover, the relative isolation of NER from 'mainland' India, hemmed in by neighbouring countries and with little access to the closer, but a shut out foreign world stifled energies in the era of a socialist economy of import substitution. Even with the opening up of the economy, the low base of industrial growth and political problems in NER did not make it a priority for the Central government decision makers in New Delhi. The relatively meagre national representation in Parliament (25 members in the lower house, *Lok Sabha* and 14 in the upper house *Rajya Sabha*) left the region inadequately positioned to influence decision making and the only cooperation with neighbours existed only for the purpose of feeding into NER's counter insurgency moments. It is with the declaration of the LEP in the mid-1990's, that for the first time, regional diplomacy has since come to be the focus of India's strategy to unbox the NER region.

Looking East through NER

It is generally accepted that the India's LEP was not pursued in a well-planned and structured manner and the policy has over the past two decades evolved in phases and directions. It is only with the inclusion of Myanmar as a full member in the ASEAN in 1997 that the development of physical connectivity between NER and Southeast Asia as a prerequisite to utilize the opportunities provided by LEP resonated in policy circuits (Rahman 2010). As the *North Eastern Region Vision2020* (2008) Report for the North Eastern Region issued by the Ministry of Development of the North East Region (DONER) states that, ironically, the LEP has benefited the NER negligibly and remains a slogan only. Another report by DONER titled, *Aspects of Look East Policy and the North Eastern States*, states that while LEP had been part of India's Foreign Policy since early 1990s, a North East perspective emerged at the official level only in October, 2007 in a meeting of the then Foreign Minister, Shri Pranab Mukherjee and the Chief Ministers of the North Eastern States on the initiative of the Ministry of DONER (2011: 1).

The LEP laid out in early 1990s was a broad contour of policy and in conceptualization and did not envisage any specific role of the NER and remained an Indian Regional initiative and did not conceptualize any sub-regional one as part of it. It was with the inclusion of Myanmar in the ASEAN and the change of mindsets in New Delhi that the North East India was to become the key to India's Look East strategy. The setting up of the Department of North East Region, in 2001, to coordinate and give impetus, to New Delhi's development efforts in the NER, that was later converted into a Ministry in 2004, were very instrumental in creating more concrete energies directed towards the NER as a geographical bridge to South East Asia. The change was also possible due to sub-regional initiatives and the Government of India's need to draw attention and strength the idea of geographic proximity with South East Asia. And thus, attention was to be focused on infrastructure, tourism and development in the North East as the 'Gateway' to SE Asia. But the potential infrastructure projects and existing possibilities for the process of enhancing connectivity had to wait for the turn of the new millennium. Over the years, three aspects of LEP-NE connect have emerged; Connectivity and Physical infrastructure to facilitate trade; Trade and investment protocols; Soft aspects of bi-lateral / multilateral relationships such as in tourism and enhanced people to people interaction through sports, culture, academic and medical research etc (DNER2011:1).

The slow and sketchy implementation of policy two decades after its first declaration is the result of the fact that in-spite of the advantages that North East India offers – like abundant natural and human resources, close access to both domestic markets and international markets, and as entry point into South East Asian markets – the pace of change has been very slow reflecting lack of priority. Similarly, the sluggish pace of industrialisation and socio-economic growth on NER has been further affected by poor infrastructure and connectivity as well as unemployment, low economic development and security concerns in NER.

Especially the lack of visible success, for the NER policy initiatives of the past decades have various contributory factors, some of which have been discussed in preceding pages. But one of the key factors is the result of the dissonance between the national and the sub-national, between the regional initiative and its sub-regional implementation. Essentially that national goals and objectives of desirable policy initiatives while not in disagreement with sub-national aims are many times out of sync with capabilities and strengths of the NER. In various commentaries, the NER was not able not benefit from enormous opportunities of the LEP because of their weak economic base, lack of proper infrastructure, slow growth of connectivity. As Prabhakar (2004: 4608) mentions that the NER states are unable to connect with each other physically not only due to poor transport links and also due to the lack of intellectual and emotional connections among neighbours, or even with and among each other due to their respective insularity flowing from political contexts. Langer (2013) writing on the LEP suggests that energy deficit and lack of infrastructure are the key reasons that NER is neglected and suggests that the lack of basic infrastructure for back end facilities to trade calls for urgent construction of roads, or else, the benefits would accrue to the 'others', a euphemism for non-locals who are often alleged to grab these opportunities.

It is a telling fact that out of India's total export volume of about \$254.4 billion, the Northeast's share is about \$0.01 billion (Langer 2013). Coal and tea make up 95 percent of the NER's exports and that out of the 40 Land Customs Stations in the region, only 20 are functional at a given time. The NER by itself is not a producer of mass consumer goods, and most of the natural resources generated in the NER such as oil, gas and coal are used internally but by mainland India. Externally, NER offers little to India's Regional Trading partners but the focus on infrastructure and law and order could help generate entrepreneurship and NER could potentially become a transit point for trade from the rest of India. Especially, the dissonance between the national and the sub-national come to fore as the *North East Vision 2020* (2008) document stresses on industry and trade, a sector in which the region has virtually none and that most of its produce are minerals and agro-products (Langer 2013).

The *North East Vision 2020* lists a few priorities for the LEP from the perspective of NER which are more reflective of the sub-regional demands. The recommendations include need to increase border trade in agriculture or agro-products; to remove existing restrictions on border trade through designated entry points; need to promote interaction with neighbouring countries through sports, music and other cultural and academic activities to ameliorate persistent security concerns. Trade facilitation with neighbouring countries can improve trade access for NER States, upgrading and activating existing land-customs stations (LCS) and finally, in the long run, the NER needs to plug into the growing trade with ASEAN countries particularly in items like wood products, ores and rubber products (MDNER 2008: 285-286). BCIM-EC provides hope for this out of box thinking on building NER's linkages with neighbouring regions.

Role of NER in BCIM-EC

In order to build a durable involvement of the NER in India's foray into the East and for North East India must ensure that NER benefits from various models and initiatives for building Regional Trading Arrangements. It is imperative that the policies empower the NER to play a creative and positive role representing various stakeholders from the region. This regionalization from below can empower NER to play a positive role in BCIM-EC. There are suggestions that the BCIM-EC has remained a non-starter like many of the Government of India initiatives in regional trading arrangement. However, Professor Patricia Uberoi (2013) suggests that the picture is more nuanced and complex. From the perspective of this study, Uberoi raises a fundamental point and asks, "how to make the BCIM a more effective and sustainable instrument of regional integration, geared to the complementary objective of improving livelihoods in India's NE border regions" (2013: 3). She then goes on to point out that these two objectives are not in harmony both, in either discourses or in practice. This state of affairs is also symptomatic of India's overarching LEP. Further, Uberoi (2003:13) points out that the NER is,

> ...only intermittently, and not consistently, the focus of attention in articulations of India's LEP. And while individual scholars from the region have contributed substantially to the BCIM dialogue, neither academic

> institutions and chambers of commerce in the NER, nor state governments of the region, nor the North Eastern Council which collectively represents the NER states have had a formal role in BCIM Forum activities. These, as noted, are conducted from institutions located in New Delhi.

It would be cogent, at this stage, to clarify that in evaluating participation of various stakeholders from NER in India's LEP forums has been an exercise in pessimism. Most observers from NER have been of the opinion that there is little meaningful participation of NER stakeholders in terms of their inputs in decision making in New Delhi. While NER participation has come to be a feature at the annual K2K forum, it has not basically changed NER's equations with the BCIM[4]. Thus, the inertia that plagues decision making in New Delhi which has been slow on the uptake of regional cooperation (i.e. LEP) is even slower with the sub-regional aspects of cooperation (i.e. BCIM-EC). If we examine the tenor and direction of the BCIM-EC with our focus on NER, we notice that while the BCIM-EC starts with the focus on 3-T's of Trade, Transport and Tourism, in 2013, the 3-T's have transformed into Trade, Transport and Energy. In the past, regional handicrafts, human development issues, people-to-people contacts, environment, climate change and resource-sharing issues have also been since brought to the table. Simply stated, there can be a range of issues that inform the priorities in any regional trading arrangement but the soft pedalling of sectors in the BCIM that would benefit the NER essentially results in the slow pace of benefits from such arrangements and reduces stakes for the region. Professor Patricia Uberoi (2013: 14) further states that,

What we see is that the 'soft' social, cultural and environmental cooperation agendas (and tourism promotion as well) are seen as relatively peripheral to the hard core issues of trade, connectivity and (latterly) energy cooperation, and to the task of building the institutional support through which these hard core objectives can be carried forward by the four governments.

Moving beyond such cherry-picking of issues with the BCIM-EC agenda and its dissonance with the sub-regional demands of India's NER, there are two fundamental issues of de-securitisation and connectivity that the BCIM-EC and other initiatives in India's LEP need to be addressed adequately. The first crucial issue is the desecuritisation of borders, to facilitate the kind of regional trading arrangements that have been envisaged by experts like Baruah (2003:15):

> ...some of the rigidities of political borders – tariffs, customs and other restrictions – will have to go. As national economies respond to the pressures of globalisation... regions have emerged as a key level of governance, innovation and policy-making. There is significant pressure for region building – a "political project in which leaders, build up a territorial form of reference and forge a territorial system of action"... Can Northeast Indian and its transnational neighbours forge such a territorial system of action?

The second is the reality that for NER presents an ideal gateway to the BCIM region, and to draw maximum benefits from NER, the BCIM needs to address issues of smooth physical and technological connectivity. The issue of physical connectivity is of crucial importance as historically India's trade routes with South East Asia have been primarily through the seas rather than continental. Even in contemporary times, it is cheaper and safer to trade with South East Asia through the sea. But in developing land links to bring benefits for NER India's initiative in its Look East policy have to calibrate with the BCIM-EC and this link seems to have finally driven home the point that India's LEP must work through both land and sea (Bhaumik 2014: 4). The two visits and joint statements in 2013 by Chinese Prime Minister Li Keqiang and later PM Manmohan Singh's visit have transformed the Track-II BCIM into a Track I engagement between India and China leading to their commitment to explore developing an Economic Corridor through land. This may also open possibilities of India and China working together on even the maritime Silk Route which is has been a favourite theme of President Xi Jinping.

While the issues of connectivity and physical infrastructure remain primary benchmarks in promoting initiatives regarding BCIM sub-regionalism in the NER of India, there needs to be a more nuanced approach to also underline their historical linkages with the larger sub-region and its extended neighbourhood. For example, as it first step, Meghalaya's traditional linkages with Bangladesh can be brought into focus rather than a more abstract 'integration' with larger South East Asia. It has been stated earlier that historical realities have to be accounted for and one of the starker reality is of ethnic community linkages/divisions across national borders, as example of the more numerous Nagas in Myanmar would illustrate that, without taking into consideration, communities in the NER, the impetus for a coming together would remain largely state driven and not people driven and may subsist and not thrive. The investments in the NER, without considering tax breaks and other incentives, are concentrated in environmentally sensitive industries like coal, petroleum and cement and not so much in environmental friendly agro-industries. These issues are of immense importance in the context of determining the nature of economic development as lessons from other sub-regions have underscored that development comes at a cost and it is a subject of much discussion in the politically conscious NER which fears it would become merely a thoroughfare for India's Look East Policy. These concerns of local stakeholders will have to be addressed and accommodated.

Future Challenges

There remain a number of NER related challenges that affect and will continue to impact on India's LEP in general and BCIM-EC in particular. These challenges can be described as both internal and external. Among the internal challenges, the history of intractable conflicts in the NER which have not been resolved but are stalemated and the low levels of industrialization and infrastructure are crucial determining factors (Bhaumik 2014: 3). It would also be pertinent to mention that the physical terrain of the region is difficult and often gets overlooked when we talk of physical infrastructure of road or rail connectivity, especially considering that this region is one of the wettest places in the world. Among other internal factors that need to be underscored, Bhaumik asserts that decision-making in mainland India remain divided on using the prism of 'volatility' in NER with regard to opening it to the outside world. A section of the security establishment remain particularly fearful of opening a less integrated region of India to China while the pro-trade lobbies point to the arguments of the continued dumping of Chinese goods through the NER asking to regularize these flows of commodities by opening border trade points (2014: 8).

The external challenges are largely in the nature of foreign policy challenges for India. These are especially in terms of it complicated relations with Bangladesh and Myanmar that have seen their ebb and flow over time. For any meaningful sub-regional trading arrangement to fructify, Bangladesh would need to facilitate the transit linkages for NER. For that to happen, India and Bangladesh relations would have to be bullish and stable to conceived of and execute some bold initiatives. Not all domestic constituencies favour such thinking and these have to be cultivated. The trajectory of Myanmar in its transition to democracy remains full of uncertainty and their coming elections in 2017 will be decisive. Meanwhile, the state of the multiple ethnic conflicts and the manner in which Myanmar deals with them would also be important challenges to determine India's foray East (Ibid: 8). The apparent drift in favour of Daw Aung San Suu Kyi's National League for Democracy remains limited with possibilities of military continuing to remain as force to reckon with. These factors must be accounted for in exploring possibilities of linking NER to the BCIM-EC.

The efforts through this paper has been to highlight role of NER and its strengths and limitations in the building blocks of regional trading arrangements for BCIM-EC. The arguments have been located in the larger context of India's celebrated Look East Policy with a particular focus on the BCIM-EC treating as central and critical component of India's LEP. The objective was to provide discussions to shape harmonious policy in both the national and the regional level that could benefit NER by making it part of thriving economic development in BCIM-EC countries and to strengthen its linkages with the ASEAN countries. There are a however a wide range of obstacles that must inform extant understanding and approaches. The objective of ensuring peace and stability in NER and its border regions, issues of illegal, migration and flow of goods, while opening up routes for trade and people-to-people exchanges will have to be addressed as they form the larger canvass to facilitate materializing the full potential of NER's participation in BCIM-EC and turning this vision into thriving reality for mutual benefit.

References

Baruah, Sanjib (2003), *Between South and Southeast Asia: Northeast India and the Look East Policy*, CENISEAS Papers 4, Guwahati: Centre for Northeast India South and Southeast Asia Studies, OKD Institute of Social Change and Development, pp. 46.

Bhattacharya, Biswa and Prabir De (2006), "Promotion of Trade and Investment between People's Republic of China and India: Toward a Regional Perspective", *Asian Development Review*, 22 (1), Asian Development Bank, Manila.

Bhaumik, Subir (2014), Look East Through Northeast: Challenges and Prospects for India, ORF Occasional Paper#51. June.

Ghoshal, Baladas (2013), China's Perception of India's 'Look East Policy' and Its Implications, IDSA Monograph Series, No. 26 October.

Griffiths, Martin and Terry O'Callaghan (2004), *Key Concepts in International Relations*, New York: Routledge.

Haokip, Thongkholal (2012), "Is There a Pan-North-East Identity and Solidarity?", *Economic and Political Weekly*, September 8, 47 (36), pp.84-85.

Langer, Avalok (2013), "Look East, But through Northeast", *Tehelka*, 4 (10), January.

Ngaihte, S Thianlalmuan (2013), "The Reality of North-East as an Entity", *Economic and Political Weekly*, December 14, 48 (50), pp.13-15.

MDNER (2008), *North Eastern Region Vision2020* , Ministry of Development of North East Region, Government of India.

MDNER (2011), *Aspects of Look East Policy and the North Eastern States*, Ministry of Development of North East Region, Government of India, February.

Prabhakra, M. S. (2004), "Is North-East India Landlocked?", *Economic and Political Weekly*, 39 (42), Oct. 16-22, pp. 4606-4608.

Rahim, Q.A.M.A. (1997), "Sub-Regional Cooperation in Eastern South Asia", *Pakistan Horizon*, 50 (3), July, pp. 25-30.

Rahman, Sabina Yasmin (2010), "The North East in India's Look East Policy", *International Politics Energy Culture* available at [web] http://inpec.in/2013/05/14/the-north-east-in-indias-look-east-policy/

Raipuria, Kalyan (2002), "ASEAN and SAARC: Select Futuristic Scenarios", *Economic and Political Weekly*, 37 (35), August 31, pp. 3581-3582.

Research and Information System for Developing Countries (2011), Expansion of North East India's Trade and Investment with Bangladesh and Myanmar: An Assessment of the Opportunities and the Constraints, RIS, 2011.

Uberoi, Patricia (2013), *The BCIM Forum: Retrospect and Prospect*, Institute of Chinese Studies, Institute of Chinese Studies Working Paper # 1

Zedillo, Ernesto (2001), "Globalization and the Changing Roles of States", 2001 Annual Meeting of the Trilateral Commission, London, (Accessed 1 June 2014) URL: http://libertyparkusafd.org/lp/Hamilton/speeches%5CGlobalization%20and%20the%20Changing%20Roles%20of%20States.htm

Endnotes

1. The Secretary-General of the Association of Southeast Asian Nations, Rodolfo C. Severino, speaking at the European Policy Center in Brussels, compared the question "Will ASEAN be like the EU?" is like the one that Professor Higgins asks in My Fair

Lady: "Why can't a woman be more like a man?" — a plaintive question uttered in extreme frustration. To ask such a question of ASEAN and the EU is similarly futile and could be frustrating. In many ways, ASEAN is not like the EU, probably never will be, as women will always be different, in many ways, from men. We all know the forces that impelled the EU's formation and shaped its character. We all know the historical, cultural and ideological foundations that have made it possible for the EU to take the shape and direction that it has. It is these unique forces, circumstances and foundations that have made the EU unique. Cited From, Will ASEAN be like the EU?, available at http://www.aseansec.org/3112.htm

2. South Asia Sub-regional Economic Cooperation (SASEC), Mekong Ganga Cooperation (MGC), Greater Mekong Sub-region (GMS), BCIM Forum, SAARC, Asia Pacific Trade Agreement (APTA), ASEAN, East Asia Summit.
3. North Eastern Council (NEC) was created in 1971 the Ministry of Development of North Eastern Region (MDONER) was constituted in 2001. The establishment of the North Eastern Hill University (NEHU) in 1973 and presence of academic bodies like the North East India History Association (NEIHA) and North East India Political Science Association (NEIPSA), testifies to the consolidation of the NE concept in the academic sphere.
4. This was also brought out in conversations with academics and journalists from North East India.

7

Analysis of Trade Relations in BCIM Sub-Regional Cooperation

Li Yanfang

At the very outset, it in important to underline that in addition to other complex inter- and intra-societal interconnection within the BCIM, inter-state trade and investment have become one of the most critical elements in their regional cooperation. Their long-term concerns on political and security issues as also their development and other national strategies —which are their basic driving force for regional economic cooperation — mainly include the endogenous market forces determining economic ties amongst these countries. This chapter attempts an in-depth analysis of these BCIM economic ties, especially trade relationships, and these qualitative and quantitative analysis seek to make a comprehensive evaluation of their regional economic cooperation exploring the scope, structures and other aspects of four countries/inter-regional trade and investment. This chapter also aims to provide a more solid basis for building not just an effective mechanism for the construction of BCIM-Economic Corridor but also suggest future areas for higher-level research in expanding their economic cooperation.

Genesis of BCIM-Economic Corridor

The earliest conception of BCIM-Economic Corridor can be traced back to the nineteenth Century. At that time, British planned to set up a direct land route from Calcutta to Yunnan to gain greater access to China. After occupying Yangon in 1824, the British planned once again to build a channel across Irrawaddy River into China (Field & Tuer, 1885). British even carried out surveys for route exploration and railway construction from Yangon to Mandalay (Davies, 1905). The idea of contemporary BCIM sub-regional economic cooperation stemmed from China-India-Bangladesh-Myanmar Regional Economic Cooperation Forum in 1999 which has since 2011 renamed as BCIM Regional Cooperation Forum. Although the significance of BCIM economic cooperation has been mentioned repeatedly, these four countries have not really initiated works on the construction of Economic Corridor. Only achievement so far remains the last May 2013 joint statement by prime ministers of China and India that included their commitment to construct BCIM-Economic Corridor.

With BCIM sub-regional economic cooperation beginning to settle into a certain visible pattern, the study on BCIM-Economic Corridor has passed enough thought process to call for a scrutiny on its strengths and weaknesses as an economic cooperation proposition. This chapter seeks to do so roughly by using the following three frameworks:

The *first* is the study of international economic corridor theory and international experience. International Economic Corridor is actually a sub-regional economic cooperation. It was first put forward in the 8th ministerial conference of the Greater Mekong Sub-regional Economic Cooperation (GMS) held in 1998. It implies a mechanism of connecting production, trade and infrastructures in a particular geographic area. Its main purpose is to combine the transportation corridor construction with the economic development strategies, and provide convenience for international cooperation by BCIM. At present, the studies on GMS and its three corridors provides important experience for BCIM Economic Corridor construction.

The *second* framework is the current geo-economic situation and the prospect of BCIM regional economic cooperation. This includes review of the development process of BCIM Economic Cooperation Forum since 1999 (Ren Jia & Chen Lijun, 2004). Studies on the current situation of each country's economic development in BCIM region (Rahman, Rahman & Wasel, 2007), economic cooperation (Tariqur Rahman & Muhammad Amin, 2009), tourism cooperation (Chen Jidong, 2009), energy cooperation (Rahman, 2013) and cooperation in other fields in BCIM region. Studies on bilateral cooperation between intra-regional countries/ regions has been increasing and include works on Sino-Myanmar political and economic relations (Shee, 2002), Sino-India economic and trade cooperation (Bhattacharya, 2005) India-Myanmar Cooperation (Yhome, 2009), Sino-Bangladesh cooperation (Islam, 2012), and the economic and trade cooperation between the northeast region of India and Bangladesh, Myanmar (RIS, 2011). From the existing data, it can be seen that these studies mostly focus on the Sino-India economic and trade relations, and lacked the study of other bilateral and multilateral trade and investment development.

The *third* framework includes studies of BCIM-Economic Corridor construction, the significance of corridor construction (Wen Fude, 2014), the selection of corridor area (Chen Jidong, 2005), the analysis of factors influencing the future economic cooperation mechanism (Li & Peng, 2005), and prospect and strategy (Chen Lijun, 2014). However, the key issues for BCIM Economic Corridor construction, such as the reaction and appeal of each country toward constructing this Economic Corridor, the specific cooperation bases of each country in all fields, the problems existing in the economic corridor construction and resolutions, especially the construction of mechanism promoting the development of economic corridor.

Since year 2000, the BCIM governments, experts and relevant international organisations have all begun to put more emphasis on feasibility of regional economic cooperation. Yet there is lack of adequate research in various fields of BCIM sub-regional cooperation and its basis, mechanism, and development potential have not yet achieved any landmark achievements. In December 2013, four countries of BCIM signed a joint research program about BCIM-Economic Corridor in Kunming, and formally established a working mechanism of promoting cooperation and advancing the economic corridor construction.

Development of BCIM-Economic Corridor

(i) Analysis on BCIM macro-economic development

BCIM-Economic Corridor is an economic belt of organised cooperation, based on complementary advantages and mutual development. With Kunming, Mandalay, Dhaka, Calcutta and other major cities as its nodes and with traffic, energy, communication and other international big channel as its links it connects people, capital, materials, information. The core regions of BCIM include China's Yunnan, India's West Bengal and all northeastern states, as well as the whole territory of Bangladesh and Myanmar, covering about 1.65 million square kilometres, with a population of more than 400 million. Their cooperation will gradually and eventually expand throughout these four countries, as a strong regional cooperation organisation covering an area of more than 13.4 million square kilometres (9% of the world), with a population of nearly 2.8 billion (accounting for 39.9% of the world's population), which will connect China to the South Asian, East Asian and Southeast Asian markets.

As regards their macro-economics, the total amount of GDP in 2012 of these four countries is $1 trillion, accounting for 14.3% of global GDP. From 2000 to 2012, the annual GDP growth of Bangladesh, China, India and Myanmar were respectively 6%, 10%, 6.9% and 11.1%, that is, the average GDP growth maintained above 6% (See Table 1). So, this region belongs to one of the world's high economic growth regions. The development level of these four countries, however, remains highly uneven. In terms of their GDP, China and India are respectively the second and the eighth largest economies of the world, while Bangladesh and Myanmar remain at 59th and 69th place respectively. Likewise, the per capita GDP of this region is only about $3,700. In 2012, the per capita GDP of Bangladesh, China, India and Myanmar was respectively $832, $6,091, $1,503 and $691, putting them respectively at 160th, 88th, 142th and 159th ranks in the world. The foreign trade of these four countries stands at $4.7 trillion, accounting for 13.1% of the world where China alone contributes 10.7%. The Bangladesh, China, India's trade dependence was 50.6%, 47% and 50.6% respectively, while the Myanmar's had just over 30%. Put together, FDI net inflows of four countries were more than $280 billion in total, occupying 18.6% of the world, among which, China contributed 16.8%. In the industrial structure as well, China stands as world's first manufacturing powerhouse followed by India that has become the world's largest offshore service outsourcing country since 2001. Bangladesh and Myanmar, however, are still typical agricultural countries where the proportion of Myanmar's primary industry in its GDP remains just above 30%.

Table 1: The Main Macroeconomic Indexes of BCIM Four Countries in 2012

Items	*Bangladesh*	*China*	*India*	*Myanmar*
Population (million people)	154.7	1350.7	1236.7	52.8
GDP (current price, 1 billion US dollars)	128.8	8227.1	1858.7	57.8
Per capita GDP (US dollars)	832.6	6091	1503	1094
GDP growth rate of 2012	6.2%	7.8%	4.7%	5%
Average GDP growth rate from 2000 to 2012	6.0%	10%	6.9%	11.1%
Proportion of three industries	17.5:28.5:54	10:47:43	17:26:57	32:31:37
Total foreign trade volume (1 billion US dollars)	58.8	3867.0	778.5	18.1
Proportion of foreign trade in GDP	50.6%	47.0%	41.9%	31.3%
FDI net inflows (BoP, 1 billion US dollars)	1.18	253.47	24.00	2.24

Data sources: UNCTAD and World Bank.

At present, the core regions of BCIM, namely, Bangladesh, Myanmar, China's Yunnan and India's West Bengal and northeastern states, belong to the most underdeveloped areas. These regions roughly cover nearly 6.7% of the world's population, while they account for only about 2% of the world total GDP, and the regional per capita GDP is less than $1,300. In addition to Bangladesh and Myanmar rank as least developed in the world. Similarly, the development levels of China's Yunnan province and India's northeastern states are significantly lagging behind their own national levels. Yunnan province is a relatively backward province in China, covering a land area of about 4% of the whole country, and accounting for about 3.5% of the country's population (see Table 2). Similarly, the India's eight states involved in this study are also a relatively poor region in India, covering a land area of about 8.9% of the total area of India, and accounting for about 11% of Indian population (see Table 3). Regarding the GDP development, Yunnan province's GDP accounted for only about 2% of China's total GDP, and its per capita GDP was only 58% of the national average level. If counting the radiation region – China's southwestern four provinces and cities, namely Guizhou, Sichuan, Tibet and Chongqing, the proportion of this regional GDP rose to about 10% of the whole country, and its per capita GDP increased to $4,300, accounting for about 70% of the national average level. Similarly, for 2012-13, the total GDP of India's northeastern states was less than 3% of India's total GDP, and its per capita GDP was only about $870, nearly $700 less than the national average level. If one includes relatively wealthier West Bengal, the total GDP in this region was about $145 billion, accounting for 8.2% of India's total GDP. Its per capita GDP was about $1,074, less than the national average by nearly $500 per annum. In recent years, the average GDP growth rate of these eight states of India's northeastern region is about 6%, which again is slightly lower than the average growth rate of all India.

Economic growth in both Bangladesh and Myanmar's depends mainly on agriculture. China's Yunnan province,

India's West Bengal and its eight northeastern provinces are also traditionally agricultural provinces. Among them, the proportions of three industries in Yunnan are 16.2%, 42% and 41.8%, and its industrialization level is lower than China's domestic average level. For Indian northeastern provinces as well (except for Meghalaya and Sikkim), the proportion of industry is all below 30% (see Table 3). Although the service industry of these states account for a relatively high percentage, the labor force is mainly engaged in agricultural production. In fact, in addition to that the low levels of industrialisation, development of the emerging industry, service industry and other emerging industries in the intra-regional countries and regions are also backward. In 2012 the foreign trades of Yunnan province stood at $21 billion, accounting for 0.5% of China's total foreign trades, not matching its 2% proportion of GDP. Its degree of dependence on foreign trade was about 12.8%, lagging behind the national average level of 47%. In 2012, the actual utilised foreign investment of Yunnan province was nearly $2.2 billion, accounting for 2% of the total amount of the national actual utilised foreign investment. If one includes the other four provinces of Southwestern China, the proportion of foreign trades of this region in the national totals increases to 3.7%, and the proportion of the utilised foreign investment was raises to 22.3%. For India, the economic opening level of India's northeast remains lower. The proportion of its foreign trades in India's totals was almost negligible. Eastern parts of West Bengal's performance has been slightly better; for 2010-11, its exports accounted for 2.83% of total exports of India. For investment, from March 2000 to August 2013, the FDI inward stock of West Bengal and northeastern provinces stood at $6.5 billion, accounting for about 3.2% of India's total FDI inflows.

Table 2: The Main Macroeconomic Indexes for China's Southwestern Five Provinces/City in 2012

Index	*Yunnan*	*Sichuan*	*Guizhou*	*Tibet*	*Chongqing*
Land area (ten thousand sq.km.)	39.4	48.5	17	120	8.24
Population (million people)	46.6	80.8	34.8	3.1	29.5
Population density	118.3	166.5	204.9	2.6	357.4
GDP (current price, one hundred million US dollars)	1633.2	3778.2	1077.6	110.2	1815.3
Per capita GDP (US dollars)	3541.9	4713.6	3119.7	3664.4	6245.6
Total exports (1 billion US dollars)	10.0	38.5	4.9	3.4	38.6
Total imports (1 billion US dollars)	11.0	20.7	1.7	0.7	14.6
Actual utilized FDI (1 billion US dollars)	2.19	10.55	1.46	0.17	10.53

Data sources: 2012 China Statistical Yearbook.

Table 3: The Main Macroeconomic Indexes for India's Northeastern States from 2012 to 2013

Index	*West Bengal*	*Assam*	*Manipur*	*Meghalaya*
Land area (sq.km.)	88752	78438	22000	22429
Population (million people)	90.8	31.2	2.9	2.7
Population density	1029.3	397.4	121.9	132.2
GDP (1 billion rupees)	5705.2	1310.1	104.4	160.6
Per capita GDP (Rupee)	62831	42036	36290	60156
Urbanization rate	31.9%	14.1%	30.2%	20.1%
Proportion of three industries	22.9:17.7:59.5	23.8:23.6:52.7	25.1:27.5:47.5	14.5:33.1:52.4

Index	Mizoram	Nagaland	Sikkim	Tripura
Land area (sq.km.)	21081	16579	7096	10486
Population (million people)	1.1	2.0	0.6	3.7
Population density	51.8	119.5	85.6	350.1
GDP (1 billion rupees)	63.5	123.8	88.9	202.6
Per capita GDP (Rupee)	54689	59535	142625	55004
Urbanization rate	51.5%	28.9%	24.9%	26.2%
Proportion of three industries	17.1:22.3:60.6	25.3:17.1:57.6	9.1:60.3:30.6	21.0:27.3:51.7%

Data sources: India's Interior Ministry and the Reserve Bank of India, in which, the data of Mizoram are the annual data of 2011-2012.

Note: West Bengal is officially defined to belong to India's eastern region.

Analysis of BCIM Trade Development

(i) Trends in trade development

From the national level, since year 2000, BCIM foreign trade has made rapid development, but their opening up trajectories have been uneven. China has been already become world's first big trade country, whose imports, exports and foreign trade volume respectively account for respectively 10.2%, 11.2% and 10.7% of the global imports, exports and total foreign trade. India ranks tenth, and its imports, exports and foreign trade volume respectively stand respectively at 2.7%, 1.6% and 2.2% of the global imports, exports and total foreign trades. The foreign trade development of Bangladesh and Myanmar is relatively backward and the proportion of the foreign trade in these two countries in the world is almost negligible. Especially Myanmar has just begun its market reforms, and the foundations of its foreign trade are very weak. For comparison, China's imports and exports accounted for 77.4% and 86.3% of the total imports and exports of these four BCIM countries; India's accounted for 20.8% and 12.2%; Bangladesh's accounted for 1.4% and 1.1%; Myanmar accounted for 0.39% and 0.37% only.

As regards the whole BCIM region, the growth of its foreign trade is very impressive. It is interesting to note that its growth rate is higher than the global average level. From 2000 to 2012, the imports of this region increased from $289.3 billion to $2.3487 trillion and its exports increased from $299.6 billion to $2.3737 trillion. The total BCIM trade volume increased from $588.9 billion to $4.7224 trillion. These three values thereby increase almost 8 times, while the global imports, exports and total foreign trades increased about 2.8 times in the same period. In year 2000, the BCIM imports and exports respectively accounted for only 4.5% and 4.7% of the global imports and exports. By 2012, these two figures increased to 13.1% and 13% (See Table 4). Among them, the proportions of China's imports and exports respectively contributed about 10 to 11 percentage points. Overall, these regional foreign trade trends were in a surplus state for most years since 2000 (only 2011 appeared a deficit of 14.2 billion US dollars). The main reason for this was that China's huge surplus made up for the export decline of the other three countries.

(ii) Country-wise Trade Developments

(a) Trade Development of Bangladesh

Bangladesh imports and exports were never very large. However, recent years have witnessed a steady growth in trade of Bangladesh, providing a strong support for its economic development. Among new trends, the most obvious evidence has been Bangladesh's increasing dependence on foreign trade which has gone up from 35.34% in 2000 to 50.6% in 2012. Although it was only equivalent to the global average level in 2002, its longitudinal development process shows that the country's economic opening up has constantly improved and the degree of dependence of its domestic economy on the international market is also rising.

Except for year 2002 (affected by American market fluctuations) and before and after 2009 (affected by the global economic slowdown), Bangladesh's import and export have experienced high growth. From 2000 to 2012, the country's total foreign trade volume increased from $15.27 billion to $58.85 billion, an increase of nearly 3.9 times. Over the same period, country's average annual import and export growth rates were more than 10%, and in 2011 both growth rates were as high as 29%. Considering the market, Bangladesh had established trade relations with more than 130 countries and regions. Its main export markets were the United States, Germany, Britain and France and its main import markets were China, India, Singapore, Japan, etc. Bangladesh's major export products included primary products (like jute, tea, aquatic products and other agricultural products), manufactured goods (like clothing, knitwear, leather and footwear, etc.). In total exports, garment exports are usually make the largest contribution, and have occupied more than 75% of its total exports for a long time. The main imported products for Bangladesh include means of production, textiles, petroleum and petroleum-related products, iron and steel and other base metals, edible oil, cotton, etc.

Because of the industrial development and foreign trade structures and other domestic reasons, Bangladesh's import and export have been generally in a deficit state. Especially in recent two years, this country has imported large quantities of food and fuel, widening the international trade deficit value. The deficit of this country in the 1990s was $2.2 billion a year but since 2000, the deficit value has expanded to $2.49 billion a year. By 2011 and 2012, the deficit value had further expanded respectively to $8.5 billion and $5.8 billion.

(b) The trade development of China/Yunnan

Since the year 2000, China's foreign trade has been growing continuously. Although the total foreign trade volume had dropped sharply in 2009, it quickly recovered in 2010, and China continues to create new records in foreign trade. China's foreign trades in 2012 and 2013 respectively reached 3.8 trillion and $4.1 trillion. However, as far as growth rates are concerned, the past two years growth rates of China's foreign trade were about 7% and 8%, which is far below the average growth rate of nearly 25% that occurred during 2001-05. In addition, the degree of China's dependence on foreign trade has seen a continuous decline: from the peak of 63% in 2005 to about 47%, though China still remains a country with medium degree trade dependence. China's foreign trade surplus in 2000 was $24.1 billion, while in 2008 this value was as high as $298 billion. In 2011 this surplus declined to $155 billion, but after 2012 it rebounded again. The European Union, the United States, ASEAN, Hong Kong and Japan are major trade partners of China. However, only in recent years, China's trade volume with the European Union and Japan has experienced a decline, while China's exports to ASEAN have been growing rapidly. The largest proportion of trade commodity is mechanical and electrical equipment and machinery equipment; the imported goods are mainly mechanical and electrical equipment, mineral fuels, machinery equipment and the ores.

In this backdrop in the recent years, foreign[1] trade of China's Yunnan province has also grown rapidly. Except for the slight decline affected by the global economic slowdown of 2009, Yunnan's foreign trade has basically maintained a high growth levels. In 2013, the imports and exports of Yunnan province amounted to $25.83 billion, accounting for 0.62% of the national total foreign trades, marking an increase of 22.9% over the previous year. Yunnan's growth rate was higher than the national average of 15.3%. Its exports amounted to $15.96 billion, marking an year-on-year increase of 59.3%. However, Yunnan's imports amounted to $9.87 billion, marking an year-on-year decline of 10.2%. In addition to the growth of the total amount, the total trade volume of Yunnan province with the main partners has also been growing. According to statistics available, trade between Yunnan and ASEAN amounted to $10.9 billion, a growth of 61%, with a proportion in the whole provincial foreign trades increasing from 32.2% in 2012 to 42.2%; the trade volume with the European

Union and the United States were $1.74 billion and $1.24 billion, increasing by 57.1% and 1.3 times. The proportion in the whole provincial foreign trade increased from 7.8% last year to 11.5%.

As regards Yunnan's bilateral trade with the South Asian countries, it amounted to $780 million, increasing by 35.6%. Yunnan mainly exports mechanical and electrical products, agricultural products, textiles and clothing, electric power and non-ferrous metals, and mainly imports mechanical and electrical products, metal ores, agricultural products, timber etc.[1] In year 2001, foreign trade of China's Yunnan province neighbouring South Asia amounted to $1.99 billion, accounting for about 7.7% of the GDP of Yunnan province, with nearly 31 percentage points lower than the national 38.5%. By year 2013, Yunnan province's foreign trade had increased to $25.83 billion, accounting for about 13.64% of Yunnan's GDP. However, given the high growth rate for overall China, Yunnan's gap with the national economy was not shrinking but growing larger. Compared with 45.41% nationwide level for year 2001, it was lower by nearly 32 percentage points by 2013.

(iii) Trade Development in India's Northeast

Since early 1990s, structural reform with the goal of liberalization, globalization and privatization (LPG), India has made remarkable achievements in economic development, and in evolving export-oriented policies that have since accelerated its foreign trade growth. Since year 2003, the scale of Indian foreign trade has continued to expand. In year 2000, India's foreign trades stood at $95.3 billion, of which the imports and exports were respectively $52.9 billion and $42.3 billion. By year 2012, India's foreign trade volume had reached $778.5 billion, of which its imports and exports were respectively $488.9 billion and $289.5 billion. For recent period during 2002-06 the average annual growth rate has been above 20%. India's foreign trade growth rate though fluctuates yet on the whole it still maintains a growth rate of more than 5%. At present, India's main trading partners are the United Arab Emirates, China,

America, Saudi Arabia and Switzerland, etc. India's main export commodities include oil, jewellery, means of transport, machinery and equipment, medical products and fine chemicals, metal products, garment, electronic products, iron, ore, sands, etc. India's main import commodities include crude oil and refined oil, pearl and semi-precious stones, gold, non-electronic machinery, electronic products, organic chemicals, iron and steel, coal and coke, metal ore and scrap metal etc. Apart from the slowing down and fluctuations in its annual growth, the biggest problem for India's foreign trade has been its trade deficit. From 2000 to 2012, trade deficit appeared to grow year after year and the deficit has continued to grow bigger. In 2000, the trade deficit was only $10.6 billion, while by 2012 the deficit had widened to $199.4 billion.

All the provinces in India's northeastern region mostly have typical internally-oriented economic channels and structures. Except for a small amount of low-value high-volume border trade, the relevance of foreign trade between these provinces of India and neighbouring economies is not really very large. Export for the period during 2006-2011 from West Bengal showed much faster growth. These increased from $12.63 billion to $25.07 billion which was an average annual growth rate as high as 18.9%, accounting for 2.83% of total exports of Indian republic. The main export products of this region are leather, flowers, tea, of which the leather exports accounted for 55% of all India's leather exports. It is also noteworthy that software outsourcing exports of West Bengal accounted for 3% of all India total IT export by value. Besides West Bengal, Meghalaya also had a small amount of exports, whose exports during 2010-11 stood at $84 million. As many as eight species of main 20 species of medicinal plants are grown in this from area.[2]

(iv) Trade Development of Myanmar

Since the military government came to power in Yangon in August 1988, Myanmar's foreign trade development level has been extremely low because of economic boycott most

Western sanctions. In year 2011, Myanmar began its transition to democracy and market reforms, but its foreign trade growth hasn't improved much. According to the data of the World Bank, Myanmar's total foreign trade in 1990 was even less than $600 million.. It reached $18.2 billion in 2011 from where it again began to slide with a clear decrease in 2012. Overall the trade had saw a certain increase, but the dependence on foreign trade of Myanmar is still very low, only about 30% by the end of 2012. Over 90% of Myanmar's total foreign trade is from neighbouring Asian countries.

Myanmar's top five trading partners are China, Thailand, Singapore, Japan and South Korea. Myanmar's main export commodities are natural gas, rice, corn, beans, rubber, minerals, timber, gems and aquatic products, etc. Myanmar's main import commodities are industrial raw materials, machinery and equipment, spare parts, metal products and consumer goods, etc.[3] Overall, Myanmar's foreign trade structure is not very streamlined. Its exports are mainly resource commodities, while the imports are commodities with higher technology and value addition. With rapid growth of its domestic economy, the use volume of natural gas is increase gradually, and its ability of depending on natural gas as the largest source of foreign exchange earning to maintain a trade balance is becoming weaker. Meanwhile, Myanmar's export of other resource products is also facing new challenges due to the rise of resource nationalism. Because of this, Myanmar's foreign trade in 2012 appeared to have a deficit once again since 2002, with a value of this deficit reaching $300 million.

Table 4: BCIM Import and Export Development Status

Unit: one hundred million US dollars

	Exports to the world								
	2000	*2005*	*2006*	*2007*	*2008*	*2009*	*2010*	*2011*	*2012*
Bangladesh	63.9	93.3	116.9	131.4	162.2	159.2	202.6	257.9	265.0
China	2492.0	7619.5	9689.4	12200.6	14306.9	12016.5	15777.6	18983.9	20487.8
India	423.6	1003.5	1212.0	1459.0	1818.6	1767.7	2204.1	3014.8	2895.6
Myanmar	16.5	39.7	46.8	64.0	69.7	66.8	86.6	92.4	89.0
Total exports of these four countries (1)	2996.0	8756.0	11065.1	13855.0	16357.4	14010.2	18270.9	22349.0	23737.4
Total global exports (2)	64314.9	103771.3	119920.8	138845.2	159688.3	124096.8	151386.2	181249.5	182146.8
(1) / (2)	4.7%	8.4%	9.2%	10.0%	10.2%	11.3%	12.1%	12.3%	13.0%

Imports from the world									
	2000	*2005*	*2006*	*2007*	*2008*	*2009*	*2010*	*2011*	*2012*
Bangladesh	88.8	126.3	156.9	176.2	226.1	206.9	263.7	343.2	323.5
China	2250.9	6599.5	7914.6	9561.2	11325.6	10055.6	13960.0	17433.9	18182.0
India	529.4	1408.6	1782.1	2186.5	3157.1	2664.0	3500.3	4624.0	4889.8
Myanmar	24.0	19.5	25.8	33.2	43.0	43.5	47.6	90.2	92.0
Total imports of these four countries (3)	2893.1	8153.9	9879.4	11957.1	14751.8	12970	17771.6	22491.3	23487.3
Total global imports (4)	64369.6	103382.3	118876.2	137062.9	158425.2	122110.5	148549.1	177946.4	178991.0
(3) / (4)	4.5%	7.9%	8.3%	8.7%	9.3%	10.6%	12.0%	12.6%	13.1%
Total trade volume in the world									
	2000	*2005*	*2006*	*2007*	*2008*	*2009*	*2010*	*2011*	*2012*

Data sources: based on UNCTAD data computing tabulating.

BCIM's Foreign Direct Investment

(i) Overall development of BCIM-FDI

In recent years, BCIM's Foreign Direct Investment (FDI) has made impressive progress. From 2000 to 2012, the FDI inflows of this region increased from $45.1 billion to $149.8 billion, increasing 3.3 times, and the outflows of FDI increased from $1.4 billion to $92.8 billion, an increase of nearly 65 times. As proportion of the total global FDI, BCIM total inflows increased from 3.2% to 11.1%, and its proportion in the global FDI outflows climbed quickly to 6.7% for 2012 from 0.1% in year 2000. Specific to the BCIM countries, FDI inflows accounted for respectively 0.07%, 8.9%, 1.9% and 0.17% of the global FDI inflows; Bangladesh and Myanmar's proportion in global FDI outflows was almost 0%, while China and India respectively accounted for 6.1% and 0.6% (See Table 5). Therefore, China's and India's, especially China's FDI inflows and outflows occupied an absolutely important position in the sum total of foreign capital introduction and investment. China's FDI inflows and outflows respectively accounted for 80.8% and 90.7% in the overall regional FDI inflows and outflows, and India accounted for 17% and 9.2%.

(ii) Country-wise/region-wise FDI trends

(a) FDI development in Bangladesh

The FDI inflows into Bangladesh are usually quite small. In 2012, the country's total FDI inflows and outflows were only $990 million and $53 million respectively. This accounted for a proportion of only 0.6% in the FDI total inflows of these four countries and with a negligible proportion in the region's FDI total outflows. The main sources of foreign capital for destination Bangladesh are South Korea, Malaysia, Egypt, Britain, Holland, Thailand and Hong Kong of China, and the main fields invested are telecommunications, textile, bank, energy and petroleum and agricultural field. As regards recent FDI trends, the net inflows under a capital balance account, for year 2012, stood at $1.8 billion for country's net FDI inflows, and foreign investment in the stoke were $7.5 billion.

(b) FDI trends for China/ Yunnan

In 2012, China attracted impressive $121.08 billion of FDI, ranking second in the world after the United States. China's FDI outflows likewise reached $84.2 billion for 2012. For the first time China became world's third largest foreign investor. China's most foreign investments were from Hong Kong, Macao and Taiwan, Japan and South Korea, Britain and the United States and the European Union countries. Approximately, 60% of the China's investment flowed into Hong Kong, British Virgin Islands and Cayman islands. China's foreign investments were mainly focused onto high-end manufacturing industries and modern service industries, wherein the communication equipment, computers and other electronic equipment manufacturing industries, and electrical machinery and equipment manufacturing industry became the main industries attracting most of its investment in its manufacturing industry. Similarly, industries with China's outward investment were widely distributed and, in various categories, wherein those with a stock of over $ 10 billion were leasing and business services, financial services, mining, wholesale and retail, manufacturing, transportation/storage and postal industry, construction industry etc.[4]

In the case of China's Yunnan province, in 2012, this province utilised over $2.189 billion worth of FDI, accounting for 1.96% of the nationwide actual utilised FDI for that year. This was consistent with its proportion of 2% in national GDP. The actual FDI in Yunnan also continues to increase piecemeal. For instance in year 2013, there were 40 new approved foreign investment enterprises, and the actual foreign investment value stood at $821.2 million, an year-on-year increase of 15.6%. By December 2013, the number of Yunnan's foreign investment enterprises had reached 440, and the actual foreign investment amounted to $3.38 billion.[5] Yunnan's foreign investments mainly came from Asia, of which 79.8% of the capital was from Hong Kong, while 80% of Yunnan's outward investment flows were aimed at Vietnam, Myanmar, and Laos in ASEAN. Yunnan's FDI is mainly in the third industry, accounting for nearly 70% of foreign capital in place. Among them, the proportion of foreign investment in real estate industry, the wholesale and retail industry had a larger increase. Energy and mineral resources have since emerged as the main commodities of Yunnan overseas investments.

(c) FDI development of India's Northeast

Since 1991, the Indian government has gradually relaxed the restrictions on foreign capital. From 2000 to 2013, the FDI attracted by India reached $206 billion, with the main investors being Holland, Mauritius, Singapore, Japan, the United States and Britain, etc. The investment sectors are mainly services, computer software and hardware, communication, infrastructure, automotive and other industries. For nearly a decade now, the foreign investments attracted by service industry have accounted for over 20% of India's total foreign investments. The main destinations of India's outward investments are Holland, Singapore, the British Virgin Islands and Mauritius, accounting for respectively 28.85%, 15.2%, 10.3% and 7% of India's total outward investments.

India's northeastern region, however, has had a very low degree of opening up to the outside world and it lacks the ability of attracting foreign investment. From March 2000 to August 2013, the FDI inflows stock of West Bengal province and India's other northeastern provinces had reached $6.5 billion, accounting for only 3.2% of India's total FDI inflows. Among them, West Bengal and Sikkim provinces individually were $2.5 billion each (accounting for about 1.2% of India's FDI total inflows). Others provinces like Assam, Manipur, Meghalaya and Tripura were each $80 million, and Nagaland was $7.8 million. FDI in Meghalaya, Manipur and Assam mainly invested in power generation and services; in Sikkim, West Bengal, Tripura and Assam mainly invest in electric power, mining, low-end manufacturing and service industry etc.[6]

(d) FDI development in Myanmar

Since 1998, Myanmar has promulgated the "Foreign Investment Law of Myanmar" and "Regulations for the Implementation of Foreign Investment of Myanmar". Compared to the Ne Win period, the new military regime has made great progress in attracting foreign capital. Nevertheless, the total amount of utilised foreign capital remains still rather small. In the more recent period of reforms starting from 2011, Myanmar's ability of attracting foreign capital has enhanced significantly. From 2000 to 2012, Myanmar's FDI inflows increased from $210 million to $2.24 billion. The main sources of Myanmar's FDI are from China, Thailand, Hong Kong, South Korea and other Asian countries and regions.

At the end of year 2013, there were a total of 32 countries and regions investing in 554 projects in Myanmar, with a total investments of $42.09 billion. Six countries and regions with maximum investment in Myanmar respectively include China ($14.18 billion), Thailand ($9.568 billion), Hong Kong ($6.381 billion), Britain ($2.989 billion) and Singapore ($2.216 billion). Among them, China, Thailand and Hong Kong accounted for 70% of Myanmar's total foreign investment. Secondly, much of the FDI is mainly concentrated on Myanmar's resource-based industry like its gas-fields. The foreign direct investment attracted by the power generation sector, oil and gas, mining and other resource-based industries accounts for 86% of Myanmar's total foreign investment.

Intra-BCIM Economic and Trade Relations

(i) Analysis on intra-BCIM trade

As these four countries began advocating BCIM cooperation since 1999, the economic and trade ties of four countries have continued to deepen. However, this kind of sub-regional economic and trade ties remain still very inadequate from any practical point of view. The imports and exports of four countries within the region in year 2000 were only $6.2 billion and $4.8 billion respectively.

Table 5: BCIM FDI Development Status

Unit: one hundred million US dollars

	2000	*2005*	*2006*	*2007*	*2008*	*2009*	*2010*	*2011*	*2012*
Situations of global and four countries' FDI inflow									
Global	14131.7	9896.2	14805.9	20027.0	18164.0	12164.8	14085.4	16515.1	13509.3
Bangladesh	5.8	8.5	7.9	6.7	1 0.9	7.0	9.1	11.4	9.9
China	407.2	724.6	727.2	835.2	1083.1	950.0	1147.3	1239.9	1210.8
India	35.9	76.2	203.3	253.5	471.4	356.6	211.3	361.9	255.4
Myanmar	2.1	2.4	2.8	7.1	8.6	9.7	12.8	22.0	22.4
Situations of global and four countries' FDI outflow									
	2000	*2005*	*2006*	*2007*	*2008*	*2009*	*2010*	*2011*	*2012*
Global	12403.2	9037.6	14274.7	22720.5	20053.3	11497.8	15049.3	16780.4	13909.6
Bangladesh	0.02	0.03	0.04	0.21	0.09	0.29	0.15	0.13	0.53
China	9.2	122.6	176.3	265.1	559.1	565.3	688.1	746.5	842.2

India	5.1	29.9	142.8	172.3	211.5	160.3	159.3	124.6	85.8
Myanmar	0	0	--	--	--	--	--	--	--
Proportion of FDI inflow of four countries in the world									
Bangladesh	0.04%	0.09%	0.05%	0.03%	0.06%	0.06%	0.07%	0.07%	0.07%
China	2.9%	7.3%	4.9%	4.2%	6.0%	7.8%	8.2%	7.5%	8.9%
India	0.25%	0.77%	1.4%	1.3%	2.6%	2.9%	1.5%	2.2%	1.9%
Myanmar	0.02%	0.02%	0.02%	0.04%	0.05%	0.08%	0.09%	0.13%	0.17%
Proportion of FDI outflow of four countries in the world									
Bangladesh	0.00%	0.00%	0.00%	0.00%	0.00%	0.00%	0.00%	0.00%	0.00%
China	0.07%	1.4%	1.5%	1.2%	2.8%	4.9%	4.6%	4.5%	6.1%
India	0.04%	0.33%	1.0%	0.8%	1.1%	1.4%	1.1%	0.7%	0.6%
Myanmar	0.00%	0.00%	0.00%	0.00%	0.00%	0.00%	0.00%	0.00%	0.00%

Data sources: the same as above.

Note: China's investment doesn't include Hong Kong and Macao. Although the specific data of Myanmar is insufficient, the fact that its total amount is too small doesn't affect the study.

Table 6: The Proportion Change of the Trade within BCIM Region in Global Trade

Unit: one hundred million dollars

Exports within the region and its proportion in world exports									
	2000	*2005*	*2006*	*2007*	*2008*	*2009*	*2010*	*2011*	*2012*
Bangladesh	0.8	2.2	4.8	4.8	5.1	4.3	7.0	10.7	11.5
China	29.6	122.7	188.8	291.0	381.2	363.7	511.8	631.7	613.2
India	15.5	90.2	96.2	117.2	135.7	127.6	207.3	205.8	201.9
Myanmar	2.9	9.1	10.7	14.6	16.0	15.3	15.2	20.4	19.5
Exports within the region (1)	48.8	224.2	300.5	427.6	538.0	510.9	741.3	868.6	846.1
Exports of four countries (2)	2996.0	8756.0	11065.1	13855.0	16357.4	14010.2	18270.9	22349.0	23737.4
World exports (3)	64314.9	103771.3	119920.8	138845.2	159688.3	124096.8	151386.2	181249.5	182146.8
(1) / (2)	1.6%	2.6%	2.7%	3.1%	3.3%	3.6%	4.1%	3.9%	3.6%
(1) / (3)	0.08%	0.22%	0.25%	0.31%	0.34%	0.41%	0.49%	0.48%	0.47%

Imports within the region and its proportion in world exports

	2000	2005	2006	2007	2008	2009	2010	2011	2012
Bangladesh	19.6	38.3	49.0	58.1	71.9	63.9	87.9	117.7	110.6
China	15.0	101.2	106.3	151.1	210.4	145.0	220.8	255.0	205.8
India	22.2	138.3	181.3	254.5	353.0	330.0	442.7	583.2	561.8
Myanmar	5.2	6.9	9.1	11.7	15.2	15.3	13.0	30.7	31.3
Imports within the region 4)	62.0	284.7	345.7	475.4	650.5	554.2	764.4	986.6	909.5
Imports of four countries (5)	2893.1	8153.9	9879.4	11957.1	14751.8	12970	17771.6	22491.3	23487.3
World imports (6)	64369.6	103382.3	118876.2	137062.9	158425.2	122110.5	148549.1	177946.4	178991.0
(4) / (5)	2.1%	3.5%	3.5%	4.0%	4.4%	4.3%	4.3%	4.4%	3.9%

Data sources: based on UNCTAD data computing tabulating.

By year 2012, their imports and exports increased to $90.9 billion and $84.6 billion respectively, an increase of 14 times and 17 times respectively. The imports of Bangladesh, China, India and Myanmar accounted for 12.2%, 22.6%, 61.8% and 3.4% respectively of the total regional imports. The exports of four countries accounted for 1.3%, 72.5%, 23.9% and 2.3% respectively of total regional exports. China occupied the first place in the export, while India imports was in the leading place.

The overall intra-regional imports and exports were nevertheless very small, occupying an insignificant proportion in the imports and exports of these four BCIM countries. These were even more insignificant proportion of the global imports and exports. For example, intra-regional imports and exports in year 2000 occupied 2.1% and 1.6% of imports and exports of four countries respectively, and 0.1% and 0.08% of the total global imports and exports. Till 2012, the intra-regional imports and exports took up 3.9% and 3.6% of ones of four countries respectively, and 0.51% and 0.47% of the total global ones respectively, and the trade volume within the region made up 3.7% and 0.49% of the trade volume of four countries and world trade volume respectively.

(ii) Development of Trade between BCIM States

(a) Bangladesh's trade with China, India, Myanmar

In 2012, total imports and exports of Bangladesh to other BCIM countries stood at $11.06 billion and $1.15 billion, occupying 12.2% and 1.3% respectively in intra-regional imports and exports. The proportion of imports dropped 0.4 percentage points compared with that in 2000, and the proportion of export dropped nearly 20% percentage points. Bangladesh has since emphasised to streamlining intra-regional imports, but has had very little influence on intra-regional exports, and the influence of Bangladesh on intra-regional trade has declined over the years.

For Bangladesh, the significance of intra-BCIM sub-regional trade has gradually increased. From year 2000 to

Table 7: The Trade Development between Bangladesh and China, India, Myanmar

Unit: one hundred million dollars

Bangladesh exports to China, India, Myanmar									
	2000	*2005*	*2006*	*2007*	*2008*	*2009*	*2010*	*2011*	*2012*
China	0.17	0.68	2.6	1.4	1.3	1.3	2.8	4.3	4.7
India	0.64	1.5	2.2	3.4	3.8	2.9	4.2	6.4	6.7
Myanmar	0.06	0.19	0.34	0.60	0.45	0.74	0.63	0.88	0.12
Total exports to this region	0.87	2.37	5.14	5.4	5.55	4.94	7.63	11.58	11.52
Total exports to the world	63.9	93.3	116.9	131.4	162.2	159.2	202.6	257.9	265.0
Proportion of intra-regional exports	1.4%	2.5%	4.4%	4.1%	3.4%	3.1%	3.8%	4.5%	4.3%
Bangladesh imports from China, India, Myanmar									
	2000	**2005**	**2006**	**2007**	**2008**	**2009**	**2010**	**2011**	**2012**
China	9.9	21.4	29.4	32.2	35.6	35.5	47.6	66.7	62.0
India	9.5	16.5	19.2	25.4	35.5	27.7	39.3	49.4	47.9

Myanmar	0.38	0.40	0.34	0.39	0.84	0.69	1.0	1.6	0.76
Total imports from this region	19.8	38.3	48.9	58.0	71.9	63.9	87.9	117.7	110.6
Total imports from the world	88.8	126.3	156.9	176.2	226.1	206.9	263.7	343.2	323.5
Proportion of intra-regional imports	22.3%	30.3%	31.2%	32.9%	31.8%	30.9%	33.3%	34.3%	34.2%
Bangladesh trade volume to China, India, Myanmar									
	2000	**2005**	**2006**	**2007**	**2008**	**2009**	**2010**	**2011**	**2012**
China	10.07	22.08	32	33.6	36.9	36.8	50.4	71	66.7
India	10.14	18	21.4	28.8	39.3	30.6	43.5	55.8	54.6
Myanmar	0.44	0.59	0.68	0.99	1.29	1.43	1.63	2.48	0.88
Trade volume with this region	20.65	40.67	54.08	63.39	77.49	68.83	95.53	129.28	122.18
Trade volume with the world	152.7	219.6	273.9	307.7	388.3	366.1	466.2	601.1	588.5
Proportion of intra-regional trade	13.5%	18.5%	19.7%	20.6%	20.0%	18.8%	20.5%	21.5%	20.8%

Data sources: the same as above.

2012, the proportion of Bangladesh imports from this BCIM sub-region as percentage of its total imports have increased from 22.3% to 34.2%. However, the proportion of Bangladesh's intra-regional exports for the same period have also increased from 1.4% to 4.3%. More specifically, Bangladesh's exports to China, India, and Myanmar were initially small, occupying respectively 1.8%, 2.5% and 0.05% in its total exports. In contrast, increasing dependence of Bangladesh on imports from China, India, and Myanmar, respectively occupies 19.2%, 14.8% and 0.2% in its total imports. There is an increasing concern with regards to the rising significance of China, India and Myanmar markets to Bangladesh export which have undergone subtle changes over the years. In year 2000, the foreign trade volume of Bangladesh with China, India and Myanmar made up 6.6%, 6.6% and 0.3% in the total foreign trade volume of Bangladesh. In 2012 these proportions changed to 11.3%, 9.3% and 0.15% respectively. That is, after thirteen years, the importance of Chinese market for Bangladesh had surpassed that of India's markets. In addition, the trade between Bangladesh and Myanmar also appeared to decline sharply as proportion of Myanmar's total trade volume with Bangladesh dropped by about a half. So with regards to Bangladesh, while China's bilateral trade had gained trade of India and Myanmar with Bangladesh had witness a relative decline.

(b) China's Trade with Bangladesh, India, Myanmar

In 2012, Chinese imports and exports to BCIM region were $20.58 billion and $61.32 billion respectively, accounting for 22.6% and 72.5% respectively of the intra-regional total imports and exports of BCIM. By 2012, the proportion of China's imports had dropped by 1.5 percentage points than where it was in 2000, but for the same period, the proportion of China's exports to the BCIM region had increased by nearly 12 percentage points. Obviously, China had a larger influence on this region's exports, but the contributions that China had to the intra-regional imports has decreased. However, compared to China's overall trade its trade volume

Table 8: The Trade Development between China and Bangladesh, India, and Myanmar

Unit: one hundred million dollars

China's exports to Bangladesh, India, and Myanmar									
	2000	*2005*	*2006*	*2007*	*2008*	*2009*	*2010*	*2011*	*2012*
Bangladesh	9.0	24.0	30.9	33.5	45.6	44.4	67.9	78.1	79.7
India	15.6	89.3	145.8	240.5	315.9	296.7	409.1	505.4	476.8
Myanmar	5.0	9.4	12.1	17.0	19.8	22.6	34.8	48.2	56.7
Total exports to this region	29.6	122.7	188.8	291	381.3	363.7	511.8	631.7	613.2
Total exports to the world	2492.0	7619.5	9689.4	12200.6	14306.9	12016.5	15777.6	18983.9	20487.8
Proportion of intra-regional exports	1.2%	1.6%	1.9%	2.4%	2.7%	3.0%	3.2%	3.3%	3.0%
China's imports from Bangladesh, India and Myanmar									
	2000	*2005*	*2006*	*2007*	*2008*	*2009*	*2010*	*2011*	*2012*
Bangladesh	0.19	0.79	0.99	1.1	1.3	1.4	2.7	4.5	4.8
India	13.5	97.7	102.8	146.2	202.6	137.1	208.5	233.7	188.0

Myanmar	1.2	2.7	2.5	3.8	6.5	6.5	9.7	16.8	13.0
Total imports from this region	15.0	101.2	106.3	151.1	210.4	145.0	220.9	255.0	205.8
Total imports from the world	2250.9	6599.5	7914.6	9561.2	11325.6	10055.6	13960.0	17433.9	18182.0
Proportion of intra-regional imports	0.7%	1.5%	1.3%	1.6%	1.9%	1.4%	1.6%	1.5%	1.1%

China's trade volume with Bangladesh, India, and Myanmar

	2000	2005	2006	2007	2008	2009	2010	2011	2012
Bangladesh	9.19	24.79	31.89	34.6	46.9	45.8	70.6	82.6	84.5
India	29.1	187	248.6	386.7	518.5	433.8	617.6	739.1	664.8
Myanmar	6.2	12.1	14.6	20.8	26.3	29.1	44.5	65	69.7
Trade volume with this region	44.5	223.9	295.1	442.1	591.7	508.7	732.7	886.7	819.0
Trade volume with the world	4743.0	14219.1	17604.0	21761.8	25632.6	22072.0	29737.7	36417.8	38670.0
Proportion of intra-regional trade volume	0.9%	1.6%	1.7%	2.0%	2.3%	2.3%	2.5%	2.4%	2.1%

Data sources: the same as above.

for BCIM region was very low, and for years its growth was relatively limited. In 2012, Chinese imports and exports within this region accounted for only 1.1% and 3% respectively of Chinese imports from the world, an increase of 0.5 and 1.8 percentage points higher than the one in 2000. Specifically, the markets of Bangladesh, India, and Myanmar had almost no importance for China's foreign trade. Chinese imports from Bangladesh, India, and Myanmar respectively occupied 0.03%, 1% and 0.07% in its total imports, and Chinese exports to Bangladesh, India, and Myanmar respectively occupied 0.4%, 2.3% and 0.3% in China's total exports. What's more, China also kept the trade surplus in its favour and against these three countries for this entire period. In 2012, China's trade surplus against this region reached as high as $40.7 billion. In year 2000, China's foreign trade volume with Bangladesh, India, and Myanmar took 0.19%, 0.6% and 0.13% of its total foreign trade volume. However, by 2012, the proportions had increased respectively to 0.22%, 1.7% and 0.18%. The importance of Indian market for Chinese foreign trade increased and India's economic engagement with China was much larger than China's economic engagement with Bangladesh and Myanmar.

(c) India's Trade with Bangladesh, China, Myanmar

In 2012, India's imports and exports to BCIM region were $56.2 billion and $20.2 billion, accounting for 61.8% and 23.8% of the intra-regional imports and exports of four countries respectively. The proportion of imports for 2012 had increased by 26 percentage points compared with imports for year 2000, while for the same period, the proportion of India's exports was down nearly 8 percentage points. As we can see, India had great influence on the imports of this region, but the contribution that India had to the exports of this region decreased. The trends in trade growth of India with these three countries of BCIM sub-region has been relatively low. In 2012, Indian intra-regional imports and exports accounted for 11.5% and 7% of its imports and exports to the world respectively, an increase of 7

Table 9: The Trade Development Between India and Bangladesh, China, and Myanmar

Unit: one hundred million dollars

Indian exports to Bangladesh, China, and Myanmar									
	2000	*2005*	*2006*	*2007*	*2008*	*2009*	*2010*	*2011*	*2012*
Bangladesh	7.7	17.2	16.7	20.6	32.4	21.8	30.2	34.1	49.4
China	7.3	71.8	78.3	95.0	100.9	103.7	17.4	167.2	147.3
Myanmar	0.43	1.2	1.2	1.6	2.4	2.1	2.7	4.6	5.3
Total exports to this region	15.43	90.2	96.2	117.2	135.7	127.6	50.3	205.9	202.0
Total exports to the world	423.6	1003.5	1212.0	1459.0	1818.6	1767.7	2204.1	3014.8	2895.6
Proportion of intra-regional exports	3.6%	9.0%	7.9%	8.0%	7.5%	7.2%	2.3%	6.8%	7.0%
Indian imports from Bangladesh, China, and Myanmar									
	2000	*2005*	*2006*	*2007*	*2008*	*2009*	*2010*	*2011*	*2012*
Bangladesh	0.78	1.8	2.4	3.1	3.4	2.6	3.6	6.0	6.0
China	19.3	130.0	171.1	243.6	340.0	315.2	428.1	564.2	542.0
Myanmar	2.2	6.6	7.8	7.8	9.5	12.3	11.0	13.0	13.9

Total imports from this region	22.28	138.4	181.3	254.5	352.9	330.1	442.7	583.2	561.9
Total imports from the world	529.4	1408.6	1782.1	2186.5	3157.1	2664.0	3500.3	4624.0	4889.8
Proportion of intra-regional imports	4.2%	9.8%	10.2%	11.6%	11.1%	12.4%	12.7%	12.6%	11.5%
Indian trade volume with Bangladesh, China and Myanmar									
	2000	*2005*	*2006*	*2007*	*2008*	*2009*	*2010*	*2011*	*2012*
Bangladesh	8.5	19	19.1	23.7	35.8	24.4	33.8	40.1	55.4
China	26.6	201.8	249.4	338.6	440.9	418.9	445.5	731.4	689.3
Myanmar	2.63	7.8	9	9.4	11.9	14.4	13.7	17.6	19.2
Trade volume with this region	37.73	228.6	277.5	371.7	488.6	457.7	493	789.1	763.9
Trade volume with the world	953.0	2412.1	2994.1	3645.4	4975.7	4431.7	5704.4	7638.9	7785.4
Proportion of intra-regional trade volume	4.0%	9.5%	9.3%	10.2%	9.8%	10.3%	8.6%	10.3%	9.8%

Data sources: the same as above.

percentage points and 3 percentage points respectively compared with 2000. Specifically, markets of Bangladesh, China and Myanmar are not essential for India. In 2012, India's imports from these three countries accounted for 0.12%, 11.1% and 0.28% of its total imports, and its exports to these countries accounted for 1.7%, 5.1% and 0.18% of the total exports. From 2000 to 2012, the importance of these three markets for India had changed a little. In year 2000, Indian foreign trade volume with Bangladesh, China, and Myanmar occupied 0.89%, 2.8% and 0.28% of its total foreign trade volume. In 2012, the proportion changed to 0.7%, 8.8% and 0.25%. The importance of Chinese market for India's foreign trade had improved, but there was a slight decline in India's economic engagement with Bangladesh and Myanmar. From year 2000 to 2012, although India had always kept a trade surplus against Bangladesh, yet India continues to have trade deficit against China and Myanmar, especially a huge one against China, causing that India's intra-regional trade deficit became larger. In 2012, Indian intra-regional trade deficit reached $36 billion.

(d) Myanmar's trade with Bangladesh, China, and India

In year 2012, Myanmar imports and exports to BCIM region were respectively $3.14 billion and $1.95 billion, accounting for 3.4% and 2.3% of the total intra-regional imports and exports of these four countries respectively. In year 2012, the proportion of imports was down nearly 5 percentage points compared with 2000, while the proportion of exports was down 3.5 percentage points. As we can see, Myanmar almost has no influence on the imports and exports of BCIM sub-region, and even so, the contribution that Myanmar has to the intra-regional trade has declined. Contrary to its slow development in global trade, Myanmar which largely depends on BCIM intra-regional trade has witnessed that trade decline for this period. In period during 2001-2012, Myanmar's imports and exports to this region occupied 34.1% and 21.9% of its imports and exports to the world, an increase of 12.5 and 4.8 percentage points. Specifically, the markets of Bangladesh, China and India

Table 10: The Trade Development between Myanmar and Bangladesh, China, and India

Unit: one hundred billion dollars

Myanmar exports to Bangladesh, China and India									
	2000	*2005*	*2006*	*2007*	*2008*	*2009*	*2010*	*2011*	*2012*
Bangladesh	0.33	0.62	0.70	0.94	1.0	0.99	0.82	1.2	1.1
China	1.0	2.8	3.3	4.5	4.9	4.7	4.8	6.3	6.1
India	1.5	5.8	6.8	9.2	10.1	9.6	9.6	12.9	12.3
Total exports to this region	2.83	9.22	10.8	14.64	16	15.29	15.22	20.4	19.5
Total exports to the world	16.5	39.7	46.8	64.0	69.7	66.8	86.6	92.4	89.0
Proportion of intra-regional exports	17.2%	23.2%	23.1%	22.9%	23.0%	22.9%	17.6%	22.1%	21.9%
Myanmar imports from Bangladesh, China and India									
	2000	*2005*	*2006*	*2007*	*2008*	*2009*	*2010*	*2011*	*2012*
Bangladesh	0.0008	0.02	0.02	0.03	0.04	0.04	0.96	0.15	0.16
China	4.7	6.2	8.2	10.5	13.6	13.8	11.3	27.1	27.6

India	0.5	0.67	0.89	1.2	1.5	1.5	1.6	3.5	3.6
Total imports from this region	5.2	6.9	9.1	11.7	15.1	15.3	13.9	30.8	31.4
Total imports from the world	24.0	19.5	25.8	33.2	43.0	43.5	47.6	90.2	92.0
Proportion of intra-regional imports	21.7%	35.4%	35.3%	35.2%	35.1%	35.2%	29.2%	34.1%	34.1%
Myanmar trade volume with Bangladesh, China and India									
	2000	*2005*	*2006*	*2007*	*2008*	*2009*	*2010*	*2011*	*2012*
Bangladesh	0.33	0.6	0.7	1.0	1.0	1.0	1.8	1.4	1.3
China	5.7	9	11.5	15	18.5	18.5	16.1	33.4	33.7
India	2	6.47	7.69	10.4	11.6	11.1	11.2	16.4	15.9
Trade volume with this region	8.0	16.1	19.9	26.4	31.1	30.6	29.1	51.2	50.9
Trade with the world	40.5	59.2	72.6	97.2	112.7	110.3	134.2	182.6	181.0
Proportion of intra-regional trade volume	19.8%	27.2%	27.4%	27.2%	27.6%	27.7%	21.7%	28.0%	28.1%

Data sources: the same as above.

have had different levels of importance for Myanmar. For year 2012, Myanmar's imports from these three countries accounted for 0.17%, 30% and 3.9% of its total imports, and its exports to these three countries accounted for 1.2%, 6.8% and 13.8% of its total exports. These data showed that Myanmar largely depended on China in imports and on India for its exports. From 2000 to 2012, the importance of these three markets of Bangladesh, China and India for Myanmar has also changed. In 2000, Myanmar's foreign trade volume with Bangladesh, China and India accounted for 0.8%, 14.1% and 4.9% respectively of its total foreign trade volume. In 2012, this proportion changed to 0.7%, 18.7% and 8.8%. The importance of Chinese and Indian markets for Myanmar's foreign trade has increased, but the importance of Bangladesh's market has a slight decline. In most years, Myanmar kept an intra-regional trade surplus. But while Myanmar kept a slight trade surplus against Bangladesh and India for a long time, its trade deficit against China has continued to be big. This has led to a trade deficit of more than $1 billion for two consecutive years since 2011.

(iii) Competitiveness & Complementarity in Intra-Regional Trade

In general, their mutual trade and investments have been seen as key to building economic and trade ties amongst BCIM countries. This section will examine multifaceted strands of competitiveness and complementarity in bilateral trades and how that impacts upon their sub-regional cooperation. Also, what are the mechanisms of this emerging regional cooperation that impact on their economic and trade ties? This section will analyse the comparative advantages of each intra-regional countries through the index of revealed comparative advantage (RCA), export similarity index (ESI) and trade complementarity index (TCI), and thus seek to understand details of the trade competition and complementarity amongst these countries. Also, most of the data of this section comes from UNCTAD (United Nations Conference on Trade and Development) database. According to the *Standard International*

Trade Classification (SITC), international trade commodities can be divided into SITC0~9, that is, ten categories of commodities, which can be further subdivided according to factor intensities. Among them, SITC 0~4 categories of commodities are resource-intensive primary products; SITC5~7 categories of commodities are capital- and technology-intensive manufactured products; SITC 6~8 categories are labor-intensive manufactured products; and SITC 9 category includes other unclassified products.

(a) Competitiveness of Individual BCIM Country

The measure indexes for the competitiveness analysis of each country are usually similarity index of export products and the index of revealed comparative advantage (RCA). The difference is that the former is generally used for the comprehensive competition among countries, while the latter is usually used to analyse their competition in the industry or product.

(b) Analysis of Export Similarity Index

The export similarity index (ESI) can be used to measure the similarity of commodities of two countries in the world market or in the market of a third country. This paper adopts the export similarity index proposed by Finger and Kreinin (1979) to measure the export similarity index of BCIM countries. If the product structures of country A and country B exporting to country N are the same, the export similarity index is 100; if the product structures of country A and country B exporting to country N are completely different, the index is 0. When the index gradually increases over time, and more close to 100, this means the export structure of both countries tends to be the same, and the competition between the two countries in N country is increasingly fierce; on the contrary, when the index decreases over time, and gradually close to 0, that means the competition of both countries in N country is gradually reducing, and the trade relations are complementary. The specialisation degree of two countries is rising.[7]

Table 11: Similarity index of trade between each country in BCIM region

Countries	*1995*	*1996*	*1997*	*1998*	*1999*	*2000*	*2001*	*2002*	*2003*
Sino-India	67.30	63.90	62.14	61.66	58.86	60.73	60.20	57.12	56.40
Sino-Myanmar	27.30	33.43	38.19	43.44	52.47	51.85	47.09	43.19	40.29
Sino-Bangladesh	66.85	65.73	63.77	59.24	56.64	54.17	53.43	50.01	46.52
India-Myanmar	39.43	47.00	48.96	50.49	50.55	47.13	45.39	45.62	44.31
India-Bangladesh	53.37	50.14	46.98	44.96	42.91	43.20	41.72	40.45	37.87
Myanmar-Bangladesh	29.43	35.78	39.74	43.80	53.11	59.31	44.68	42.22	39.38
Countries	*2004*	*2005*	*2006*	*2007*	*2008*	*2009*	*2010*	*2011*	*2012*
Sino-India	56.65	55.57	55.21	53.93	55.00	59.25	53.42	55.48	55.46
Sino-Myanmar	34.73	32.28	32.13	31.70	30.60	31.38	25.75	30.32	29.26
Sino-Bangladesh	43.04	43.24	41.90	41.04	40.44	41.16	41.51	42.47	44.03
India-Myanmar	47.85	48.75	52.13	53.08	51.47	50.41	60.47	58.68	61.95
India-Bangladesh	37.77	37.75	36.90	35.86	33.52	37.68	34.14	35.59	36.89
Myanmar-Bangladesh	35.30	33.63	34.38	35.92	33.59	33.70	23.48	27.45	26.10

Data sources: the same as above.

Table 11 shows the trade similarity index of BCIM countries in the world market. As shown in the table, the similarity indexes of products in exports of four countries to the world market presented three types: the first was that the current trade similarity indexes of Sino-India, Sino-Bangladesh, and India-Bangladesh were high, but in the long term there appears a downward trend, indicating that the competition of products of these three groups of countries in the world market were gradually weakening; the second was that the trade similarity index between India and Myanmar was rising, indicating the export products of both counties had an increasingly intense competition, and the similarity of industry structures of both countries stood out; the third is that the trade similarity indexes of Sino-Myanmar and Myanmar-Bangladesh increased first and then decreased. All three indexes began decreasing when they reached the highest point in 2000, indicating the trade competition of both groups of countries increased first and then decreased, which meant that the structures of export products of both groups differed increasingly, and there existed a large potential to continue the bilateral trade.

(c) Analysis of revealed comparative advantage (RCA)

The index of revealed comparative advantage (RCA) is an important index for studying the competitiveness of a certain product or industry in the international market. Its calculation formula is as follows:

$$RCA_{xi}^{k} = \frac{X_i^k / X_i}{X_w^k / X_w} \quad \text{(Formula 1)}$$

RCAk xi means the index of revealed comparative advantage (RCA) of k-type product or industry in i country. *Xk i, Xk w* respectively shows that the exports of k-type product or industry in i country and world export trade and Xi, Xw represents the export volume of i country and the world. Generally, when R*CAk xi*<0.8, it means that the k-type product or industry of i country has a extremely low international competitiveness; when 0.8< R*CAk xi*<1.25, it means that the k-type product or industry of i country has a relatively weak international competitiveness; when the 1.25< *RCAk xi*<2.5, it means that the k-type product or industry of i country has a relatively strong international competitiveness; when *RCAk xi*>2.5, it means that the k-type product or industry of i country has a extremely strong international competitiveness.[8]

According to the Formula 1 above, we calculated the RCA of BCIM countries as shown in Table 12. Bangladesh's most globally competitive product is SITC 8, followed by SITC 0, and 6. Since year 1995, the comparative advantage of Bangladesh's SITC 8 category of commodities has always been large, and the RCA of this category is over 5 for a long time. This category of commodities had the strongest comparative advantage in Bangladesh, and also had the strongest international competitiveness in this region. The comparative advantage index of SITC 0, 6 categories of commodities gradually decreased from 1 in 1995 to 0.8 in 2012, indicating the international competitiveness of these two categories of commodities are weakening. The revealed comparative advantage (RCA) index of the other seven categories of commodities of Bangladesh were always below 0.5. These categories of commodities almost had no comparative advantage and stayed a competitive disadvantage in the international market for a long time.

As regards China, its products with long-term comparative advantage focused on SITC 6, and 8, and the international competitiveness of SITC 7 category of products is gradually becoming strong. The RCA of China's STIC 6, and 8 categories of products had always maintained above 1.25, especially the RCA of STIC 8 products is particularly high. It confirms how China has a very strong comparative advantage in labor-intensive products. However, the comparative advantages of SITC 8 products has began to weaken in recent years, which is consistent with that the competitiveness of China's textiles in the international market started to slide down. The RCA of SITC 7 products increased gradually, and its comparative advantage became increasingly strong. China's SITC 7 products were the products with the strongest comparative advantage in BCIM four countries, which showed that Chinese manufacturing level had an extremely strong competitive advantage in the BCIM four countries.

For India, the products with long-term comparative advantage lies in SITC 0, 2, 6, and 8 categories of products. The international competitiveness of SITC 3, and 5 products were becoming strong, while the comparative advantage of SITC 4 products is gradually weakening. Since year 1995, the RCA of India's SITC 0, 2, 6, and 8 products wandered between 1.1 and 2.5, indicating Indian part resource-intensive products (SITC 0+2) and labor-intensive products (SITC 6+8) always have a certain international competitiveness. The comparative advantage of India's resource-intensive products is next only to Myanmar, and the competitiveness of the labour-intensive products also is next only to China. The RCA of India's SITC 3, and 5 products has gradually increased since year 1995, from the initial completely comparative disadvantage to the relatively weak comparative advantage, indicating the SITC 3, and 5 products would have a strong development potential; In addition, the RCA of India SITC 4 products is down year by year, and this category stayed at a relatively comparative disadvantage position in the international market.

As regards Myanmar, its products with the most international competitiveness concentrate in SITC 0, 2, and 3. The RCA of Myanmar's resource-intensive products (SITC 0+2+3) has been higher than 2 for a long time, and has a fully comparative advantage, especially the RCA of SITC 0, and 2 products is always higher than the other three countries, which is closely related with the rich resources of Myanmar. Myanmar has the richest resources in BCIM region and the resources are its natural comparative advantage.

Table 12: Index of Revealed Comparative Advantage (RCA) of all Commodities in BCIM Four Countries

Country	*Standard International Trade Classification*	*1995*	*1998*	*2001*	*2004*	*2007*	*2008*	*2009*	*2010*	*2011*	*2012*
Bangladesh	0	1.30	1.07	1.02	1.06	1.09	1.01	0.73	0.83	0.84	0.80
	1	0.04	0.14	0.10	0.27	0.26	0.31	0.35	0.48	0.44	0.39
	2	0.63	0.56	0.39	0.39	0.69	0.55	0.54	0.61	0.54	0.50
	3	0.04	0.02	0.03	0.02	0.08	0.05	0.06	0.05	0.03	0.04
	4	0.02	0.04	0.05	0.07	0.03	0.04	0.03	0.06	0.08	0.08
	5	0.34	0.12	0.12	0.12	0.10	0.18	0.15	0.13	0.14	0.18
	6	1.02	0.73	0.89	0.68	0.65	0.70	0.70	0.82	0.87	0.85
	7	0.03	0.02	0.02	0.03	0.05	0.04	0.04	0.04	0.04	0.04
	8	5.35	5.91	6.19	6.84	7.28	7.71	7.02	7.25	7.44	7.24
	9	0.32	0.07	0.03	0.04	0.04	0.07	0.06	0.02	0.03	0.10
China	0	0.95	0.88	0.84	0.60	0.50	0.43	0.44	0.46	0.46	0.44
	1	0.82	0.48	0.35	0.24	0.15	0.14	0.15	0.16	0.16	0.16
	2	0.70	0.56	0.51	0.31	0.21	0.22	0.19	0.18	0.18	0.17
	3	0.49	0.45	0.32	0.22	0.12	0.12	0.12	0.11	0.09	0.08
	4	0.58	0.32	0.13	0.06	0.06	0.07	0.05	0.05	0.05	0.05
	5	0.66	0.59	0.52	0.42	0.47	0.53	0.45	0.50	0.56	0.52
	6	1.35	1.17	1.21	1.21	1.26	1.35	1.22	1.22	1.30	1.33
	7	0.56	0.67	0.88	1.17	1.31	1.40	1.46	1.47	1.49	1.48
	8	2.93	2.92	2.59	2.24	2.26	2.30	2.17	2.22	2.31	2.42
	9	0.08	0.00	0.06	0.05	0.05	0.03	0.03	0.02	0.03	0.01
India	0	2.40	2.38	2.08	1.70	1.60	1.65	1.09	1.23	1.34	1.61
	1	0.41	0.53	0.47	0.45	0.45	0.57	0.64	0.59	0.43	0.50
	2	1.17	1.20	1.23	1.91	2.07	1.85	1.61	1.69	1.23	1.60
	3	0.23	0.07	0.49	0.71	1.11	1.01	0.93	1.10	1.05	1.00
	4	1.54	1.00	1.47	1.11	0.69	0.63	0.64	0.67	0.64	0.61
	5	0.88	0.99	1.12	1.09	1.07	1.08	0.91	0.96	0.95	1.12
	6	2.38	2.47	2.65	2.48	2.07	2.01	1.96	2.20	1.94	1.90
	7	0.20	0.17	0.21	0.26	0.31	0.40	0.45	0.43	0.44	0.43
	8	1.59	1.72	1.58	1.56	1.33	1.18	1.57	1.14	1.27	1.38
	9	0.56	0.84	0.78	0.32	0.31	0.40	0.90	0.45	1.08	0.20

Myanmar	0	5.45	5.19	3.85	3.14	3.31	3.38	3.02	2.87	3.10	3.11
	1	0.04	0.05	0.40	0.34	0.38	0.36	0.37	0.10	0.31	0.26
	2	10.55	8.78	5.20	7.28	6.31	5.94	5.84	2.49	3.85	3.78
	3	0.02	0.01	2.47	2.81	2.29	1.96	2.35	2.17	2.15	2.09
	4	0.05	0.13	0.03	0.00	0.32	0.29	0.23	0.00	0.28	0.24
	5	0.11	0.02	0.01	0.01	0.02	0.03	0.02	0.00	0.02	0.03
	6	0.39	0.37	0.25	0.37	0.39	0.34	0.39	1.73	1.40	1.55
	7	0.02	0.05	0.02	0.01	0.02	0.02	0.02	0.00	0.01	0.02
	8	0.73	2.13	2.60	1.86	1.86	1.93	1.76	0.44	0.72	0.68
	9	0.05	0.15	0.04	0.04	0.00	0.00	0.00	2.63	0.00	0.00

Data sources: the same as above.

(d) Trade Complementarity Index (TCI)

The Trade Complementarity Index (TCI) can be used to measure the matching degree and the trade complementarity between two countries. Its calculation formula is generally divided into single product (or industry) and national whole and synthesis. The calculation formula of the trade complementarity index of single product (or industry) is:

$$TCI_{ij}^{k} = RCA_{xi}^{k} \times RCA_{mj}^{k} \quad \text{Formula 2}$$

TCIk ij means the trade complementarity index of i country and j country on k-type product (or products). *RCAk xi* means the comparative advantage of k-type product in i country measured by exports. *RCAk* m_j means the comparative advantage of k-type product in j country measured by imports. This formula can be divided into two parts: one part is *RCAk xi* whose calculation formula is the same with formula (2). The bigger the *RCAk xi* value is, the more comparative advantage k-type product of i country has; the other part is $RCA_{mj}^{k} = \dfrac{M_j^k / M_j}{M_w^k / M_w}$, Mk j, Mk w means the imports of k-type product in j country's imports and in the world import trade. M_j, M_w respectively represents the trade volume of j country and the world. The bigger the *RCAk* m_j value is, the more obvious the trade complementarity of k-type product of i country and j country is[9]. The calculation formula of comprehensive trade complementarity index is as follows:

$$TCI_{ij} = \sum_{k}(RCA_{xi}^{k} \times RCA_{mj}^{k}) \times \frac{X_{w}^{k}}{X_{w}} \text{ Formula 3}$$

TCI_{ij} means the comprehensive trade complementarity index of i country and j country, and it regards the share of each kind of product in global trade as the weight. The average value of trade complementarity indexes of all products can be obtained through weighted calculation. The bigger the TCI_{ij} value is, the higher the matching degree between the exports of i country and imports of j country is, and the stronger the bilateral trade complementarity is. Generally, the critical value determining whether the trade complementarity is strong or weak is 1. If the trade complementarity index is greater than 1, it means that the trade complementarity of both countries is strong, on the contrary, weak.

Complementarity Analysis of BCIM Trade and Investments

(a) Trade Complementary between China and Bangladesh

As shown in table 13, whether regarding Bangladesh or China as exporter, Sino-Bangladesh comprehensive TCI, for a long time, has been less than 1, indicating that the trade complementarity of both countries is always low. But China and Bangladesh have strong trade complementarity and matching degree in SITC 0, 2, 6, and 8 categories of commodities. Bangladesh as exporter, the TCI of SITC 2, and 8 products of Bangladesh exporting to China has always been more than 1, especially the TCI of SITC 8 is greater than 2 for a long time and appeared an increase trend; the TCI of China's SITC 0, and 6 products exporting to Bangladesh had always maintained above 1 with China as exporter, especially the TCI of SITC 6 products is always higher than 2. It is obvious therefore that their trade complementary.

Table 13: Trade Complementarity Index Between China and Bangladesh

Country	Standard International Trade Classification	1995	1998	2001	2004	2007	2008	2009	2010	2011	2012
Bangladesh exports China imports	0	0.84	0.42	0.35	0.32	0.25	0.23	0.17	0.22	0.24	0.27
	1	0.01	0.02	0.02	0.03	0.05	0.07	0.08	0.11	0.12	0.12
	2	1.05	1.14	1.05	1.08	2.13	1.96	2.01	2.08	1.83	1.65
	3	0.02	0.01	0.02	0.02	0.06	0.04	0.05	0.04	0.03	0.04
	4	0.09	0.08	0.05	0.13	0.05	0.06	0.05	0.07	0.09	0.10
	5	0.44	0.18	0.15	0.12	0.10	0.18	0.14	0.12	0.13	0.16
	6	1.37	1.06	1.12	0.64	0.50	0.49	0.60	0.60	0.58	0.57
	7	0.03	0.02	0.03	0.03	0.05	0.05	0.04	0.05	0.04	0.05
	8	2.61	2.69	2.96	5.01	5.98	6.43	5.11	5.40	5.28	5.23
	9	0.06	0.01	0.01	0.00	0.00	0.01	0.00	0.01	0.03	0.10
	Comprehensive	*0.70*	*0.61*	*0.61*	*0.76*	*0.84*	*0.85*	*0.78*	*0.80*	*0.76*	*0.76*
China exports Bangladesh imports	0	1.64	1.67	1.38	1.01	1.22	0.95	0.95	1.06	1.03	1.05
	1	0.32	0.20	0.10	0.07	0.02	0.03	0.03	0.04	0.04	0.04
	2	0.80	0.97	1.02	0.63	0.43	0.43	0.40	0.36	0.33	0.30
	3	0.38	0.33	0.20	0.18	0.08	0.10	0.05	0.06	0.05	0.04
	4	2.73	2.60	1.59	0.67	0.80	0.55	0.51	0.52	0.52	0.57
	5	0.63	0.54	0.53	0.39	0.52	0.67	0.55	0.59	0.69	0.68
	6	3.26	2.86	2.87	2.34	1.97	2.14	2.22	2.28	2.70	2.78
	7	0.28	0.33	0.53	0.76	0.83	0.95	1.08	0.92	0.83	0.84
	8	1.41	1.08	1.16	1.23	0.91	0.94	0.87	0.83	0.75	0.79
	9	0.03	0.00	0.01	0.01	0.02	0.00	0.00	0.00	0.00	0.00
	Comprehensive	*1.06*	*0.94*	*0.94*	*0.91*	*0.83*	*0.86*	*0.89*	*0.85*	*0.86*	*0.85*

Data sources: the same as above.

(b) Trade Complementarity between India and Bangladesh

As shown in table 14, from year 1995 to 2012, the India-Bangladesh comprehensive TCI wandered between 0.4 and 0.6 with Bangladesh as exporter, indicating the matching degree of Bangladesh's export commodities with Indian market is not high; the India-Bangladesh comprehensive TCI is always above 1.1 with India as exporter, indicating the trade complementarity of India's products exporting to Bangladesh is significant. Specifically, the TCI of SITC 8 commodities of Bangladesh exporting to India is increasing, and has been more than 1.8 for a long time. The TCI of SITC 0, 2, 4, and 6 commodities of India exporting to Bangladesh is always above 1, especially the TCI of SITC 4 commodities is up to 17.59, indicating the India-Bangladesh trade complementarity on SITC 0, 2, 4, 6, and 8 commodities is extremely strong, especially the TCI of SITC 2, 8 commodities is increasingly expanding, and its trade complementarity is gradually becoming strong. The trade matching degree is expected to gradually increase on these two categories between India and Bangladesh.

Table 14: Trade Complementarity Index Between India and Bangladesh

Country	*Standard Int'lTrade Classification*	*1995*	*1998*	*2001*	*2004*	*2007*	*2008*	*2009*	*2010*	*2011*	*2012*
Bangladesh exports India imports	0	0.41	0.52	0.51	0.40	0.36	0.23	0.24	0.23	0.18	0.19
	1	0.00	0.02	0.01	0.03	0.02	0.02	0.02	0.04	0.04	0.04
	2	1.10	0.86	0.96	0.75	1.01	0.64	0.66	0.66	0.56	0.57
	3	0.08	0.05	0.03	0.02	0.16	0.09	0.11	0.09	0.06	0.08
	4	0.09	0.36	0.61	0.55	0.10	0.11	0.13	0.23	0.29	0.31
	5	0.54	0.16	0.15	0.13	0.08	0.19	0.13	0.11	0.12	0.15
	6	1.36	0.90	1.34	1.10	0.72	0.76	0.83	1.06	1.04	0.83
	7	0.02	0.01	0.01	0.02	0.03	0.03	0.02	0.02	0.02	0.02
	8	1.89	1.94	2.96	3.06	2.48	2.40	2.35	2.31	2.42	2.92
	9	0.53	0.28	0.10	0.13	0.09	0.14	0.14	0.07	0.10	0.26
	Comprehensive	0.61	0.49	0.64	0.59	0.47	0.43	0.46	0.47	0.46	0.50
India exports Bangladesh imports	0	4.14	4.52	3.41	2.87	3.95	3.61	2.36	2.86	2.99	3.83
	1	0.16	0.22	0.13	0.13	0.06	0.11	0.14	0.13	0.10	0.13
	2	1.33	2.06	2.44	3.93	4.29	3.61	3.35	3.46	2.30	2.84
	3	0.18	0.05	0.32	0.58	0.80	0.82	0.39	0.58	0.53	0.52
	4	7.28	8.09	17.59	12.20	9.49	4.59	6.08	7.57	6.82	7.18
	5	0.84	0.90	1.13	1.03	1.19	1.37	1.12	1.14	1.18	1.47
	6	5.77	6.05	6.31	4.80	3.23	3.20	3.58	4.08	4.03	3.95
	7	0.10	0.09	0.13	0.17	0.20	0.27	0.33	0.27	0.24	0.24
	8	0.77	0.63	0.71	0.86	0.54	0.48	0.63	0.43	0.41	0.45
	9	0.24	0.21	0.19	0.07	0.12	0.00	0.00	0.00	0.00	0.00
	Comprehensive	1.54	1.54	1.48	1.35	1.23	1.21	1.12	1.23	1.18	1.24

Data sources: the same as above.

(c) Trade Complementarity between Myanmar and Bangladesh

Table 15: Trade complementarity index between Myanmar and Bangladesh

Country	*Standard International Trade Classification*	*1995*	*1998*	*2001*	*2004*	*2007*	*2008*	*2009*	*2010*	*2011*	*2012*
Bangladesh exports Myanmar imports	0	0.84	2.26	0.71	1.10	1.36	1.12	0.69	0.52	0.86	0.78
	1	0.32	0.41	0.12	0.71	0.68	0.79	0.90	0.03	0.96	0.84
	2	0.11	0.06	0.10	0.09	0.14	0.11	0.12	0.10	0.12	0.12
	3	0.02	0.02	0.05	0.03	0.11	0.06	0.07	0.06	0.04	0.05
	4	0.37	0.45	0.30	0.75	0.23	0.26	0.21	0.38	0.55	0.45
	5	0.33	0.10	0.11	0.13	0.11	0.20	0.16	0.11	0.13	0.17
	6	1.37	1.03	1.80	1.24	1.16	1.29	1.42	1.51	1.81	1.85
	7	0.03	0.02	0.02	0.02	0.03	0.03	0.03	0.03	0.03	0.03
	8	3.29	2.09	1.67	2.92	2.88	3.00	2.80	1.51	2.29	2.24
	9	0.21	0.02	0.01	0.03	0.00	0.00	0.00	0.08	0.00	0.00
	Comprehensive	0.75	0.61	0.53	0.62	0.60	0.59	0.59	0.43	0.57	0.56
Myanmar exports Bangladesh imports	0	9.42	9.83	6.31	5.31	8.16	7.37	6.56	6.67	6.92	7.38
	1	0.02	0.02	0.11	0.10	0.05	0.07	0.08	0.02	0.07	0.07
	2	11.95	15.07	10.33	14.99	13.08	11.58	12.12	5.09	7.20	6.69
	3	0.02	0.01	1.58	2.28	1.64	1.59	0.98	1.14	1.08	1.09
	4	0.25	1.07	0.42	0.01	4.46	2.14	2.22	0.00	3.01	2.88
	5	0.11	0.02	0.01	0.01	0.03	0.04	0.03	0.00	0.03	0.03
	6	0.93	0.90	0.60	0.72	0.62	0.55	0.72	3.21	2.92	3.23
	7	0.01	0.02	0.01	0.01	0.01	0.01	0.01	0.00	0.01	0.01
	8	0.35	0.79	1.17	1.02	0.75	0.79	0.71	0.16	0.23	0.22
	9	0.02	0.04	0.01	0.01	0.00	0.00	0.00	0.00	0.00	0.00
	Comprehensive	1.37	1.41	1.07	1.25	1.32	1.27	1.17	1.20	1.34	1.35

Data sources: the same as above.

As shown in table 15, the comprehensive TCI between Bangladesh exports and Myanmar imports has always been below 0.75, and the index is gradually decreasing, indicating the matching degree between Bangladesh's exports and Myanmar's market is low, and appears a decrease trend in recent years, thus their trade complementarity has gradually weakened. The comprehensive TCI between Myanmar exports and Bangladesh imports has always fluctuated at about 1.2, indicating the matching degree between Myanmar's exports with Bangladesh's domestic demand is high. Their trade complementarity is significant and tended to be stable. In terms of specific commodities, the TCI of SITC 6, and 8 categories of Bangladesh exporting to Myanmar is always higher than 1.0. The TCI of SITC 0, 2, 3, and 4 categories of Myanmar exporting to Bangladesh has been higher than 1.0 for a long time. This not only indicated that Bangladesh and Myanmar have a strong trade complementarity on SITC 0, 2, 3, 4, 6, and 8 categories, but also fully reflected that Bangladesh-Myanmar trade is built on both comparative advantages, that is, the Myanmar's export resource-intensive primary products (SITC0+2+3+4) matched with Bangladesh's domestic demand and Bangladesh's export labor-intensive products (SITC 6+8) matched with Myanmar's import demand.

(d) Trade Complementarity between China and India

As shown in table 16, the Sino-India comprehensive TCI with China as exporter has decreased year on year basis, indicating the matching degree between China's exports and India's domestic demand is low and has decreased year on year basis. Their bilateral trade complementarity has been weak. The Sino-India comprehensive TCI has fluctuated at about 1.0 for a long time with India as exporter, indicating Indian exports basically matched with China's import market. Their trade complementarity tend to be stable but not high. In terms of specific commodities, the TCI of China's SITC 6 category exporting to India kept above 1.4 for a long time. The TCI of India's SITC 2, and 6 exporting to China always kept a higher level (more than 1.2 for a long time), especially, the maximum TCI of SITC 2 category could be up to 6.61, indicating the trade complementarity between China and India on SITC 0, 2, and 6 categories is significant.

Table 16: Trade Complementarity Index between China and India

Country	*Standard International Trade Classification*	*1995*	*1998*	*2001*	*2004*	*2007*	*2008*	*2009*	*2010*	*2011*	*2012*
China exports India imports	0	0.30	0.43	0.42	0.23	0.17	0.10	0.15	0.13	0.10	0.11
	1	0.07	0.06	0.03	0.03	0.01	0.01	0.01	0.01	0.02	0.02
	2	1.23	0.87	1.26	0.59	0.30	0.26	0.23	0.19	0.19	0.20
	3	0.94	1.22	0.35	0.16	0.24	0.23	0.24	0.21	0.18	0.17
	4	2.28	2.87	1.51	0.45	0.20	0.23	0.22	0.19	0.17	0.19
	5	1.06	0.77	0.65	0.47	0.40	0.55	0.40	0.45	0.48	0.44
	6	1.80	1.45	1.82	1.96	1.38	1.46	1.44	1.60	1.57	1.29
	7	0.40	0.36	0.53	0.85	0.91	0.94	0.98	0.87	0.84	0.77
	8	1.04	0.96	1.24	1.00	0.77	0.72	0.73	0.71	0.75	0.98
	9	0.13	0.00	0.19	0.18	0.11	0.06	0.07	0.06	0.09	0.04
	Comprehensive	0.83	0.71	0.79	0.83	0.71	0.71	0.70	0.68	0.65	0.60
India exports China imports	0	1.54	0.94	0.72	0.51	0.37	0.38	0.26	0.33	0.38	0.54
	1	0.12	0.07	0.08	0.05	0.08	0.13	0.14	0.13	0.12	0.16
	2	1.95	2.45	3.29	5.25	6.43	6.61	5.96	5.74	4.17	5.32
	3	0.12	0.05	0.36	0.55	0.86	0.86	0.80	0.96	0.93	0.93
	4	5.62	2.04	1.39	1.95	1.23	1.07	0.93	0.81	0.68	0.74
	5	1.16	1.44	1.46	1.17	1.11	1.06	0.86	0.90	0.88	1.00
	6	3.21	3.62	3.35	2.35	1.57	1.41	1.69	1.62	1.30	1.26
	7	0.21	0.17	0.24	0.30	0.37	0.47	0.54	0.49	0.49	0.48
	8	0.78	0.78	0.76	1.14	1.09	0.98	1.15	0.85	0.90	1.00
	9	0.11	0.15	0.16	0.03	0.02	0.04	0.08	0.17	0.93	0.19
	Comprehensive	1.03	1.02	0.98	0.97	0.98	0.98	0.98	0.99	0.93	0.96

Data sources: the same as above.

(e) Trade Complementarity between China and Myanmar

As shown in Table 17, on the whole, the comprehensive TCI between China exports and Myanmar imports has fluctuated between 0.78 and 0.96, indicating the matching degree of China's exports with Myanmar market has not high for a long time, and the trade complementarity is to increase. The comprehensive TCI between Myanmar exports and China imports has been above 1 for a long time, indicating the Myanmar's exports met the China's domestic market demand. In terms of specific commodities, the TCI of China's SITC 6, 7 categories exporting to Myanmar is increasing and surpassed 1 and 2 respectively. The TCI of Myanmar's SITC 2, and 3 exporting to China were higher than critical value 1, especially, the TCI of SITC 2 category always kept an extremely high level, with a minimum value of 8.46. This not only indicated that China and Myanmar

Table 17: Trade Complementarity index between China and Myanmar

Country	*Standard International Trade Classification*	*1995*	*1998*	*2001*	*2004*	*2007*	*2008*	*2009*	*2010*	*2011*	*2012*
China exports Myanmar exports	0	0.62	1.86	0.59	0.62	0.62	0.48	0.41	0.29	0.47	0.43
	1	6.87	1.42	0.42	0.62	0.39	0.36	0.40	0.01	0.35	0.36
	2	0.13	0.06	0.13	0.07	0.04	0.04	0.04	0.03	0.04	0.04
	3	0.26	0.53	0.61	0.24	0.16	0.16	0.14	0.14	0.12	0.11
	4	9.08	3.53	0.74	0.62	0.47	0.53	0.35	0.31	0.33	0.27
	5	0.64	0.46	0.50	0.47	0.51	0.59	0.48	0.44	0.52	0.50
	6	1.81	1.65	2.45	2.21	2.24	2.47	2.48	2.26	2.72	2.90
	7	0.49	0.57	0.70	0.89	0.95	1.03	1.18	1.02	1.07	1.09
	8	1.80	1.03	0.70	0.96	0.89	0.90	0.87	0.46	0.71	0.75
	9	0.05	0.00	0.02	0.04	0.00	0.00	0.00	0.07	0.00	0.00
	Comprehensive	0.96	0.85	0.86	0.89	0.88	0.90	0.92	0.78	0.88	0.88
Myanmar exports China imports	0	3.50	2.05	1.34	0.94	0.77	0.78	0.71	0.77	0.88	1.04
	1	0.01	0.01	0.07	0.04	0.07	0.08	0.08	0.02	0.08	0.08
	2	17.61	17.89	13.94	20.02	19.58	21.16	21.58	8.46	13.03	12.56
	3	0.01	0.01	1.82	2.17	1.78	1.67	2.01	1.89	1.91	1.95
	4	0.20	0.27	0.03	0.00	0.58	0.50	0.34	0.00	0.30	0.30
	5	0.15	0.03	0.01	0.01	0.02	0.03	0.02	0.00	0.02	0.02
	6	0.52	0.54	0.32	0.35	0.30	0.24	0.34	1.27	0.94	1.03
	7	0.03	0.05	0.02	0.01	0.02	0.02	0.02	0.00	0.02	0.02
	8	0.36	0.97	1.24	1.37	1.53	1.60	1.29	0.32	0.51	0.49
	9	0.01	0.03	0.01	0.00	0.00	0.00	0.00	1.03	0.00	0.00
	Comprehensive	1.13	0.97	0.89	1.16	1.23	1.31	1.30	0.94	1.15	1.13

Data sources: the same as above.

had a high complementarity on SITC 2, 3, 6, and 7 categories, but also showed the complementary products were different: China's manufactured products (SITC 6+7) and Myanmar's resource-intensive primary products (SITC 2+3) achieved trade complementarity.

(f) Trade Complementarity between India and Myanmar

As shown in Table 18, whether regarding India or Myanmar as exporter, the India-Myanmar comprehensive

Table 18: Trade Complementarity Index between India and Myanmar

Country	*Standard International Trade Classification*	*1995*	*1998*	*2001*	*2004*	*2007*	*2008*	*2009*	*2010*	*2011*	*2012*
India exports Myanmar imports	0	1.56	5.05	1.46	1.77	1.99	1.83	1.03	0.77	1.37	1.58
	1	3.43	1.56	0.56	1.16	1.19	1.45	1.65	0.04	0.93	1.10
	2	0.21	0.13	0.30	0.43	0.42	0.37	0.34	0.28	0.27	0.37
	3	0.12	0.08	0.95	0.81	1.54	1.28	1.12	1.39	1.38	1.32
	4	24.25	10.99	8.15	11.23	5.62	4.42	4.11	4.50	4.28	3.45
	5	0.86	0.77	1.07	1.24	1.16	1.20	0.98	0.84	0.89	1.07
	6	3.20	3.50	5.39	4.54	3.67	3.69	3.99	4.06	4.05	4.12
	7	0.18	0.15	0.17	0.19	0.23	0.30	0.37	0.30	0.31	0.32
	8	0.98	0.61	0.43	0.67	0.53	0.46	0.63	0.24	0.39	0.43
	9	0.37	0.28	0.29	0.23	0.00	0.00	0.00	1.65	0.00	0.00
	Comprehensive	1.09	1.17	1.19	1.19	1.16	1.15	1.09	1.12	1.13	1.15
Myanmar exports India imports	0	1.72	2.52	1.93	1.20	1.10	0.76	1.01	0.81	0.68	0.75
	1	0.00	0.01	0.03	0.04	0.04	0.03	0.02	0.01	0.03	0.03
	2	18.48	13.52	12.77	13.96	9.27	6.95	7.02	2.71	3.98	4.34
	3	0.05	0.02	2.69	2.02	4.78	3.69	4.78	4.22	4.14	4.41
	4	0.21	1.19	0.40	0.00	1.13	0.88	0.95	0.00	0.99	0.96
	5	0.18	0.02	0.01	0.01	0.02	0.03	0.02	0.00	0.02	0.02
	6	0.52	0.46	0.38	0.60	0.43	0.37	0.46	2.25	1.69	1.50
	7	0.02	0.03	0.01	0.01	0.01	0.01	0.01	0.00	0.01	0.01
	8	0.26	0.70	1.24	0.83	0.64	0.60	0.59	0.14	0.23	0.27
	9	0.08	0.58	0.12	0.14	0.00	0.00	0.00	8.00	0.00	0.00
	Comprehensive	1.04	0.82	0.99	0.93	1.23	1.08	1.14	1.50	1.21	1.27

Data sources: the same as above.

TCI has been higher than 1 for a long time, indicating the trade complementarities between these two countries is always high. In terms of specific commodities, the trade complementarity varied as the exporter has varied. The TCI of Indian SITC 0, 1, 4, and 6 categories exporting to Myanmar has been higher than 1 for a long time. The TCI of Myanmar's SITC 2, and 3 categories exporting to India has been higher than 2 for a long time. This indicated that India and Myanmar had a significant trade complementarity on SITC 0, 1, 2, 3, 4, and 6 categories. The TCI of Indian SITC 4, 6 categories exporting to Myanmar and Myanmar's SITC 2 category exporting to India has always been higher than 2, indicating that both countries have a more significant trade complementarity on SITC 2, 4, and 6 categories.

Development Analysis of Intra-Regional FDI

Compared with the relatively rapid development of the intra-regional trade, the mutual investment in the BCIM sub-region still remains extremely low. Similar to the bilateral trade amongst these four countries, China and India occupied enormously large proportion in the inflow and outflow of the intra-regional FDI. Because Bangladesh and Myanmar only have a little investment within this region, this paper only analyses China's and India's status in intra-regional FDI and investment. Judging from China's situations, China's actual utilised investments from Bangladesh, India and Myanmar have had large fluctuations, and have been in a state of negative growth since 2008. In year 2012, the investments of these three countries in China were only $50 million, a decrease of $43 million compared with 2008. In fact, from year 2000 to 2012, the investments of these three countries in China can be almost negligible compared with China's total foreign capital. As we can see from Table 14, over the years, the proportion of China's actual utilised investments from Bangladesh, India and Myanmar in its total utilised FDI wandered between 0.03% and 0.09%, and this proportion has always kept 0.05% and below since 2010. We can see from Table

20 that, China's investment in Bangladesh, India and Myanmar accounted for a very small proportion of its total outward investment, but relatively China's investment in three countries was far greater than the investment of three countries in China. Indeed, except for the special circumstances in 2009, it can be seen that China's investment in Bangladesh, India and Myanmar also had a large fluctuations. The proportion of its investment in three countries in its total outward investment decreased from 2.5% in 2005 to 1.4% in 2012, indicating that in recent years the importance of investment in Bangladesh, India and Myanmar relative declined, but in terms of total investment amounts, China's investment in three countries reached $1 billion in 2012, which is a new record. Specifically, in China's total utilised FDI, the proportion of investment from Myanmar and Bangladesh has been decreasing, and was only 4.5% and 7.5% respectively in 2012, while India's proportion raised to 88%.

In China's total intra-regional investments in BCIM, the proportion of its investment in India also declined during 2001-2012 though trends in 2013-2015 have shown an upswing in China's promised investments in India. The proportion of China's investments into Bangladesh have also increased, while the proportion of its investment in Myanmar has increased from 50% to 70%. In terms of China's investment in BCIM, its investment in Bangladesh have concentrated mainly on the textile and apparel and related machinery, equipment and other related sectors. China's investment in India has been limited mainly to the electronics, communication and light industries, while the investment in Myanmar was mainly energy, mineral, natural resources and other fields. As regards India, development of its intra-regional FDI has also been very limited. From 2000 to 2013, India's actually utilised amounts of FDI coming from Bangladesh, China, Myanmar stood at $0.298 billion, accounting for 0.14% of its actually utilised cumulative amounts of FDI in BCIM. However, India's investments in these three countries stand at $1.1 billion, accounting for 1.3% of its total cumulative amounts of

Table 19: The Investments of Bangladesh, India and Myanmar that China Actually used

Unit: one million dollars

	2000	2005	2006	2007	2008	2009	2010	2011	2012
Bangladesh	0.66	0.06	1.2	1.9	2.1	3.6	1.1	4.9	2.3
India	10.4	21.4	52.4	34.0	88.1	55.2	49.3	42.2	44.1
Myanmar	2.3	3.7	7.4	3.3	3.3	3.4	3.5	10.2	3.8
The actual use of intra-regional FDI	13.36	25.16	61	39.2	93.5	62.2	53.9	57.3	50.2
Proportion of intra-regional FDI using	0.03%	0.03%	0.08%	0.05%	0.09%	0.07%	0.05%	0.05%	0.04%

Data sources. Chinese Statistical Bureau.

Table 20: China's Investment in Bangladesh, India, and Myanmar

Unit: one million dollars

	2005	2006	2007	2008	2009	2010	2011	2012
Bangladesh	0.2	5.3	3.6	4.5	10.8	7.2	10.32	33.0
India	11.2	5.6	22.0	101.9	-2488	47.6	180.1	276.8
Myanmar	11.5	12.6	92.3	232.5	376.7	875.6	217.8	748.9
Total investment in this region	22.9	23.5	117.9	338.9	- 2100.5	930.4	408.22	1058.7
Proportion of intra-regional investments to total investments	2.5%	0.2%	0.7%	1.3%	-3.8%	1.6%	0.6%	1.4%

Data sources: China's outward investment communiqué in 2012

outward investment. China was the most important investment partner for India in this region, occupying 0.14% and 1.1% in the cumulative amounts of India's FDI inflow and outflow. Bangladesh and Myanmar accounted for only 0% and 0.2%. Taking investment as an example, India's cumulative investment in China had ranked the 12th place in total India's cumulative investment, while Myanmar and Bangladesh ranked respectively the 75th and 123rd place. India's investments in Bangladesh are mainly concentrated on electric power, electric transmission lines, telecommunications, textile, pharmaceutical and so on. Its investment in China focused on information technology, pharmaceuticals and biotechnology fields, and its investment in Myanmar was mainly in energy, hydropower and agricultural infrastructures.

Table 21: The Investments of Bangladesh, China and Myanmar that India actually used from 2000 to 2013

Unit: one million dollars

Source of foreign investment	*Inflow cumulative amounts of FDI*	*Proportion in India's inflow amounts of FDI*
Bangladesh	0.03	0%
China	289	0.14%
Myanmar	8.96	0%
The total use amounts of intra-regional FDI	298	0.14%
Actually utilized investment amounts in the world	204658.20	100%

Data sources: From the data of Reserve Bank of India

Table 22: The Investments of India in Bangladesh, China, and Myanmar

Unit: one million dollars

	Cumulative amount of investment	*Proportion occupying the India's total outward investments amounts*
Bangladesh	64.5	0.08%
China	949.4	1.1%
Myanmar	92.6	0.1%
Investments in this region	1106.5	1.3%
Investments in the world	83510	100%

Data sources: from the data of Reserve Bank of India.

Conclusion

It can be seen from the findings of empirical researches in the preceding pages of this chapter that, since the BCIM Economic Cooperation Forum opened in 1999, the economic and trade cooperation relations between four countries have became increasingly closer. Both trade and investment have witnessed a certain increase. From 2000 to 2012, the intra-regional imports of four BCIM countries grew from $6.2 billion to $90.9 billion, and exports increased from $4.8 billion to $84.6 billion, an impressive increase of 14 times and 17 times respectively. The intra-regional FDI inflow and outflows involving investment of Bangladesh, India and Myanmar in China also increased from $13 million to $50 million, and China's FDI in Bangladesh, India and Myanmar for this 2000-2012 period increased rose from $22 million to a record $1 billion. In addition, the cumulative investment amounts of Bangladesh, China, and Myanmar to India also reached $0.298 billion.

Compared with the overall economic growth and the total trade and investments growth of these four BCIM countries, their intra-regional trade grew at relatively low speed compared to trends in their global trade and investments. The effect of intra-regional trade, investment on their overall trade and total investment of these four countries, therefore, remains negligible. In 2012, the total imports and exports of BCIM four countries stood respectively at $2,348.7 billion and $2,373.7 billion, an 8 times increase compared to figures for year 2000, accounting for 13.1% and 13% respectively of the global total imports and exports. However, the intra-regional imports and exports of four countries were only $90.9 billion and $84.6 billion, respectively accounting for 3.9% and 3.6% of the total imports and exports of four countries, and accounting for 0.51% and 0.47% of global total imports and exports. In addition, the level of mutual investment in this region is very low. The intra-regional FDI introducing and FDI introducing of investment in four countries accounted for less than 0.1% and 1.5% of total investment amounts. Compared again with the total trade and investment level of four countries to the core region of BCIM namely China's Yunnan, India's Northeast and Bangladesh and Myanmar, their intra-regional trade and investment was abysmalto begin with as well. The proportions of trade and investment of this core regions

– Bangladesh, Myanmar, China Yunnan and India's eight states, can be said to remain negligible.

Let us finally look at the economic and trade relationships between these four BCIM countries and also examine enumerate their attendant problems.

Bangladesh and Myanmar depended largely on the intra-regional trade, while China and India almost have very little dependence on this sub-region. The intra-regional trade volume of Bangladesh for 2012 was $12.2 billion, accounting for 20.8% of its total trade volume, in which, its exports to China, India and Myanmar respectively occupied 1.8%, 2.5% and 0.05% of its total exports, and its imports from above three countries respectively held 19.2%, 14.8% and 0.2% of its total imports, indicating this country depended more largely on the intra-regional imports than on the intra-regional exports, and has a great import demand from China and India. China's intra-regional trade volume for 2012 stood at $81.9 billion, accounting for 2.1% of its total trade volume, in which, its imports from Bangladesh, India and Myanmar occupied 0.03%, 1.0% and 0.07% of its total imports, and its exports to above three countries held 0.4%, 2.3% and 0.3% of its total exports, indicating that the current intra-regional trade has no importance for China in quantitative terms. India's intra-regional trade volume was about $76.4 billion, accounting for 9.8% of its total trade volume; its imports from Bangladesh, China and Myanmar occupied respectively 0.12%, 11.1% and 0.28% of its total imports, and its exports to above three countries held 1.7%, 5.1% and 0.18% of its total exports, indicating except for China's market the importance of Bangladesh's and Myanmar's markets is very low for India. Myanmar's intra-regional trade volume was about $5.1 billion; its imports from Bangladesh, China, and India accounted for 0.17%, 30% and 3.9% of its total imports, and its exports to above countries held 1.2%, 6.8% and 13.8% of its total exports, indicating that Myanmar depended largely on China in imports and on India in exports. Analysed from the trade balance perspective, only China's intra-regional trade of these four countries has maintained a surplus, while Bangladesh and India maintained a deficit for years. Myanmar maintains an intra-regional trade surplus for most years during 2001-2012. While there appeared slight surplus against Bangladesh and India, its trade deficit against China has become increasingly large.

There also exists a certain competition in the intra-regional trade of these four countries. On the global market, Sino-India, Sino-Bangladesh, and India-Bangladesh have a relatively high trade similarity index. But, in the long-run, this competition shows a downward trend. The trade similarity index between India and Myanmar is rising, proving that the competition of export commodities of two countries in the world market has become increasingly fierce. For the period 2001-2012, Sino-Myanmar and Myanmar-Bangladesh trade similarity index has increased first and then decreased, indicating that the difference of export product structures between the two groups of countries continued to expand, and there appeared a large potential to continue the bilateral trades. The changes in their comparative advantage structures in different commodities in the four BCIM countries are very complex. At present, the intra-regional resource-intensive products with strong international competitiveness belonged to Myanmar and India. The comparative advantage of labour-intensive commodities from strong to weak are China, India, Bangladesh and Myanmar. Only China has comparative advantages in capital- and technology-intensive commodities. Overall, although the BCIM four countries has certain competitiveness in labor-intensive products, there still existed an extremely complementarity in resource-intensive products for four countries. Therefore, there still existed great cooperation space for four countries. The comprehensiveness of trade and the complementarity between BCIM four countries has also varied because of the different exports. For the two groups of Sino-Bangladesh and India-Myanmar, regardless of which country is the exporter, its comprehensive trade complementarity remains unchanged. The Sino-Bangladesh comprehensive trade complementarity is not significant, while India-Myanmar comprehensive trade complementarity is always good. India-Bangladesh, Myanmar-Bangladesh, Sino-India and Sino-Myanmar comprehensive trade complementary degree and matching varied according to different exporters. The trade complementarity of various types of commodities in BCIM four countries has its own features, and differences are obvious in the terms of specific categories of goods and sectors.

The development of FDI in BCIM sub-region has two major problems: One is that the intra-regional FDI is small, and the growth trends are unstable. As of 2012, the investments of Bangladesh, India and Myanmar into Chinese market were only $50 million, accounting for a very small proportion in China's total FDI inflows, and the proportion has remained below 0.05%, a decrease of 0.04 percentage points compared with the peak, and a decrease of 1.1 percentage points compared with 2005. The total cumulative investment of Bangladesh, China, and Myanmar into Indian market accounted for 0.14% of India's total cumulative FDI inflow. Conversely, India's investment into this sub-region accounted for 1.3% of its total cumulative outward investments. In this, investments into China constituted a major part of the sub-region. The most part of India's intra-regional investment into Bangladesh and Myanmar were into agriculture, energy and infrastructure construction, and the productive investments into industry were generally low.

To sum up, firstly the overall economic and trade development scenario of the BCIM countries remains driven by their uneven levels of development and varying advantages. China and India are clearly relatively more developed and seen widely as emerging markets. Bangladesh and Myanmar, on the other hand, are among the most backward countries in the world. Second, the trade structures amongst BCIM four countries are mutually varying with both competitive and complementary strands. The current intra-regional trade, however, proves one fundamental point: that even in past decade of evolving BCIM has not fully exploited their trade potential. Thirdly, their mutual bilateral trade, investments and their ability of attracting investments from outside this region (except for China) have also remained weak, indicating that the development of untied intra-regional market to make BCIM attractive for outside world has also not been achieved. Fourthly, the comparative analysis of time series data shows that their dependence on the intra-regional trade and investment is weakening in different degrees which is not a good sign. Above conclusions proved that the BCIM intra-regional development lacks market force, and this lack of endogenous force which calls for building of the BCIM-Economic Corridor.

Future Trends

Any analysis on the future of BCIM-Economic Corridor begs the questions as to what is basically required to successfully build it and its attendant institutions and infrastructure.

Firstly, the positive side of this insufficient trade and growth or lack of endogenous power shows that this region has great potential for development. The BCIM region constitutes of countries with fastest economic growth in the world and is a land bridge connecting the Pacific and Indian oceans. It can not only integrate the two emerging biggest developing economies (China and India), but its impact can also cover East Asia, Southeast Asia, South Asia, and the Indian Ocean rim. Firstly, the superiority of its geo-economic location is obvious. Secondly, the proposed Economic Corridor not only has a large population, but also has rich biodiversity, hydrology, minerals, energy sources, forest resources and marine resources. Right now, in the face of global economic slow down it is the dynamic of regional economic integration that is giving support to both domestic and international trends. This sub-region as yet doesn't have any strong regional integration organisation to catapult it to its perceived future and substitute its functional interactions into institutions that can help it in development of its available resources.

Secondly, the lack of endogenous power also shows that the economic potential of BCIM-Economic Corridor needs many technical conditions to be realised. That is, in situation of lacking internal market forces, the BCIM regional development would need mechanisms to intervene, which is one of the reasons for promoting BCIM-Economic Corridor. Due to the lack of endogenous power, the economic cooperation of the region needs more external facilitation in which the government forces remain vital. The construction of Economic Corridor at Track-I level is especially important. Four BCIM governments should exclude the political, safety and security factors from interfering and work on the basis of interconnection, apply themselves to the trade and investment facilitation, reduce the tariff, and strengthen the institutionalisation of economic cooperation. They must exert the comparative advantages of different countries to realize the advantage complementarity of BCIM economies and trade, avoid deterioration of competition between Member States, and actively explore the space of economic and trade cooperation. This requires that all four countries adjust comprehensively the intra-regional industrial structures. China should especially consider investing in raw material processing and light industry in Bangladesh, India and Myanmar, and use certain degree of domestic imports and substitution to cultivate the long-term consumption ability in these countries, thus eventually improving the overall trade of the region. In addition, they need to pay more attention to the priority needs of the economic and trade development for all four countries. For instance, development of Bangladesh urgently needs growth of trade; the development of Myanmar urgently needs FDI; the northeast region of India and China's southwest (Yunnan) require foreign trade and foreign investment simultaneously.

Finally, the poor intra-regional mechanisms and weak intra-regional market forces also need BCIM to carefully deliberate the specific routes of the BCIM-Economic Corridor. There are two types of regionalism that can guide its construction. Traditional regionalism emphasises the intra-regional trade creation and economic integration, but the new regionalism advocates openness, and emphasises that the regional organisations must not only stress the internal cooperation, but also strengthen the transverse link with external areas, and encourages the intra-regional countries to actively participate in intra-regional and extra-regional cooperation. For economic and trade development, the new regionalism emphasises the regional productive integration and the role of investment. The results of empirical analysis shows that due to the lack of the intra-regional economic and trade, industry development, investment capacity and orientation, it will be a long haul to construct a perfect internal market in BCIM region. In that case, how about changing a way of thinking? That is, to use the mechanism construction of economic corridor that can provide this sub-region various international public products, such as, interconnected infrastructure, dialogue mechanism, relevant platform for investment facilitation and trade facilitation, as well as the intra-regional governance for the traditional and non-traditional security. All this should help improve regional ability of sustained opening up and reforms so as to improve the level of industrial development and economic growth of each of the four countries, and then to improve regional internal creativity, realising the benign intra-regional and extra-regional linked development. In reference to the performance evaluation standards of ASEAN regional economic integration, what BCIM-Economic Corridor construction needs to attempt is not how to construct a closed market driven by an endogenous forces, but how to make it embedded in the larger global integration of production systems and global value chains.

Endnotes

1. Yunnan Bureau of Statistics, 2013 Statistical Bulletin of National Economy and Social Development of Yunnan, (accessed on 9 August 2016), http://www.stats.yn.gov.cn/TJJMH_Model/newsview.aspx?id=2748024
2. IBEF, State Report, accessed on 9th August 2016, at http://www.ibef.org/states.aspx.
3. Academy of International Trade and Economic Cooperation of the Ministry of Commerce, "Guide for Foreign Investment

Cooperative Country (Region) –Myanmar" http://fec.mofcom.gov.cn/gbzn/gobiezhinan.shtml?COLLCC=1333079570&.

4. Ministry of Commerce of the People's Republic of China, et al, 2012 Statistical Bulletin of China's FDI, (Beijing: China Statistical Publishing House, 2012)
5. Department of Commerce of Yunnan Province, Profile of 2013 Yunnan's Foreign Investment and Cooperation, (accessed on 9th August 2016) http://www.bofcom.gov.cn/bofcom/432921734090326016/20140228/367917.html
6. IBEF, State Report, accessed on 9 August 2016 at http://www.ibef.org/states.aspx.
7. Lin Mei, Yan Sen, "The Economic and Trade Relations between China and Malaysia: Analysis of Competitiveness and Complementarity", Southeast Asian Affairs, 2011(1): 25-35.
8. Yue Yunxia, "The Comparative Study of Economic and Trade Competitiveness between China and Mexico" , Journal of Latin American Studies, 2008(3): 48-54.
9. Yu Jinping, "The Comparative Advantage and Trade Complementarity between China and East Asian Countries and Regions" [J] World Economy, 2003, 26(5): 33-40.

8

Energy Dynamics of BCIM-EC: Connectivity for Transactions

Manan Dwivedi

In the terms of the narrative of conventional International Politics, the hard power demeanour of the power centric approach still rules the roost in the realm of international relations. The quintessential lore of 19th century smokeless power, small bore rifles and quick firing artillery all the way to the age of Revolution in Military Affairs, have posed prominent ordeals for politics. The emerging trends in the realm of developments triggering consciousness regarding shrinking energy reserves has shifted the power discourse to resources. It is this that has since raised urgency with regard to exploring alternate natural resources and suppliers and supply lines. In the wake of urbanization and industrialization of our immediate neighbourhood has witnessed rising demand resources with fluctuations in oil prices graphically reflecting the crisis.

The BCIM region is marked by the newly emerging nation states such as People's Republic of China, India, as also Bangladesh and Myanmar too; all requiring far more energy. This heralds the advent of a new sub-regional artifice of some geo-economic strategic significance impacting at least regional energy markets. These few nations however can also be harnessed to establish new conduits for their energy starved principalities. With the region becoming open to new international practices and the attendant idiom of regional cooperation, such a sub-regional 'Regime'[1] can do wonders for a specific realm like energy. This will be needing immensely augmented quota of energy supplies for domestic households as also for their industrial utilities. This is especially true of China and India that are called the emerging markets and economies with increasing purchasing power with their masses. Both regionally and globally in a post American world order, BCIM is likely to expand its influence in setting the regional energy trajectories. Increasingly, their interventions in world energy markets will be compelled by their domestic constituencies.

It is in this backdrop that this paper examines the emerging contours of intra and inter-regional energy equations of BCIM and its impact on the regional development and equations as also strengths and challenges of this process unfolding in coming times.

Geo-Strategic Significance of Energy

In India, the dynamics of energy security and its fulfilment has been amply realised by the New Delhi denomination since the times of Prime Minister Manmohan Singh. Dr. Singh is on record for having said that "the quest for Energy Diplomacy has become an important and significant part of the functioning of Indian Diplomacy and the country's relation with the vast swathe of nations across the Globe."[2] Apart from ensuring energy security for the nation's population, the idea has come to be integral part of very conception and practise of India's foreign policy and security policies. It is here that the environmental, developmental and economic dimensions have a key role to play in the attendant debate and in the building of the Indian narrative on energy. This promises to bind BCIM further as also boost BCIM-EC to play a role in setting regional geo-economic trends where BCIM can itself become a fulcrum of larger regional dynamics in other sectors.

Historical analysis can be a very useful guide to direct any analysis of international issues and global trends. The way the scholars have read the attendant scenarios, several major military endeavours and manoeuvres were directly or indirectly attached to energy motives. Contemporary times have seen manoeuvres in international relations being guided by 'Oil politics'.[3] More specially, as all the military equipment runs on oil, namely the ships, tanks and fighter aircraft, so there remains a direct linkage between energy security, and national security.[4] The political and strategic fall out was that great powers have often played off nations against one another in order to wield a effective influence on every country. The all-pervading strategic and military significance of natural resources for regional and global domination cannot be underrated. It is from this standpoint also that the fulcrum of this chapter revolves around the energy dynamics of the BCIM-EC involving the energy production modes of Hydro, solar and nuclear power, their suppliers and supply lines.

China, India, Bangladesh, Myanmar have all been gifted by nature with a shared habitat and water and energy resources. Common rivers run through the region which can be effectively utilized for harnessing energy output for supporting their industrial vibrancy and energy self-sufficiency. In the contemporary context, both the India and China have been highly dependent upon the Middle East for the Oil and natural gas supplies though Tar sand and Shale gas and other alternative fuel supplies are being actively explored by both nations. United States meanwhile has succeeded in breaking free from the quintessential dependence on the Middle East Oil through its Shale gas revolution. This may impact on the energy competition both by as also inside BCIM. Shebonti Ray Dadwal of New Delhi-based Institute for Defence Studies and Analysis points out that,

> The US' claim that it will become energy independent shortly on the back of the revolution in its shale resources technology has been followed by

> Washington's announcement of its 'rebalancing to Asia' policy. These two factors have set off a debate on the tectonic shifts that may accrue in the geopolitical landscape of the world's energy sector as well as global geopolitics.[5]

These recent debates on the American energy sufficiency have led to the idea that nations such as India and China, that are major consumers and large scale importers of oil and natural gas, will be impacted by the American energy autonomy and boom. This means that these nations will be too hard pressed to refashion their own bilateral and multilateral equations with the Middle East in order to settle their domestic energy demands. Or they may also have to look for alternative energy resources to reduce their dependency on the mud and tar of the Middle East. To extrapolate its impact for the BCIM, big powers like US will continue to influence the larger global trends. BCIM remains mired in their own internal developmental processes of varying contours. This also protects them from the larger global dynamics as BCIM remains more localized and relatively disconnected. This makes BCIM much more of a sequestered and localized context of BCIM-EC sub-region.

BCIM's Individual Actors: Myanmar

Myanmar happens to be surging nation replete with global and regional offers of prosperity especially from its nearby sub-national principalities such as Yunan. In the case study of Myanmar and as a partner nation in the larger rubric of the energy rich region BCIM, Myanmar's domestic markets have been opened up over last one decade. This has its own consequences. The trade practices have been liberalised leading to the opening up of the national economy with a positive spin for the regional equation amongst BCIM countries. Shebonti Ray Dadwal writes that,

> Not surprisingly, Myanmar's energy sector has elicited the most attention. With reserves assessed between 7.8 trillion cubic feet (tcf), the government's 2011 bidding round

offered 18 onshore blocks, eight of which were awarded to foreign firms, while the January 2013 round, which put up 18 onshore and 30 offshore blocks on offer, have attracted significant interest from international oil companies, including the majors. Another round for 20 more by the end of 2013 has been announced.[6]

She further contends that, "However, till recently, Myanmar's gas was sold only to Thailand, though from July 2013, China too will receive 6.5 tcf of gas for 30 years from its Rakhine blocks, jointly owned by Myanmar, South Korea's Daewoo and India's OVL and GAIL following the completion of a pipeline."[7] The energy rich Myanmar is strategically poised and posited between two of the Asian powers which also happen to be the first and third largest economies of Asia with a larger footprint at the global level being engaged in a cooperative and a deft quid pro Quo. It can alter the geo-economic and strategic landscape of the BCIM-EC and the entire sub-region if it is perceived as a sub-regional Regime. The 'internationalisation' of an individual nation's natural worth is being made through the envisaged cooperation of a resource rich Myanmar despite its political limitations. Shebonti Ray-Dadwal further writes that,

> With no transparency, accountability or public disclosure of how the revenues accruing from the sale of energy were managed or used, the perception is that they were utilised to prop up the military rule or went into the personal coffers of the junta.[8]

In spite of concerns about its democratic reform and rule of law situation, there exist strong accountable, workable and transparent procedure and norms in Myanmar's political and revenue receipt system. This can spawn a glitch free and globally acceptable framework and pattern which incentivizes engagement by energy deficit economies. This explains how impressive energy gains by Myanmar are being recorded and utilised. The rule by the military junta is also explained as one reason why the norm setting and procedural cleansing has not become part of the 'routinised administrative ritual.' New Myanmar has been belabouring for a democratic transition since the days of the house arrest of Aang Saan Sui Kyi. The political and internal systemic constraints too play a key role in the upkeep, development and a long term objective sustenance of the Oil and gas developmental and business project of Myanmar and the larger BCIM-EC sub-regional belt.

Bangladeshi as a Case Study

Bangladesh too has a key role to play in the BCIM's dynamics as it is an energy rich country which has successfully mitigated its human development limitations. The stereotypical South Asian reservations which these micro states have had against their bigger and relatively resourceful neighbour India can be relegated to the backburner as a pragmatic cause for the larger BCIM. Biru Paksha Paul writes that,

> The relationship between energy consumption and output is still ambiguous in the existing literature. The economy of Bangladesh, having spectacular output growth and rising energy demand as well as energy efficiency in recent decades, can be an ideal case for examining energy-output dynamics. We find that while fluctuations in energy consumption do not affect output fluctuations, movements in output inversely affect movements in energy use.[9]

The case study of Bangladesh is a rather quaint one as a micro state of the region as it has recorded quick, responsive and managed economic success which is directly related to the energy use factors and the energy demand and supply dynamics. When Bangladesh became independent in the early 1970s, its viability as an independent nation state was universally questioned as it had the onerous task to tide over its disability of low per capita income and a high and unregulated density of population. Nawrim Samrina writes about the notion of energy security in Bangladesh that,

> In the past, energy development programs in Bangladesh suffered from a lack of long-term planning. Decisions made about energy sector projects, in particular, were influenced by foreign investors and political party agendas. For the population of the Chittagong Hill Tract area, habitation has become untenable due to the Kaptai hydropower plant, which has resulted in the submersion of 40 percent of the area's arable land.[10]

In its initial years since liberation, the state of Bangladesh was faced with the clash of the contending idioms of development and indignity. The choices had to be made by the Dhaka in order to make the nation run on an energy driven path of progression. As time progressed adhocism and a want of planning withered away from the larger energy planning profile. Gradually, a rational, pragmatic optimisation of the nation's energy resources such as hydro power projects took shape. Also, the strategic implications of natural gas too emerged as a key factor in the BCIM's larger dynamics. Natural gas too remains as the sole fore runner of the energy demands in the country. Nawrin Samrina further writes,

The national energy balance of Bangladesh clearly depicts that natural gas is Bangladesh's only significant indigenous source of commercial energy. It is the principal source of energy for the country's power, industry, commercial, and domestic sectors. Natural gas provides over 90 percent of Bangladesh's electricity, and is also the feedstock and fuel of the urea and ammonia fertilizer plants.[11]

Natural gas forms Bangladesh's staple fare of the energy demand and needs with serious reservations being aired and discussed widely. The rationale of either clinging to a strictly localized demand oriented domestic usage of natural oil or letting it become an income generator of foreign exchange for a needy Bangladeshi economy, is a core political theme in the political elite of Bangladesh. The BCIM cause can only be subserved if Dhaka's internal political uncertainty and attendant reservations about exporting and exchanging energy with other BCIM players is tided over by a more pragmatic and convergence oriented political decision making. BCIM grid can be a nice first step towards this shift.

Bangladesh's Energy Minister, Mosharraf Hossain, commented that "if exporting is found to be economically beneficial, the government will definitely decide to allow it."[12] Finance Minister Saifur Rahman also stated that the administration of Prime Minister Zia might go for natural gas export "provided that it is beneficial for the country" and that "no resource in the true sense is a resource if it remains under the soil."[13] The larger argument runs like this: that in the name of regional cooperation and the upgradation of the common interest, nations need to emerge out of the 20th century idiom of existing in a self-preservatory region with nations, concentrating upon the idea of being, "consumers of security".

And finally, the state of Bangladesh exists in middle of South and south East Asia. This makes a gainful collaborative alignment of its interests and trade-offs with SAARC, BIMSTEC and BCIM nations that may facilitate upgradation of its regional interest and initiatives. Also, it is generally understood that a mutual exploitation of the hydel and other resources amongst multiple stakeholder nations may make it a more profitable exercise especially for energy production, processing, marketing and distribution. Such a shared distributive and utilization mechanism within BCIM will always be far more profitable especially for their immediate surrounding regions of China and India.

India as a Major Player

In the case study of India, the benefits from such shared development and use of region's Hydel power, say in case of Bhramputra river system, can open up the South East Asia's gateway for India especially for its North East

Region. Asma Masood writes in a New Delhi-based Institute of Peace and Conflict (IPCS) publication,

The region is a crucial gateway to Southeast Asia. Delhi can continue to harness the geostrategic location of Myanmar. Bangladesh is a promising shipping hub for India's spoils in oil. Commitment with smaller, indispensable neighbours and a future world economic leader lend to regional stability and order.[14]

The idea of being a 'benign' hegemon in the sharing of the hydel resources and facilitating the legal and bureaucratic hurdles in hydel power sharing with Bangladesh remain the core issue for continuing lack of trust and cooperation. In the third Joint Consultative Commission (JCC) between India and Bangladesh, both these nations have renewed their commitment for sharing of waters of the Teesta and Feni rivers. In a meeting in September, 2014, the ministers from India and Bangladesh expressed the optimism that the forthcoming BCIM-EC meeting to be held in Bangladesh will impart dynamism to cooperation amongst the BCIM countries.[15] Ben Crow and Nirvikar Singh contend that,

> One can delve inside the challenges of managing Himalayan rivers as a result of climate change and the industrialization and economic growth of India and China. We discuss a range of conceptual issues relevant for negotiations over the management of Himalayan rivers. We introduce the concept of multi-track diplomacy, and apply it to the case of international river management, in the context of innovations incorporated in five international treaties signed in 1996 and 1997.[16]

The management of rivers and their Hydel power output and outcomes can be effectively harnessed for the greater advantage of the BCIM sub-region. For instance, this can help the rural belts to be electrified and the industrial base can be ignited for the larger development of the BCIM. Bilateral treaties between these BCIM nations can be redirected towards a BCIM oriented larger sub-regional energy and hydel power interests. This is similar to spawning a BCIM Hydel power project which moves further from their existing bilateralism. But, of course, it is from their experiences of bilateralism that multilateral efforts for energy cooperation in BMIC can emerged. Mahendra P Lama contends that,

> In Bangladesh, the National Energy Policy 1995 (NEP), has been designed to ensure proper exploration, production, distribution and rational use of energy sources to meet the growing energy demand of different zones, consuming sectors and consumer groups on a sustainable basis.[17]

India and Bangladesh, both the nations are bedevilled by the scourge of power theft which underlines need for greater cooperate in the field of energy sharing. In India too with the growing idea of power shortages and the attendant features of 'seasonability', the need for the creation of a power based grid in the twilight zone beyond India's North East has emerged and is very much a part of the nation's Look East Policy. In India, legislation has been created to deal with the question of energy. Mahendra P Lama further contends that,

> India's power sector reforms have been at both the Union and State levels. Besides the setting up of the regulatory commissions, both at the Centre and in the States, the Electricity Act 2003 has injected fairly advanced and comprehensive policy changes.[18]

In India, their public policy emanating at the domestic and the national levels has led to the spawning of a need for a regional agreement and adaptive mechanism in order to optimise the energy scenario in the constituent nations of the BCIM region. Also, in India, local capacity building and harmonizing of energy and trade standards with the rest of the BCIM sub-region have been too called into attention as essential prerequisites for an energy-trade-tariff regime in the sub-region.[19]

Renewable Energy & India's Northeast Region

Prime Minister Narendra Modi's solar energy ambitions are immense and with sub-regional cooperation in renewable sources of energy can become the idea that can lead to the building say a Solar grid for BCIM. The British newspaper, *Guardian* writes that,

> As chief minister of Gujarat, Modi spurred companies to build more than 900MW of solar plant across the state in just a couple of years. Now, as prime minister, the question is whether he can repeat the feat across India, which receives more sunlight than any other country in the G20. The Gujarat Solar Park in Gujarat, India, is Asia's largest solar power station with an installed capacity of 1,000 MW. The answer matters across the globe: at the heart of tackling climate change is bringing power to the world's poorest people without choking the planet with rising carbon emissions.[20]

The need for alternate power and energy resources can transform the energy environment in the BCIM sub-region. These nations have an abundant exposure to sunshine and have great potential to get away from the putrid carbon emissions in the neighbourhood and opt for cleaner energy. The Gujarat's instance is an apt reminder of the opportunities in the North East too with larger implications for the BCIM-EC region. Apart from the Solar Energy perspective being ignited in the Indian state of Gujarat, Agartala another Indian province in India's North East Region has created the North East's first Solar city which has been supported by India's Ministry of Renewable Energy. It is documented in a Zee News Report that, "Agartala city would be the first 'solar city' in northeast India within the next few years." This comment was attributed to Tripura's Urban Development Minister, Manik Dey, who said this after inaugurating a 50 kilowatt solar power plant at the Agartala Municipal Council head office here. The Minister reported also said that, "Solar power is the sustainable and viable energy for both cities and remote areas. Electricity crisis would not be solved in the country unless we use non-conventional energy like solar power in a big way."[21]

In this, India's North Eastern Region can serve as an ideal staging point for the BCIM sub-region's non-conventional energy dynamics. This will also provide new opportunities for India's North East Region to expand cooperation with similar advantages of the Mekong river terrain. Such perspective from India's North Easter Region will be a significant component to the notion of energy grid in the BCIM-EC. Such argument has also been re-enforced by Mr. Barun Barpujari, Chairman, CII Assam State Council and Executive Director, Indian Oil Corporation Ltd. (AOD) who believes that integration within India's North East region was a prerequisite before the region could integrate with other countries. He also feels that sectors such as oil and gas, non-renewable energy, natural resources, agriculture etc. hold tremendous potential for cooperation between the North East and the BCIM region.[22] Similarly, the grip levels of rural electrification and power loses in India's North Eastern Region have been another issue of energy debates. The water resources of this region can be availed to tide over the glum energy scenario in the region which partakes of the neighbourhood of the BCIM–EC as well. Consultant V V K Rao writes that,

> Village electrification in the Northeastern power region, at 76.6 percent of the total villages (29,696), is lower than the national average of 84.3 percent. Nagaland and Sikkim are the only states in the region where all villages have been electrified so far. This is followed by Mizoram (99.6 percent), Tripura (95.9 percent), Manipur (95.5 percent), Assam (77.3 percent), Arunachal Pradesh (63.5 percent), and Meghalaya (63.5 percent).[23]

The hydro-power normalisation in the region can be connected with the larger BCIM-EC grid which will also boost chances for the Indian North East Region. India's Central Electricity Authority has prepared reports on the various basins in the Indian north Eastern region such as, Power Development in Dibang Basin, Lohit Basin, Meghalaya Basin, Siang Basin, Teesta Basin, Subansiri Basin, etc all in the year 2004 which make for a heady insight inside the hydro power dynamics in the region. The Reports further provide insights into how some of the geographically suitable basins can be made part of the larger BCIM-EC territory for hydel usage. The Ganges water Treaty between India and Bangladesh has been one of the primordial guiding lights for the future of the nature of energy cooperation in the sub region. In a presentation by Mir Sajjad Hussein, Member Joint Rivers Commission, Bangladesh Ministry of Water Resources, it emerges that,

Bangladesh is crisscrossed by an intricate network of rivers. The life and livelihood of the people of Bangladesh is heavily dependent on the river waters like Indian north East. There are more than 400 rivers in Bangladesh out of which 57 are transboundary and 54 rivers enter from India and the remaining 3 from Myanmar. In fact most of these rivers(51) are within the catchment areas of the three mighty rivers; the Ganges, the Brahmaputra and the Meghna. Total catchment area of these three great rivers together is about 1.72 million sqkm of which only about 7 percent lies within Bangladesh."

It is this nature of the contiguous and the shared nature of hydel power and water resources wealth which can be imaginatively utilized by India and Bangladesh as these two share their river waters. And since this is no longer a matter of national consumption or bilateral cooperation, the entire BCIM-EC sub-region can participate to maximise their relative advantages in order to spawn a sub-regional energy grid.

Nuclear Energy can too be earmarked as a factor of cooperation in the BCIM-EC sub-region. Recently, China and India have evinced an expanded interest in developing a civil nuclear agreement and India has already inked the same with a few other western nations. It is mentioned in the September 2014 joint communiqué between India and PRC that,

> As large developing countries committed to promoting the use of clean energy, India and China believe that expansion of civil nuclear energy program is an essential component of their national energy plans to ensure energy security. The two sides will carry out bilateral cooperation in civil nuclear energy in line with their respective international commitments, including working level consultations between the Department of Atomic Energy of India and the China Atomic Energy Authority.[24]

Such possible cooperation in nuclear power generation can have spin-offs of benefits for other two smaller neighbours in BCIM spawning sub-regional level mechanisms for energy cooperation.

Multilateralism and BCIM-EC

The tide of multilateralism has been a significant precursor element in the run up to the creation of the Kunming initiative and then leading to the firming up of the BCIM-Forum and BCIM-EC sub-regional initiatives. And there surely remains great potential in BCIM developing networks in special sectors like energy and agriculture etc. A Food and Agricultural Organization report informs that, the Mekong River Commission (MRC) came into existence on 5 April 1995 on agreement between the governments of Cambodia, Lao People's Democratic Republic, Thailand and Viet Nam. These four countries signed the "Agreement on the cooperation for the sustainable development of the Mekong River Basin" and agreed on joint management of their shared water resources and development of the economic potential of the river.[25] The MRC's creation has seemingly served as a substratum for the generation of a cooperation agreement between the various riparian states in the context of Hydel power cooperation and the sharing of water resources. This is bound to inspire similar initiatives inside neighbouring BCIM hydel power grids etc. Ananth Krishnan in the national daily, *The Hindu* had argued that, the BCIM-EC will run from Kunming to Kolkata, linking Mandalay in Myanmar as well as Dhaka and Chittagong in Bangladesh. The BCIM-EC plan, he says, promises to "advance multi-modal connectivity, harness the economic complementarities, promote investment and trade and facilitate people-to-people contacts."[26]

This sub-regional formulations have moved from being academic discourses to becoming state policies of rising China and emerging India which promises to make it an effective paradigm in international system characterised by the advent of the Asian century and the US Pivot to Asia. The 'coming' of the Orient becomes a stronger possibility when the nations such as India, China, Bangladesh and Myanmar, coalesce together in order to stock their mutual worth and energy with a higher objective to bridge divides with other regional actors such as ASEAN, OPEC, TPP and RCEP in the larger region.[27] But, at its core BCIM really happens to be the energy conclave and this character promises to bring together these nations as producers and consumers of energy for their rapid development. Another report in newspaper *The Hindu*, further asserts that,

> The hope is that before the holding of the third joint study meeting in India towards the end of 2014, the four countries will have agreed upon a cooperation framework – including modalities of financing projects – that will pave the way for on-the-ground work to begin. Recent talks saw the four countries come up with an ambitious proposal that included developing multi-modal transport, such as road, rail, waterways and airways, joint power projects and telecommunication networks.[28]

On the flip side, the entire BCIM-EC has also been prey to catch-phrases and tokenish phraseology, wherein, the dictum of cooperation from Kunming to Kolkata is paraded as the central pivot of the entire grouping. One of the significant glitches in the region happens to be the political instability in Myanmar. Still, as the junta in Yangon has emerged out of the self imposed isolation and sublimated with the rest in the region. Therefore, better days can be envisaged for the BCIM-EC connecting nations of South Asia and South East Asia. After all, these have been only politically motivated artificial classifications of colonial times further re-enforced by the colonial dynamic where ASEAN was created to contain the spread of communism. India too has taken a keen interest in BCIM-EC along with its main official sponsor, i.e. China. The whole grouping is primarily premised upon the rubric of economic, energy and developmental cooperation with the avowed objective of sustaining greater physical and economically conducive connectivity in the larger pragmatic interest of the sub-region. A Joint Study group to explore the feasibility of BCIM-EC was organized by the Indian Embassy in 2013. The minutes of the meetings of the Joint Group informs that BCIM will focus on

> ...improvement in infrastructure building and establishing appropriate legal and regulatory framework for development of multi-modal transport (road, rail, waterways, airways) by developing and accelerating transportation inter-connectivity. At the same time, collaboration would need to be augmented in energy and power sectors to tap substantial opportunities. Development of tele-communication networking would also need to be addressed.[29]

Apart from developing an Economic Corridor, the BMIC-EC promises to become a vibrant energy corridor intertwined with potential of resolving water sharing issues. Water, of course, remains, both directly by moving turbines as also indirectly as a critical source in all other power generation processes, an important source of energy. The BCIM-EC can develop on the lines of energy cooperation. Diplomatic spade work needs to be done before energy transfers and energy trade can be especially facilitated. This energy led cooperation can facilitate improving the infrastructure, trade regimes, tariff barriers and connectivity between the twin nations and the other two smaller nations of the order of Bangladesh and Myanmar.[30] As these nations develop, the functioning of their domestic industries and economies would demand self sufficiency in energy. The BCIM-EC has potential to develop innovative ways to carve out its individual or regional sources of energy.

BCIM-EC Towards Energy Self Sufficiency

Apart from the established global players like China and India, the other two nations of BCIM-EC, namely Bangladesh and Myanmar, may be less influential yet they have critical resources and supplier leverages. Therefore, all four share strong complementarities to build energy self-sufficiency through their resources and infrastructure-building capabilities that can be effective to meet their domestic energy and power generation needs within the BCIM-EC. The BCIM-EC can even try to be a model of energy self-sufficiency as also a 'connect' between two larger economies of the world. It is this framework that forms the core of the Kunming initiative to drive home a core sub-regional cooperation theme.[31] In the words of Mustafizur Rahman, Habibur Rahman and Wasel Bin Shadat,

> The BCIM concept draws its inspiration from the concept of Growth Zones. The idea of growth zones has been a relatively new introduction in the vocabulary of development economics. It involves cooperation between three or more countries for the development of a geographically contiguous region consisting of a part or the whole of each of the participating countries.[32]

Given their colonial history having created several artificial boundaries, several regions within different nations are bounded by contiguous populations in neighbouring countries which have commonalities of ethnicity, informal trade cooperation and other cultural interfaces. They can be brought back together in a post-nation-state and a post-territorial-sovereignty order and this is what BMIC-EC may seek to achieve through its idea of connectivity underlying their energy cooperation. Mustafizur Rahman, Habibur Rahman and Wasel Bin Shadat further inform us that the sub-region of South West China too imparts a new colour to the BMIC-EC, where-in, hydropower and energy calculations have to be courted with the other three BMIC-EC member states trying to promote connectivity in this sub-region. These three authors underline the fact that,

> Yunnan is rich in natural resources. It has about 17.7 billion tons of coal reserves. More than 150 kinds of minerals have been discovered in the province which constitutes high quality iron and ore, lead, zinc, tin, copper, nickel, indium, cadmium, silver, germanium, platinum and phosphorus ore. Installed capacity of Yunnan's power industry was estimated at 9.2 million kw of electric power comprising 6.2 million kw hydropower and 3 million kw thermal power in 2002. In the same period this sector generated a total revenue income of US$ 1.4 billion.[33]

So, from Chinese perspective as well, the BMIC-EC can be developed as a novae energy grid, where-in, bigger corporate and governmental players can invest in a liberal trade and energy regime in the sub-region. The sub-region can later emerge as an regional hub of energy transfers and trade across South and South East Asian countries. Water resources also exist here as the significant precursor element to the harnessing of energy. All this can be traded with other regional players and can lead to the emergence of BCIM as 'an energy trade hub' for the other interested players.[34] In the long run, trade aspect of BMIC-EC natural reserves can emerge as a novae parameter with energy being traded for mutual welfare benefits. One can also chart out the India-Bangladeshi and Myanmar initiative as a prelude to the Kunming Initiative. These were given impetus in 2013 by the heads of states of India and People's Republic of China agreeing to focus on BCIM-EC. The case of the Myanmar-Bangladesh-India (MBI) gas pipeline project is worth examining. A press release by the High Commission of India in Dhaka contends that,

> Some analysts say that the primary reason for the failure of the 2005 pipeline negotiations between India

and Bangladesh was the lack of convergence in the energy policies of the two countries – India's energy policies then pointed naturally towards the pipeline while Bangladesh's policies did not feature it. With an estimated reserve of 2 trillion cubic meters of gas the government of Bangladesh did not see the salience of the pipeline in 2005. This was because while India was able to recognize the importance of gas imports to meet domestic demand, Bangladesh seemed to feel that it had adequate domestic reserves and planners did not realize an impending crisis in its regional energy security in the form of depletion of gas reserves.[35]

The BCIM initiatives concerning energy cooperation had started in the year 2005 between India and Bangladesh but the variance in the tenor of the twin national energy policies and the want of clear cut guidance had led to the obfuscation of the agenda of energy cooperation. Now, the BCIM-EC initiative portends that the new sub-regional perspective on developmental, energy, trade and economic cooperation can help these countries to overcome their parochial political concerns and address their trust-deficit. The larger sub-regional framework of BCIM-EC promises to overcome the conditionalities of their bilateral equations. Such initiatives therefore can serve them to prepare healthy ground for welfare and energy-cum-trade cooperation in the BCIM-EC.

Energy Policies Inside BCIM-EC

Individual energy policies of the BCIM-EC member states need to be delved within the holistic rubric of the BCIM-EC which is where this energy grid need to be located, understood and ably implemented. In the light of the US energy debt clock, China happens to be the biggest energy consumer since 2014 followed by India at the fourth position with the United States locked at a second place in the listing akin to an international stock prices list.[36] Also, in light of the dwindling mainstream sources of conventional energy sources, alternatives like wind, nuclear and solar energy production also deserve a great deal of strategic attention. Especially, the solar energy sources that have been part of a core agenda for India's new Prime Minister Narendra Modi. This phenomenon has since emerged as the central developmental plank of New Delhi's ruling party, Bharatiya Janata Party.

Lately, there has been an immense talk of energy contestations between India and China which is expected to threaten the energy grid of BCIM-EC. Their larger natural resources rivalry inside various states has already been seen in few cases. Energy cooperation, along with developing mutual understanding in other spheres, happens to be the primal challenge for Beijing and New Delhi for which both sides have been working. For energy cooperation to occur in the BCIM-EC, it is important that both China and India dither from the feeling that either of them is intervening or adversely influencing their regional and sub-regional dominions of prosperity. However, their confrontation for energy resources is part of the larger competition for politico-strategic manoeuvrability in the maritime arena of Asia-Pacific and now the Indo Pacific has since been projected as the new framework for US 'pivot' to Asia. And then they also have to deal with demands compulsions of their respective domestic constituencies. It was reported in the *China Daily* that,

> According to its Ambassador, India's 12th Five Year Plan (2012-2016) calls for generating more power through renewable sources such as wind and solar power. At the same time, China's 12th Five Year Plan (2011-2015), which runs until 2016, focuses on a greener approach to economic growth.[37]

In the realm of energy cooperation, the Sino-Indian misunderstandings can prove to be a bottleneck. For energy cooperation to ensue in the BCIM-EC, a working infrastructure has to be developed with transnational pipelines running across all four member states. Apart from the Sino-India equations in the BCIM-EC, the developmental and human security diffidence in the HDI indicators too can serve as an impediment in the firming up of a robust energy network. But, apart from political equations, their energy needs will have to put in perspective their proximity, shared demographics and geo-economic enclaves. They will also have to take into account their respective labour market conditions and development level. A few discrepancies amongst these four nations tend to sour the pitch for a long term energy cooperation. Md. Tariqur Rehman and Muhammad Al Amin allude to this when they say that,

> Resource endowments in the BCIM region vary from country to country, which supports the precondition for the formation of this type of regional integration. China and India have comparatively better technology, a more efficient labour force, and improved physical and commercial infrastructure. On the other hand, Bangladesh and Myanmar have a large unskilled and semi-skilled labour force as well as basic and intermediate technology.[38]

All the four nations of BCIM-EC can strive for the attainment of energy self-sufficiency in the near future if their energy grid can materialise at the sub-region level. Shared nature of their socio-cultural and ethnic compositions can facilitate such a sub-regional cooperative paradigm. The entire Indian natural resources of its North East (and even of mainland India) can be extended inside the BCIM-EC arch. Their localized and national economic set ups can also develop their regional linkages leading to smooth integration of BCIM-EC. Pravakar Sahoo and Abhirup Bhunia write that,

> BCIM sub-regional cooperation can capitalise on hydrocarbons in Bangladesh, hydro-electric and mineral resources in Northeast India, natural gas reserves in Myanmar, and coal reserves in East Indian states like Odisha, Chhattisgarh and Jharkhand and China's Yunnan province. The potential for Northeast India to export energy to power-starved Bangladesh under the auspices of BCIM's institutional structure is particularly strong. Energy cooperation among BCIM

countries will have implications for China, the largest consumer of energy.[39]

The nations in the BCIM-EC especially China and India are part of the larger picture of the regional energy market where-in, a renewed stress by on the alternative and hydro power resources has ramifications for the neighbouring states of the BCIM-EC nations It has been reported in the Bloomberg News that,

> The world's largest carbon emitter is planning the energy projects to stabilize growth and adjust its energy structure after Li declared war on smog in a speech last month, vowing to shut coal-fired furnaces among other measures. The nation will also start construction of some key nuclear power projects in eastern coastal areas and "reasonable" hydropower plants.[40]

In the smog-ravaged nation like China, with abundant use of conventional energy sources like coal, this advent of renewable energy resources within BCIM-EC can enhance China's stakes in this adjacent region and emerge as part of the kernel of a sound energy strategy for China. This espouses Chinese energy cooperation with the BCIM-EC framework which is very much in the Chinese national interest. China's President Xi jinping has already been talking of reviving the ancient Silk Road which is expected to give further boost to the BCIM-EC initiatives especially between China and India. Ravi Boothlingam writes in an Issue Brief of the Institute for Peace and Conflict Studies saying,

> Chinese oil and gas pipelines are under construction from the Bay of Bengal port at Kyaukphu to reach Yunnan. They will reduce the risk to China which would otherwise have to ship the oil through the Malacca Strait... China will emerge as the larger gainer in the entire mechanism of BCIM as the governance structure of the Chinese border provinces such as Yunan suits the sub region. In India, the

North Eastern provinces are not free and autonomous to the extent the Chinese Provinces are in the Mekong region to individually and separately have diplomatic parleys with contiguous nations such as Myanmar.[41]

Though, too much stress and an emphasis on the China factor may also impede the smooth sailing of the BCIM-EC, especially its energy cooperation. So may be a middle path need to be carved out for the sub-region instead of either treating BCIM-EC as a Chinese instrument or defying China's lead in most initiatives. If India's energy excavations in its North Eastern backyard are done diligently and power sources can be explored and developed, then the BCIM-EC can prove to be a potent opportunity for India's North East Region to emerge as one 'power neutral node of an energy grid' in this region. Strategically speaking, China can count on the adjacent flock of smaller nations such as Myanmar with its newly found energy reserves in order to secure its sub-regional periphery thereby overcome its Malacca dilemma.

Conclusion

To conclude, therefore, balance of power understanding can be that for bigger states like India and China, the perpetuation of sub-regional energy grid like BCIM-EC can pave the pathway for the firming up of a neighborhood geo-economic buffer for both sides. Nevertheless, China-India are not the only factor determining the larger sustainability and energy rationale for the BCIM sub-region. The hard power attribute with traditional actors in sub-regional stage has to give way to newer idea, issues and players with gains to be made in the realm of energy and sustainability. The energy potential of BCIM-EC is thus, a step in direction of political and economic positive outcomes for all for all the four nations of the BCIM-EC.

Akin to their emerging quartet, limitations of their bilateral equations are a significant pointer to the direction of what variant of an energy connectivity awaits to blossom in their multilateral BCIM-EC framework. India unfortunately continues to bear its tag of being a benign South Asian hegemon which is a non-starter for building stronger BCIM-EC framework. Some of their extant bilateral equations like Indo-Bangladesh cooperation in the energy and power sectors also speaks well for India as a benefactor in the true tradition of global interdependence and regional bonhomie. But same India and Bangladesh have been deliberating upon River Teesta's repercussions. This shows that a compact is possible in the realm of energy cooperation which can serve as a potent mechanism for the larger energy cooperation within BCIM-EC. Somya Suryanarayan reports in the *World Security Network*,

> Talks are underway to set up a 130 km power transmission link connecting Behrampur in India and Bheramara in Bangladesh. India will supply 250 MW of power out of its central share of 15 per cent; an additional 200 MW will be supplied based on the power requirements of Bangladesh. A joint venture has been initiated between India's state-owned National Thermal Power Cooperation and the Bangladesh Power Development Board to set up a coal-fired power plant in Khulna district in Bangladesh.[42]

In the end, visions of an energy grid as a pillar in the BCIM-EC framework can serve as an ideal and pragmatic conduit for firming up regional cooperation and strength their mutual stakes and interdependence. With the immediate commercial benefits and progression towards developmental goals the spawning of the energy related sub-regional infrastructure, historical rivalries in the BCIM-EC framework can become a feature of the past. In the near term future, the BCIM-EC can serve as a bridge between the larger South East Asian and South Asian groupings. With India and China being the precursors of the entire BCIM-EC, the smaller nations of Bangladesh and Myanmar can too benefit in terms of their energy needs. For a while strategic and political miasmas can take a backseat in the light of critical energy gains. The bilateral energy arrangements which exist between nations such as India-Bangladesh, India-Myanmar, Myanmar-China can serve as an energy bulwark for the multilateral sub-region formulations. Thus, the trend of bilateralism addressing individual concerns such as energy theft, generation, distribution and utilisation, can serve as an ideal precursor for the spawning of a larger energy resources sharing at the sub-regional level.

Endnotes

1. Robert Keohane, "The Demand for International Regimes," *International organization*, Volume 36, No.2, Spring, 1982.
2. Manmohan Singh, "The New India," *The Wall Street Journal* (Eastern Edition) May 19, 2005.
3. Daneil Yergin, "The Prize: The Epic Quest for Oil,"(New York: Simon and Schuster, 1991)
4. Leonardo Magueiro, " The Age of Oil: The Mythology, History and the Future of the World's Most Controversial Resource, "(Westport, Connecticut: Praeger Publishers, 2006)
5. Shebonti Ray Dadwal, " The Geo Politics of American Energy Independence: Implications For china, India and Global Energy Market," (Online: Web), URL: http://www.idsa.in/monograph/TheGeopoliticsofAmericasEnergyIndependence.html (Accessed on 1 September, 2014)
6. Shibonti Ray Dadwal, "Myanmar Opens to Business Opportunities, But Is It Sustainable", (Online: Web), URL:http://www.idsa.in/idsacomments/MyanmarOpenstoBusinessOpportunities_srdadwal_140613.html
7. Ibid
8. Ibid 1.
9. "Energy and Output Dynamics in Bangladesh",URL: http://econpapers.repec.org/article/eeeeneeco/v_3a33_3ay_3a2011_3ai_3a3_3ap_3a480-487.htm (Online: Web) Accessed on 14 October, 2014.
10. ACDIS Occasional Paper, Nawrin Samrina, "Energy Security For Bangladesh: Prospects and Strategic implications for Natural Gas," (University of Illinois, Urbana Champaign, 2004) Page No. 1-4.
11. Ibid Page 15.
12. Walliur Rahman, "Bangladesh Edges toward Gas Export," BBC News, October 31, 2001, http://news.bbc.co.uk/hi/english/world/south_asia/newsid_1630000/1630925.stm

13. "Bangladesh in Debate over Natural Gas Export," Alexander's Gas and Oil Connections, News and Trends: East and Southeast Asia, Volume 6, Issue 24, December 19, 2001, http://www.gasandoil.com/goc/news.
14. Asma Masood, "india and the BCIM: Should the "I" Stand Up?"URL: http://www.ipcs.org/article/india/india-and-the-bcim-should-the-i-stand-up-3966.html (Online: Web), Accessed on 14 October, 2014
15. Khurram Zaman, "Dhaka Delhi Renew Teesta Pact Promise,"URL: http://www.banglanews24.com/en/fullnews/bn/98980.html, (Online : Web), Accessed on October 19, 2014.
16. Ben Crow, Nirvikar Singh, "T he Management of International Rivers as Demands Grow and Supplies Tighten: India, China, Nepal, Pakistan, Bangladesh" , E Series Publication, University of California, 2009
17. Mahendra P Lama, "India Bangladesh Energy Cooperation: Historic New Trends", (Mainstream, March, 2013)
18. Ibid
19. "Need to Build Local Capacities in the North East", URL:http://orfonline.org/cms/sites/orfonline/modules/report/ReportDetail.html?cmaid=70273&mmacmaid=70274, (Online : Web), Accessed on 19 October, 2014
20. Damian Carrington, "Can Narendra Modi Bring the Solar Power Revolution to India?" The Guardian, 30 September, 2014
21. "Agartala To Be North East India's First Solar City" URL: http://zeenews.india.com/news/eco-news/agartala-to-be-northeast-indias-first-solar-city_799221.html (Online : Web), Accessed on 19th October, 2014.
22. "North East in India to Benefit from BCIM Groups on Transportation, Trade and Tourism," URL: http://www.theshillongtimes.com/2014/07/20/ne-to-benefit-from-bcim-groups-on-transportation-trade-tourism/ (Online: Web), Accessed on 19 October, 2014
23. VVK Rao, " Hydro power in the North East: Potential and Harnessing Analysis," Background Paper Number 6, September 2006, India Water portal.
24. Ministry of External Affairs Release, "Joint Statement Between the Republic of India and the People's Republic of China on Building a Closer developmental Partnership," URL:http://www.mea.gov.in/bilateral-documents.htm?dtl/24022/Joint+Statement+between+the+Republic+of+India+and+the+Peoples+Republic+of+ China+on+Building+a+Closer

+Developmental+Partnership, (Online: Web), Accessed on 19 October, 2014

25. Aquastat, Food and Agriculture Organization of the United Nations, URL: http://www.fao.org/nr/water/aquastat/countries_regions/mmr/index.stm (Online : Web), Accessed on 19th October, 2014
26. Ananth Krishnan, "BCIM Corridor gets Push After First Official Level Talks in China," *The Hindu*, December 21, 2013
27. Beginda Pakpahan, "Will RCEP compete with TPP?" URL: http://www.eastasiaforum.org/2012/11/28/will-rcep-compete-with-the-tpp/ (Online: Web), Accessed on 12 September, 2014
28. Ibid
29. Embassy of India, "Minutes of the First Meeting of the Joint study Group of BCIM-EC" (Online: Web), URL: http://www.indianembassy.org.cn/newsDetails.aspx?NewsId=455 (Accessed on 5 September, 2014)
30. "Bangladesh, China India Myanmar Bid To Bring Energy and Economic Corridor Gathering Steam," (Online: Web), URL: http://stratrisks.com/geostrat/16666 (Accessed on 7th September, 2014)
31. BCIM forum is a Track II initiative which was floated in 1999 at a conference on regional cooperation which was held at Kunming, the capital of the Yunnan province of the Peoples' Republic of China. This sub-region comprises a number of geographical units in contiguous eastern South Asia: North-east states of India, Southern provinces of China, Bangladesh and Myanmar. Broadly, it covers the four relevant countries, hence the acronym BCIM.
32. Mustafizur Rahman, Habibur Rahman and Wasel Bin Shadat, "BCIM Economic Cooperation: Prospects and Challenges," Paper No. 64, Centre for Policy Dialogue.
33. Ibid.
34. Ashis Biswas, "Prospects of the BMIC Project,"URL: http://echoofindia.com/reflex-action/prospects-bmic-project-41562 (Online: Web), Accessed on 12 October, 2014.
35. "India- Bangladesh Myanmar: Potential for Sub Regional Cooperation,"(Online: Web), URL: http://www.hcidhaka.gov.in/pages.php?id=1448 (Accessed on 10 September, 2014)
36. Central Intelligence Agency, "Expanded Energy Data Now in the World Fact Book," URL: https://www.cia.gov/news-information/featured-story-archive/2012-featured-story-

archive/expanded-energy-data-in-world-factbook.html (Online: Web), Accessed on 12 October, 2014

37. Qin Jize, "China, India Look to Energy Cooperation," *China Daily*, April 14, 2011
38. Md. Tariqur Rehman and Muhammad Al Amin, "Prospects of economic cooperation in the Bangladesh, China, India and Myanmar region: A quantitative assessment," *Asia Pacific Research and Training Network on Trade Working Paper Series No. 73*, July, 2009.
39. Pravakar Sahoo and Abhirup Bhunia, "BCIM Corridor a Game Changer For South Asian Trade,"(Online: Web), URL: http://asiapacific.anu.edu.au/blogs/southasiamasala/2014/07/24/5554/ (Accessed on 1 September, 2014)
40. "China Premier Li Reiterates Plans to Boost Clean Energy," *Bloom Berg News*, April 21, 2014
41. Ravi Boothalingam, "China and its Peripheries: Beijing and the BCIM," (Online: Web). URL: http://www.ipcs.org/issue-brief/china/china-and-its-peripheries-beijing-and-the-bcim-216.html (Accessed on 14 September, 2014)
42. Soumya Suryanaranan, "India, Bangladesh and Energy Security," URL: http://www.strategicforesight.com/inner-articles.php?id=178#.VEEtVvmSyHM (Online: Web), Accessed on 14 October, 2014

9

Physical Connectivity of BCIM: Chinese Perspective*

Liu Wu

BCIM sub-regional cooperation has been regarded as a strategy to promote the growth and development of the peripheral regions. However, in line with their disadvantages of poor infrastructure and high costs of transportation the economies of these peripheral regions continue to suffers lower growth and development. Especially, their lack of physical connectivity discourages private investments in the peripheral regions, which in turn stands on the way of the regionalisation of production, consumption and market formation. Constructing efficient and convenient physical connectivity therefore seen as the key for pushing forward the BCIM Economic Corridor. The physical connectivity of BCIM includes road connectivity, railway connectivity, waterway connectivity and aviation connectivity as well. Each country of BCIM has its own priorities regarding the transportation and traffic routes to be built.

It is in this backdrop that this chapter examines as to what are the realistic and feasible infrastructure projects for boosting physical connectivity in the current historical

* This paper is the research result of National Planning Office of Philosophy and Social Sciences Fund general project of "Study of the Development Prospect of Sino-Myanmar Relation and its Influence Factors" (sponsor number: 13BGJ026).

situation and from there it analyses the challenges and difficulties that lies for materialising this Economic Corridor. Finally, it enlists some of the measures that needs be considered for constructing physical connectivity of BCIM Economic Corridor. Also to put it at the very outset, This chapter examines these issue from a Chinese perspective, discusses China's contribution to the connectivity cooperation with other countries in the BCIM Economic Corridor, and analyses the challenges and prospects, and put forward some suggestions for promoting the construction of connectivity of BCIM Economic Corridor.

Brief History of Connectivity

To begin with a brief history of the initiation and construction of Bangladesh-China-India-Myanmar (BCIM) Economic Corridor, this idea can be traced back to BCIM Economic Cooperation and Development Forum (BCIM Forum for short) that was set up in 1999. In last 15 years, this Forum has held 11 meetings in four countries and has transformed itself from being the initial mechanism of Track-2 discussion and exchange among scholars to Track-1 mechanism in which all the four government now participate to make decisions while Track-2 also continues as a parallel exercise. After China's Premier Li Keqiang visited India in May 2013 and suggested that China and India should jointly promote the construction of BCIM Economic Corridor the BCIM regional cooperation has entered a new stage.[1]

As regards building physical connectivity as an important tool to strengthen this sub-regional integration, this did not just exist from the very beginning but has always been the primary focus of all BCIM Forum deliberations and studies. A certain trade network had already existed in this region before the establishment of modern Bangladesh, China, India and Myanmar. The main part of this network was the silk road, which mainly consisted of Sichuan-Yunnan-Myanmar-India Road (i.e.Wuchi Road), Sichuan-Yunnan-Tibet-India Road (i.e. the Ancient Tea Horse Road), and other several trade routes. The main road of Sichuan-

Yunnan-Myanmar-India Road started from Chengdu, passed through Xi'chang, the Jinsha River, and Yongchang, and then split into two routes after entering Myanmar. The south route arrived in Manipur after travelling through Shan State, the Chindwin Mountain, the Chin Hills and the Naga Hills. The north route started from Tengchong, Yunnan Province, and after travelling through Myanmar's Myitkyina, Mogaung, and Hukawng Valley, and crossing the Naga Hills and Patkai Mountain pass, it reached India's Assam, and then went on to Pakistan, Afghanistan and other areas of the Central Asia and West Asia. At the northwest end of the Naga Hills, from the northeast Ledo Station of India's Assam, there was a very developed traffic line that travelled across the tip of the northern Myanmar to the Xinpingyang (Yunnan Province) connecting the ancient India with Myanmar.[2] The Bhamo and Myitkyina in Myanmar were connected with China to the east and India to the west respectively which also became an important link of trade route.[3]

The Sichuan-Yunnan-Tibet-India Road that went on to Nepal and India was prosperous in the Tang and Song dynasties, which was famous for the Ancient Tea Horse Road.[4] The Sichuan-Yunnan-Tibet-India Road can be divided into the Sichuan-Tibet-India Road and Sichuan-Yunnan-Tibet-India Road. The route of Sichuan - Yunnan - Tibet - India Road is as follows: Puer - Dali - Lijiang - Shangri - La - Bomda - Qamdo - Nepal and India. In China, this route is basically in line with today's Sichuan-Yunnan Railway and Yunnan-Tibet Highway. The Ancient Tea Horse Road was an important route for Southwest China's Tibet Region to connect with Sichuan and Yunnan Provinces and South and Central Asia. The Ancient Tea Horse Road is both a trade route inside China and an important trade route connecting South Asia and India. The route mainly serves for the trade between the Han people and Tibetans in Sichuan and Yunnan Provinces, and between the Tibetans and Nepalese and Indians.[5] Through the southern silk road, a trade network started from around 1st and 2nd century B.C., silk, cloth, iron ware, porcelain, salt and other artware produced in Southwest China went to today's India, Afghanistan, Bangladesh, and other parts of South Asia through Sichuan and Yunnan, while the beads, precious stones, pearls, shells, etc. came from India and other parts of South Asia went into Southwest China through the southern silk road.

As maritime trade route replaced the land route and became the main trade route between China and South Asia, especially after the British colonial power entered into the South Asian region, and started the colonial rule in the South Asian region, the trade route between South Asia and southwest China increasingly degraded. In the Second World War, the allied forces built the Yunnan-Myanmar Road, Stilwell Road, oil pipeline, and opened the Hump Course in order to unite Chinese troops in this region to expel Japanese invaders. Although the main purpose for the construction and opening of these traffic lines was to transport munitions and supplies in the Chinese war against Japanese aggression, they objectively strengthened the transport links in the region. At the end of the Second World War, the transport links in this region gradually diminished, and even terminated in some areas. The reason was that the traffic lines opened in the wartime were mainly for the purpose of serving the war needs instead of being formed as the result of social development. In the decades from the mid-1940s to 1970s, this region saw great changes in political geography: newly independent or established countries carried out the policy of seclusion, or engaged in contradiction, conflict and even war with neighbouring countries, which further hampered various traffic connections in this region.

Connectivity in BCIM: Projects and Progress

Establishing various forms of regional and subregional economic cooperation, and building regional and subregional organisations to promote the development of regional economy have become a new trend of economic development. Around the BCIM, the ASEAN Free Trade Area, Greater

Mekong Subregion, Indian Ocean Rim Association (IORA), South Asian Free Trade Area (SAFTA), and Bay of Bengal Initiative for Multi-Sectoral Technical and Economic Cooperation (BIMSTEC) are active mechanisms but there is no effective regional and sub-regional cooperation organisation for the BCIM region that overlaps South Asia and Southeast Asia that can provide a push to their regional cooperation and promote the regional economic and social development. Until 1999, scholars of Yunnan province of China proposed to enhance the economic and social exchanges and cooperation in the BCIM areas. But in the following ten years, most of the proposals were only used in the academic discussions. In May 2013, when Prime Minister Li Keqiang visited India and proposed constructing the BCIM Economic Corridor to promote the regional cooperation, the construction of BCIM Economic Corridor then began to gain new momentum.

However, in order to build BCIM Economic Corridor to promote the regional cooperation, we must understand that the most important basis is to implement the physical connectivity in the BCIM areas. As of now, transportation connectivity modes among these countries of BCIM Economic Corridor are poor, and their allied infrastructure is relatively backward. Such poor regional connectivity is not only manifested in the low level of physical connectivity amongst BCIM countries, but also in the extremely backward domestic traffic of some countries in these peripheral regions. The development of connectivity between China and other three countries of BCIM Economic Corridor in the near future will focus on the traditional traffic connectivity of the highway, railway, aviation, and water transportations among which the land connection is the most important one. However, even on the road connection, the development is not balanced amongst these countries. For example, China, because of strong economic strength and infrastructure construction capacity, and with the ambition of opening the great Indian Ocean trade channel, seeks to open the land trade roads between China and India, Bangladesh, Myanmar, thus increasing its domestic traffic infrastructure investment.

At present, among the outward highways in Yunnan Province, the international big pathways between China and Myanmar, and between China and India are all high grade highways and will soon be qualified for the expressway grading. The railways from Yunnan to India and Myanmar are also under discussion or in planning. However, since India and Myanmar have fears and doubts about China, or are worried about the instability of minority regions along the borderline, or lack of infrastructure investment, it is difficult to make the road sections of China-Myanmar and China-India land routes within the territory of Myanmar and India connect with the planned outbound traffic lines of China in the short term.

(i) Connectivity between China and Myanmar

In terms of China-Myanmar highway connection, through Asia highway No.03 Line and No.1 Line, Kunming has been connected with Mandalay and Rangoon. The specific path of this road section is as follows: Kunming – Chuxiong – Dali – Baoshan - Ruili/Muse – Meikhtila - Pyinmana, Payogya – Pegu - Rangoon.[6] In April 2007, a secondary level road from Tengchong County to Myitkyina which was mainly invested by Baoshan City was opened. The overall length of this highway is 205 km. The route runs well since its opening, and partly reassures Myanmar of the China's true intention to provide assistance or aid for the construction of Myanmar. Currently, Baoshan city wants to participate in the construction of BCIM Economic Corridor connectivity project, and supports the extension of the Tengchong-Myitkyina highway to Ledo of India.

Although China has not signed a bilateral transport agreement with Myanmar, Yunnan Transportation Management Department, by means of local pilot projects and step-by-step approach, actively implements the Entry and Exit Transport Management Agreement signed between the local government and Myanmar. In early 2008, Yunnan Province had already opened the passenger traffic routes from Ruili to Muse and Namhkam of Myanmar, and ran the international road passenger transport route bus from

Jinghong to Nampan of Myanmar. In 2009, Yunnan opened the irregular international tourist road passenger transport at Ruili port and Daluo port. China's freight vehicles can directly enter the Myanmar from Ruili and Daluo, which greatly facilitated the bilateral movement of both people and goods. However, as can be seen from the current effect of implementation, even though the Sino-Myanmar bilateral transportation distance is short, efficiency of road transport is far from satisfactory. This also causes a lot of limitations for the entry and exit transport of vehicles of both China and Myanmar.[7] Xishuangbanna, Dehong, Lincang, and Puer in Yunnan province reached the agreement with the local government of Myanmar to approve the vehicles of both sides to be engaged in passenger and cargo transportation and tourism business in the border cities.

In terms of railway connectivity between China and Myanmar, with the construction of oil and gas pipelines between China and Myanmar, these two, in principle, have reached a consensus on the construction of highway and railway along the pipeline, and China has contracted to build the pipeline in the form of BOT. The Dali-Ruili road section of Sino-Myanmar proposed in *Medium and Long Term Railway Network Planning* (adjusted in 2008) will form an international railway channel connecting China with Myanmar. This railway is an important part of the west line of Pan-Asia Railway, as well as an important route with China in the railway network planning of "eight domestic railway lines to Yunnan, four railway lines to four countries" in Yunnan province. The total length of Dali-Ruili Railway is 330 km. The designed freight transport capacity is 12 million tons per year, and the passenger transport capacity is 12 pairs of trains each day. One can reach Ruili from Kunming by train in nine hours. The section from Kunming to Dali has been opened; the section from Dali to Baoshan is expected to be built next year; the section from Baoshan to Ruili had commenced in May 2011. The China Railways Engineering Corporation signed the *MOU on Muse-Kyaukpyu Railway Transport Project* and *Supplementary Agreement of MOU on Muse-Kyaukpyu Railway Transport Project* with the Myanmar

Union Ministry of Rail Transportation in April 27, 2011 and May 27, 2011 respectively, stipulating that China Railways Engineering Corporation shall organise and implement the transport project from Muse to Kyaukpyu, which would be constructed in the form of BOT.[8] The railway will travel through Rakhine State, Magwe Region, and Shan State of Myanmar. The railway line that connects Kyaukpyu - Minbu - Ann - Minbyar - Myohoung - Kyauktaw - Sittwe will be connected with the section of Minbu - Padein - Ann. Myanmar will newly build the section of Minbu - Padein - Ann that leads to the Kyaukpyu deepwater port with the length of about 65 miles. After the completion of Kyaukpyu -Minbu - Ann Railway, it will connect the Minbu, Magwe, Mandalay, Lashio and Muse. Meanwhile, the transnational railway project that connects the Muse of Myanmar with Jiegao of China will also commence.[9]

In terms of the oil and gas pipeline between China and Myanmar, in 2004, scholars from Yunnan University had suggested to construct the Sino-Myanmar oil and gas pipeline to improve oil import security. Through negotiation, China and Myanmar jointly constructed and operated the Sino-Myanmar crude oil pipeline from Kyaukpyu of Myanmar to Kunming of which the length of phase I trunk line was 1444 km, 848 km in Myanmar and 596 km in China. The Sino-Myanmar natural gas pipeline is parallel to the crude oil pipeline of which there is 870 km within the territory of Myanmar.[10] The Sino-Myanmar oil and gas pipeline engineering project commenced in June 2010, and by June 5, 2013, the natural gas pipeline was finished. On July 28, the natural gas pipeline started to transmit gas to China. On July 31, the natural gas entered the territory of China through Ruili station. Currently more than 96% of the crude oil pipeline has been completed, and by the end of 2014, it will be able to meet the needs of oil production.

In terms of waterway transport between China and Myanmar, as early as 1988, Myanmar had already proposed the water-land transshipment plan. The route of this plan was as follows: the land route started from Kunming, and travelled through Baoshan, Ruili, to Bhamo Port of Myanmar, and via Bhamo Port, it reached the Rangoon Port by water and eventually entered into the Indian Ocean. The land route mileage of Sino-Myanmar water-land transshipment route was 923.3km (807 kilometres in China, and 116.3 kilometres outside China), and the water route mileage from Bhamo Port to Rangoon was 1,277 km, which was navigable all year round. This water-land transshipment plan finally fell into abeyance due to the external factor interference and too high requirement of the Myanmar side.

In terms of air connectivity between China and Myanmar, since April 2002 when Kunming opened the air route to Mandalay, the second largest city of Myanmar, the number air routes from China to Myanmar has been increasing constantly. Air routes of Beijing-Rangoon, Beijing-Mandalay, Nanning-Rangoon, Kunming-Rangoon, Wuxi-Rangoon, Qingdao-Rangoon, Guangzhou-Rangoon, MangCity-Mandalay have been opened successively. With the Kunming Changshui International Airport put into operation, Kunming has become the fourth largest national portal airport of China facing South Asia and Southeast Asia. The number of flights from Kunming to the regions of Myanmar have continued to increase.

(ii) Traffic Connectivity between China and India

In the aspect of highway connectivity between China and India, in July 2006, with the completion of Nathula highway in Tibet, the highway between Tibet of China and Calcutta of India was opened. The distance from Nathula of Tibet to Calcutta of India and other Indian Ocean ports is shortened by about 1,200 km. Although this route is located in high altitude area and frozen by snow most of the time, which makes it difficult to form a large channel straight into the Indian Ocean, it is no doubt that the opening of this route make the highway connectivity diversified in the BCIM regions.

In order to open the land route from Yunnan to India and Bangladesh, Baoshan of Yunnan also repeatedly proposed to build the highway roughly along the Stilwell Road from Kunming to Ledo, which was also the Sino-India Road during the Second World War. China hoped to build an Economic Corridor by means of highway and railway of Kunming-Tengchong - Myitkyina -Ledo - Kolkata. But since this route may involve the areas where China and India have territorial issue, which makes the progress slow, only the highway of Kunming-Tengchong-Myitkyina of Myanmar has already pened.

In terms of air connectivity between India and China, in December 2000, the first flight of business jet from Kunming to New Delhi marked the end of long-term absence of air connectivity between China and India. In 2002, an air route of Beijing-Shanghai-Delhi was opened. In 2006, a direct flight from Beijing to Delhi was opened. The flight line from Guangzhou to New Delhi was opened in October 2006. An air route of Kunming-Calcutta was opened in October 2007. An air route from Kunming to Calcutta was opened in 2008, and an international route directly flying from Chengdu to the "silicon valley" Bangalore of India was opened in 2010. In February 2012, a flight line from Chengdu to Mumbai was opened and in 2016 a direct flight between Kunming and New Delhi also began.

(iii) Traffic Connectivity between China and Bangladesh

China has no common border with Bangladesh. Therefore, the direct transport link between the two countries is mainly the international air route, and the land connectivity needs to be enabled through a third country. In May 2005, the Beijing-Kunming-Dhaka international air route was opened. In 2006, a chartered airplane from Dhaka to Kunming was opened between China and Bangladesh. In July 2009, a direct passenger flight from Guangzhou to Dhaka was opened. China basically achieved the airline connectivity with Bangladesh, India and Myanmar, but these airlines still cannot meet the need of regional cooperation and development of the BCIM in the future.

Myanmar, India and Bangladesh also constructed or restored some traffic connections. In 2001, India built a high-grade highway that was connected with India and Myanmar with the length of 160 miles. In April 2002, ministers of India, Myanmar and Thailand agreed to build a road from Morey of India to Mae Sot of Thailand, via Myanmar. In 2004, Bangladesh and Myanmar signed agreement to build the 'Bangladesh-Myanmar friendship road' with the total length of 133km.[11] In 2007, India and Bangladesh restored the railway link from Dhaka to Calcutta.

Challenges in the BCIM Connectivity

At present, the difficulty in the traffic connectivity between China and other three countries (Bangladesh, India and Myanmar) mainly lies in the land connectivity. But the greatest challenges are some countries' shortage of funds for construction, low political will, mutual distrust, and some countries' concern for the traditional security and non-traditional security issues in this region, rather than the worse natural and geographic conditions and worse natural climate where the BCIM traffic routes pass through.

(i) Shortage of Funds in Myanmar and Bangladesh

A comparison of the total capital volume of the BCIM region and the capital volume that can be invested to the construction of connectivity infrastructure in this region reveals that this region does not lack the capital. Objectively speaking, this region also has a huge capital need for the construction of high levels of connectivity projects, and at least few BCIM countries have huge construction ability for the construction of large infrastructure. However, the capital distribution is not even. For example, China has a huge foreign exchange reserves and enormous non-governmental capitals seeking to be invested in foreign countries. But the strong nationalist sentiment in some parts of BCIM region hinders the use of Chinese money in these regions.

To make the land traffic of the countries of BCIM Economic Corridor become a connected regional traffic network, they must build and re-build many disconnected road sections and improve the original condition of traffic network. However, since the financial resources of Bangladesh and Myanmar are limited, it is difficult to raise enough domestic construction funds at least in the short term. For example, for the highway from Kunming to Mandalay, after leaving Ruili, the highway classification in Myanmar is low, which is only equivalent to China's level 3 pavement and Level 4 roadbed. The pavement of many sections are damaged seriously, and the road condition is poor. It is extremely difficult for Myanmar, a less developed country with a thousand things waiting to be done, to raise a lot of money in a short period of time to complete the construction and repair of high-grade highway network of BCIM. For the road section from Kunming to Rangoon, which is taken as the west section of Pan-Asia railway, Myanmar is expected to build a railway with the length of 130 km from Ruili of Yunnan to Lashio of Myanmar. In April 2011, China and Myanmar signed the *MOU on the Muse-Kyaukpyu Railway Construction Project Cooperation* under which China promised to assist Myanmar to build the railroad section from Ruili to Lashio. Since the Thein Sein government of Myanmar came to power and adjusted domestic and foreign policies, the Sino-Myanmar relationship had undergone a rapid adjustment. Therefore, it is difficult to finish the construction of this railway in a short period of time.

(ii) Low Political Mutual trust between China and India

Since India is afraid that China's influence will extend to the South Asia and the Indian Ocean regions due to the reopening of Stilwell Road, it delays the recovery of this road and the linking between China and India with the excuse of security concerns including the anti-government forces existing in northeast of India. India always regards China as the biggest threat since it was defeated in the Sino-Indian border conflict in 1962. Although Sino-Indian relation improved after the Indian prime minister Rajiv Gandhi visit our country in December 1988, China and India still occasionally have had disputes in border issues because both sides still are unable to find ways and means to settle the border dispute. Therefore, the political mutual trust building of both sides is still missing. Sino-Indian relation in the short term had improved with China's national strength enhanced since the reform and opening up, but the gap between China and India has gradually widened. Therefore, India strengthens its precautions against China under the influence of the China threat theory. Particularly, China's Indian Ocean strategy in Indian Ocean region mainly aiming at the economy and the promotion of bridgehead strategy which is opening to the southwest further upsets New Delhi. As a result, India remains filled with apprehensions about China's westward strategy and any action of China in extending its impact in the Indian Ocean region. All of these makes India negatively inclined to the BCIM Economic Corridor connectivity work carried out by China.

(iii) Differences in their Priorities

Another problem in building physical connectivity between China and other three counties (Bangladesh, India and Myanmar) is their varying priorities. Because of a variety of reasons and the countermeasures against other country's influence, these three countries are slow in proceeding with the construction and repair of the important road sections that are connecting the traffic nodes and regions of each of these four countries country. Particularly, each country, with different development levels and different national goals, has different perspectives on what should be regarded as the key areas and important routes for building physical connectivity.

In the discussion of how to strengthen BCIM physical connectivity, Bangladesh representatives have often underlined that there were three feasible traffic channels connecting four countries, respectively the northern route, middle route and south route among which, the northern route was the shortest one from Yunnan of China to India, via Myanmar and Bangladesh. But it has often faced many problems. The middle route was the route adopted by BCIM car rally, as well as the easiest connected route; the south route started from Kunming, and travelled through Mandalay, Meiktila and Magwe, and finally arrived in Chittagong, which was the most convenient channel that connected the deep-water harbours of all three countries. Thus it is also the route with the greatest potential for development.[12] In addition to strengthening the traffic connectivity, the representative of India have often proposed that the power grid connectivity can also be strengthened, because BCIM were faces severe energy shortage. All four countries can learn from the experience of 'ASEAN Big Power Grid' for power connectivity to strengthen their grid interconnection, and to make use of the complementary advantages in energy and the seasonal characteristics of some of the energy supply to solve the energy shortage problem through energy trade among the BCIM countries.[13] China wants to build a comprehensive, diversified physical connectivity network in BCIM region, but recently it hopes all the more to connect both highway and railway from Kunming to Kyaukpyu Port on the Indian Ocean coast roughly along the Sino-Myanmar oil and gas pipeline as soon as possible so that the goods can be transported out of Indian Ocean through the West of China as soon as possible. This main route travels through Kunming, Dali, Baoshan, Ruili, Lashio, Mandalay, Magwe, Kyaukpyu, Chittagong, Dhaka, and Kolkatta. For China, this route can directly go into the Indian Ocean only via Myanmar where the geographical condition and earlier foundation of infrastructure are good. For the section of Lashio- Magwe outside China with the length of about 650 km, the existing railway can be used, and by constructing the railway of about 350 km, and rebuilding the railway of 650 km, China can reach the Kyaukpyu Port and enter the Indian Ocean. The section can also be connected with the South Asian part of AH41 line in Asian highway network. This suboptimal line travels through Kunming, Dali, Baoshan, Ruili, Lashio, and Mandalay, and then extends from Mandalay to the northwest, successively via Tamu, Imphal, Shillong, and Dhaka, and finally arrives in Kolkatta. Building comprehensive connectivity network is needed for the construction of high level BCIM Economic Corridor, and the coordinated development of each region of BCIM. Therefore, China is willing to build the land route of Kunming-Dali-Baoshan-Myitkyina-Ledo-Calcutta, although the territorial dispute that may be faced by China and India must be properly handled for this route.

(iv) Impact of Minority Problems

If Myanmar, which is currently in the political transitional period, wants to connect the Indian Ocean route of Kunming-Ruili-Mandalay-Magwe-Kyaukpyu, and construct the road of Kunming-Tengchong-Myitkyina-Pangsau-Ledo and the road of Kunming-Ruili-Mandalay-Dhaka-Kolkatta, this road will pass the areas with many national problems and sensitive ethic issues. The oil and gas pipeline, highway, and railway from Kunming to Kyaukpyu must pass through the areas controlled by Myanmar's armed ethnic groups of Kachin Independent Army, Palaung State Liberation Front, Shan State Army-North and Shan State Army-South, as well as several areas with severe ethnic or religious conflicts. The road from Kunming to Ledo of India mainly passes through the area controlled by Kachin Independent Army in Myanmar, and at the end of this route is the Northeast part of India. Northeast India itself is also an area with armed activities of separatism from multiple minority groups. Different from Myanmar that is trying to build a nation with uniform government decree and military order through economic and social development in the ethnic minority areas, India is afraid of the economic development of ethnic minorities in the northeast region, because some central government officials think that the economic and social development in this region will strengthen the ethnic separatist force.

The entire sections of Sino-Myanmar and Sino-India international big pathways that connect the BCIM Economic Corridor in China has been realised in China with high speed.[14] For the west corridor of Pan-Asia Railway, the domestic part of the railway from Kunming to Myanmar is under construction, and the capacity expansion project for the Kunming-Guangtong Railway is scheduled to be completed soon. But many sections within the territory of India and Myanmar are currently in a state of stagnation or slow progress due to various factors including ethnic issues.

(v) Development Prospect of Connectivity

(a) Each Country's Emphasis on Connectivity

China's 'Westward' strategy objectively requires the realisation of BCIM Economic Corridor connectivity as soon as possible. China's Overseas Development Strategy is comprehensive, which not only requires the strengthening of the traditional 'Eastward' opening-up strategy focusing on the coastal areas, but also requires the 'Westward' strategy that pushes forward the development of West China. The integration of the large pathway development strategy with Yunnan's opening up to South Asia and southeast Asia and 'China's Bridgehead Strategy Oriented to the Southwest' at the national level can form convenient channels for the provinces in western China to seek development overseas. In this way, the goal of promoting the quality and level of the West China development strategy to achieve sustainable social development and to make good use of both domestic and overseas markets and resources can be realised. Therefore, China's implementation of the Strategy of 'West China Development' and the Bridgehead Strategy requires increasing the input of policy support and funding to the connectivity, which will greatly promote the development of the BCIM Economic Corridor. Yunnan, as a frontier province in opening to the Southwest, is motivated and willing to promote construction of the BCIM Economic Corridor and the realisation of Economic Corridor connectivity is sought to be achieved as soon as possible. For example, in order to build a comprehensive BCIM land transport network, China's central government and local government in Yunnan have been considering to jointly repair the mostly abandoned Stilwell Road with India to connect the road from Kunming to Ledo in India, via Myitkyina town of Myanmar. For China, the economic benefit of this route is much less than the route that runs through Myanmar from Ruili to Kyaukpyu on the Indian Ocean coast, but from the perspective of promoting regional common and balanced development of the region, China is also willing to repair and upgrade this route as well.

The main existing channels from China to the Indian Ocean coast and South Asian countries must pass Myanmar. Therefore the success of these channels lies in the attitude of Myanmar. In order to open the great channel to the Indian Ocean coast, China has been actively planning implementing the railway and highway routes from China to Myanmar. For example, for the road from Kunming, via Simao, Jinghong, Daluo, to Taung-Gyi and Mandalay of Myanmar highway, the expressway of 462 km as part of the 672 km section in Yunnan Province has been completed, and the rest has been upgraded to the high-grade highway of above level 2.[15] Myanmar's recent political development at home now seems to cause large impact on the Sino-Myanmar connectivity projects. Sino-Myanmar gas pipeline was already completed on June 4, 2013, but gas supply has been delayed thanks to Myanmar's domestic political transition. Although China's projects in Myanmar are impacted since some of Burmese people and politicians associate them with Myanmar's domestic changes, the country's mainstream political forces have a clear consensus to maintain a friendly Sino-Myanmar relationship. Therefore, in the long run, the development of Myanmar and its cooperation with China in the field of physical connectivity are likely to continue.

Bangladesh, another BCIM developing country, also lacks major resources for development except for having its abundant labour resources. Therefore, this country seeks to use external resources to boost its economic development and social progress. Bangladesh is a smaller country without big ambitions of a great power. In its foreign policy as well, it mainly pays attention to the absolute interests, rather than relative interests. In the tide of regionalisation to promoting the rapid economic and social development of all countries, since the South Asian Association for Regional Cooperation (SAARC) process is slow, Bangladesh has not won the desired fruit in the wave of regionalisation. Therefore, it is also willing to join various other forums of regional cooperation mechanisms that can promote its social and economic development. Accordingly, Bangladesh favours realisation of BCIM physical connectivity as soon as possible, especially the Pan-Asian Highway and Western Pan-Asia Railway Traffic connectivity.

As regards India, it is very sensitive to its own great power status, especially for its superpower status in South Asia and the Indian Ocean region. This has been one very important aspect of its foreign policy since independence and India has continued to maintain its dominance in the South Asian region. This is how India has been inclined to developing bilateral relations with South Asian countries in the past. In Indian's view, any regional cooperation in the South Asia, or the northern Indian Ocean regions is likely to cause a situation in which small countries may jointly contend against India's great power status. As the most powerful country in South Asia, it had neither desire nor strong motivation to form and promote the development of the regional organisations in this region in the past. The initiative to develop SAARC from early 1980s was that of President Ziaur Rahman of Bangladesh and it was not advocated by India first, although India, together with Bangladesh, Bhutan, Maldives, Nepal, Pakistan and Sri Lanka passed the *Declaration of Dhaka* in 1985, and formulated the *Charter of The South Asian Association for Regional Cooperation*, and established the SAARC. Nevertheless, the degree of regionalisation and integration of SAARC members continues to lag far behind the regional cooperation of other parts of the world and this is primarily because of India's negative response. The biggest fruit of the cooperation of SAARC is just the signing and implementation of South Asia Preferential Trade Arrangements (SAPTA). This agreement was formally executed on December 8, 1995. But given the regionalisation development trend, India is gradually starting to promote the development of regionalisation. The establishment of SAPTA is expected to facilitate regional economic development and integration and encourage trade and investment transfer from the non-members to members though, the reduction of import barriers under SAPTA actually is a kind of discrimination against non-members.[16] For example, India had put forward the Ganges-Mekong Subregional Cooperation Initiative in June 2000 and emphasised on the construction of transport infrastructure. India had also accelerated its regional trade agreements with the regional organisations of other countries since 2003, such as the free trade agreement with Thailand in 2003 and free trade agreement and economic cooperation agreement signed with the Gulf Cooperation Council and Singapore respectively in 2004. Though these agreements still have the characteristics of bilateral relations, as can be seen from the content of the cooperation agreements signed with other countries or organisations, India still exhibits strong desire to strengthen regional economic cooperation to improve transportation. Therefore, India is also equally committed to solving the transportation bottleneck problems through the construction of regional economic integration.[17]

(b) From Hard Links to Both Soft and Hard Links of Connectivity

According to the definition of connectivity in the ASEAN Master Plan on Regional Connectivity, the connectivity includes the physical connection, the mechanism of docking and links between people. Especially, the physical connection includes transportation, information and communication technology and the energy; the mechanism docking includes trade liberalization and facilitation, liberalisation and facilitation of services and investment, multilateral certification agreement, regional transport agreement, cross-border procedures simplification, capacity building; the links between people include education, cultural exchanges, and tourism.[18] This section roughly divides the diversified connections of connectivity into two kinds: hard links which include the traditional highway, railway, shipping, and aviation as the main content, and the soft links between

Table 1: Main Focus in the Transport Connectivity at BCIM Forum Meetings

Time	*Place*	*Main points of connectivity*
October 1999, the first meeting	Kunming	To develop infrastructure and strengthen links to promote the economic cooperation
October 2000, the second meeting	New Delhi	In the meeting, establishing the traffic link, carrying out the trade by roadway, and strengthening the exchange of information were discussed.
February 2002, the third meeting	Dhaka	Emphasizing on improving traffic link and promoting convenient circulation of goods and manpower.
March 2003, the fourth meeting	Rangoon	Attaching importance to the traffic construction in BCIM region and requiring simplifying procedures and promoting customs clearance.
2October 2004, the fifth meeting	Kunming	Proposing to hold self-driving tour and car rally, open the direct air route within the region, and strengthen the people and trade contacts.
March 2006, the sixth meeting	New Delhi	Deciding to simplify the transit formalities, and promote the trade facilitation; suggesting strengthening air pathway construction; constructing the traffic route along the Asian Road and Pan-Asia Railway; and organizing the car rally from Kunming to Calcutta.
March 2007, the seventh meeting	Dhaka	To establish a number of ports and carry out transit trade, eliminate the barrier to promote the border trades; improve existing road and other available roads according to the standards of "Asian Road", promote the exit and entry facilitation to realize the continuous and non-transship border crossing of vehicles, supplies and people; improve the missing sections of Pan-Asian Railway in BCIM region.
July 2009, the eighth meeting	Naypyida w	Proposing that each country should simplify the trade formalities in the countries of BCIM, complete the respective missing sections of Pan-Asia Railway, and expand respective air routes.
January 2011, the ninth meeting	Kunming	Proposing to build the BCIM traffic cooperation mechanism and to strengthen the cooperation in the construction of highway network.
February 2012, the tenth meeting	Calcutta	In the meeting, a consensus was reached on the economic corridor of Kunming-Mandalay-Dhaka-Calcutta, and strengthening cooperation in the construction of highway, railway, water transport, etc.
February 2013, the eleventh meeting	Dhaka	Strengthening various forms of connectivity.

and with the people, information, and system as its main contents. In general, the connectivity of regional organisations begins with the traditional hard link, and gradually moves to the more complex soft connections, especially for the countries and regions which are geopolitically adjacent, the initial cooperation of which starts from hard links of transport projects, and then expands to the soft links related projects.

BCIM Economic Corridor does not have a high degree of transport connectivity, and the construction of the soft channels is even more backward. For example, the establishment of the trade system and rules within this Forum, and customs clearance facilitation are seriously lagging behind when it comes to their peripheries which is where BCIM seems to be located. As can be seen from Table 1 below, the major issues discussed in the previous meetings of the BCIM Forum and the projects promoted and implemented by four countries, the four countries pay more attention to hard link with the transport connectivity as the main content, and care less about their soft links with the personnel, information and system as the main content.

But the attitude of emphasising the hard link and ignoring the soft link in the connectivity has lately begun to change. The BCIM Forum, on the basis of continuing to strengthen the hard link in connectivity, has begun to push forward the construction of soft links as well. For example, in terms of personnel exchanges and connection in recent years, the exchanges among officials and scholars in the BCIM regions have become far more frequent; business enterprises and their personnel exchanges are also increasing, and many colleges and universities in China have enrolled students from India, Myanmar and Bangladesh and also sent students to Indian universities. China has also been establishing Confucius Institutes or Confucius Classrooms in Bangladesh, India, Myanmar to strengthen their cultural exchanges. In 2013, in the BCIM Forum that was held in Dhaka strongly underlined the need for strengthening various kinds of connectivity which had emerged as the main topic of that meeting.

Measures to Promote the BCIM Connectivity

(i) Connectivity Projects Depend on Coordination and Planning

The construction of BCIM physical connectivity is a systematic project that will lay the foundation for all other future development. It is the success of these projects that will determine the smooth progression of BCIM Economic Corridor. Therefore, top-level design must be well thought out and conducted such as to realise comprehensive planning and scientific development. The BCIM Economic Corridor connectivity project shall be regarded as a whole and the uniformly collaborated coordination agency must be organised so that in the planning, development and management, there is a channel for extensive consultation and advice seeking for building the regional connectivity. In the construction of connectivity, management and maintenance of connectivity projects and the promotion of the region's economic and social development and the improvement of the people's living standard must be emphasised. Meanwhile, the bearing capacity of the regional ecology and environment must also be considered. Particularly, in areas where the connectivity project passes through the ethnic minority areas, attention must be paid to maintain their economic interests and cultural traditions so as to reduce the resistance from these ethnic minorities.

(ii) Widen Financing Channels

BCIM Economic Corridor connectivity project requires enormous engineering, and the funding required is also huge. So we must properly use the fund both inside and outside of the BCIM region to promote the construction of BCIM Economic Corridor connectivity project. For attracting capital from outside of this region, BCIM needs to learn from regional cooperation experience of other regions, and actively invite capital from the World Bank, Asian Development Bank and other international financial institutions. Bangladesh, China, India and Myanmar are the members of the Asian Development Bank. And building the BCIM Economic Corridor connectivity project to promote economic and social development is also in line with the purposes of the Asian Development Bank which seeks to 'eradicate poverty and promote economic and social development in the Asia-Pacific Region'. Therefore, the constructions of the BCIM Economic Corridor projects should obtain the funding and support from the Asian Development Bank. The introduction of external funding can alleviate the pressure from fund shortage inside BCIM, bring in the advanced management and experience, prevent any country's monopoly in BCIM Economic Corridor project construction and investment, and dispel some countries' concerns and worries caused by their dependence on large funds of China or India.

Although the use and introduction of outside funds to promote BCIM connectivity can play an important role, most of the funds for promoting BCIM Economic Corridor construction will mainly come from the four countries. Therefore, raising and properly using the investment of the four countries within the region must be a top priority. In doing this, Bangladesh, China, India and Myanmar can encourage domestic enterprises and consortiums to directly invest in their connectivity projects. Alternatively, the enterprises and consortiums of four countries can carry out joint development projects. Second, Bangladesh, China, India and Myanmar can expand the financing model, such as issuing project construction bonds, and carrying out the cooperation with domestic and international financial institutions. Third, four countries can formulate policies oriented to the connectivity projects, and provide preferential loans to project contractors and so on. Fourth, four countries can form diversified BCIM Economic Corridor development fund to provide special funding support for the regional development of BCIM.

(iii) Building Mutual Confidence

Four countries have different degrees of aspiration for building BCIM Economic Corridor. One of the reasons is that their political trust is insufficient or absent at least between few of their bilateral equations within the BCIM.

However, the important basis of building a higher level of regional cooperation is the political mutual trust amongst BCIM nations. Therefore, strengthening the mutual trust building among the BCIM remains an important challenge that the four countries face with regards to their cooperation in the current phase and in the future. The building of mutual trust between countries can not be achieved overnight. Particularly for the Sino-India relation both of which have precious historical baggage and still have territorial dispute. Therefore, both sides need to promote their bilateral relation with wisdom and patience, and any rush of thoughts and practice could backfire. The mutual trust building among Bangladesh, China and India and Myanmar can begin from low-level political problems, and gradually expend to the high-level political problems. The regional economic cooperation with less sensitivity is more likely to succeed. China should make good use of the construction of BCIM Economic Corridor, and push forward the comprehensive cooperation and exchange with other three countries in the aspects of economy, society and culture, and on that basis, gradually expand the areas of mutual trust and enhance mutual trust expectation.

Speaking relatively, among the four countries, China's overall power is stronger. Therefore, China needs to do more work in mutual trust building and enhancing political mutual trust with other three members. First of all, China should frankly communicate with other three countries in the construction of BCIM Economic Corridor and how the connectivity projects need to be implemented so as to make India, Myanmar, and Bangladesh clearly understand China's efforts in promoting BCIM regional cooperation and its reasons and intention for actively promoting the realisation of connectivity as soon as possible. China should also help enable other countries to understand that China's interests in the construction of BCIM Economic Corridor is only limited to the trade and commerce, rather than geared by any military and security objectives in Indian Ocean as usually misunderstood by the other countries. China should also make these countries understand that China's promotion of BCIM Economic Corridor is mainly driven by its economic consideration, and the purpose is to change the backwardness of China's western provinces, narrow the gap between its western area and its coastal area in ensuring their economic and social development, and China's BCIM Economic Corridor building strategies of China are limited to promoting the economic and social development in its western China, rather than changing the geopolitics of the BCIM region.

In order to promote the development of western China and narrow the gap between the west China and its coastal area, China has a strong willingness to promote various regional cooperation for the western region and open the trade channels in the Western region which lead to neighbouring countries. Since the reform and opening up in the late 1970s, China mainly focuses on the east in the opening up to the outside world. For more than 30 years of reform and opening-up, China's eastern coast has grown into a world famous 'golden coast' which has a wide range of trade and economic ties with the rest of the world. Although the western region has got rapid development in its economy since the reform and opening up, by contrast, China's western region's economic and social development continues to lag far behind the eastern parts. The difference in the level of economic development between the eastern areas and western areas has become an obstacle that hinders the further comprehensive development of China. Such kind of difference in the level of economic development has brought about the dilemma in development mode and resource distribution between the developed coastal areas and the underdeveloped western areas. For the western areas, especially western border areas where many ethnic minorities inhabit, if for a long time the economic development here can not be improved, it is bound to affect the political stability of the ethnic minority areas and border areas, and affect China's border security. So, both for promoting economic development in western China and for stabilising minorities inhabited border regions, China requires increasing the western areas' trade and economic ties with the neighbouring countries, and make good use of foreign resources to promote the development of western China. Therefore, China endeavours to realise the physical connectivity with Bangladesh, India and Myanmar as soon as possible, and increase the level of regional cooperation through BCIM Economic Corridor.

Secondly, in order to strengthen trust and clear up doubts, China can also frankly communicate and exchange its expected connectivity projects and routes. In the road routes, for example, China can explicitly inform each country as to which of the route is optimal, suboptimal, or a third choice for China. China can honestly speak out its optimal selection and the hope of opening the route as soon as possible, and objectively explain the pros and cons of each route as well as the different roles of routes in promoting the whole BCIM Economic Corridor construction. China does not have to bottle things up, rather it should openly explain its difficulties in construction of certain roads, if any, to other three countries. From the perspective of transferring goods and personnel out from India Ocean and into the west of China, the optimal choice of China is to build the highway and railway along the Sino-Myanmar oil and gas pipeline which goes from the Sino-Myanmar border to the Indian Ocean cost, namely, Kunming-Dali-Baoshan-Ruili-Lashio-Mandalay-Magwe-Kyaukpyu railway and highway. The previously-constructed Sino-Myanmar oil and gas pipeline has laid a good foundation for the construction of this channel. This channel only involves China and Myanmar, and most of the areas passed through can be basically controlled by Myanmar's central government. This channel can then be extended to the northern Chittagong, Dhaka, and Kolkatta. After the channel is fully completed, it can not only realise the opening of southern channel of BCIM, and facilitate China's coming in and going out of Indian Ocean, but also combine the land route with the maritime shipping advantages of the Bay of Bengal, and integrate the industrial structure of the east Bay of Bengal area again to create a new gold coast in the Bay of Bengal. The south route is, however, too far down south, which cannot exert the potential of driving the economic and social development of a wider area of BCIM as soon as possible, and also it cannot realise the goal of the regional common development. This may even cause new uneven development between the coastal areas and inland areas of BCIM.

Although the optimal choice for China to enter into the Indian Ocean is the route from Ruili to Kyaukpyu, China is also willing to build the middle route that runs through the BCIM Economic Corridor at the same time for the sake of the healthy and sustainable development of BCIM Economic Corridor, as well as the northern route from Tengchong of China to Ledo town of India and then turning southward. For China, the areas passed through by the middle route are relatively more complex. This route not only runs through the area controlled by ethnic armed groups in the north Myanmar but also passes through the area where there are ethnic armed activities in the border of India and Myanmar. There is no doubt that this will increases the instability of these connectivity channels. The middle route has its advantageous and positive factors too, such as the good foundation laid by the previously BCIM car rally. From February to March 2013, Bangladesh, China, India and Myanmar had successfully held their first such car rally. The competition started from Calcutta and passed through Dhaka, Silchar (Assam), Imphal (Manipur), Mandalay and Ruili (Yunnan province). Before the game, the delegation of car rally had already known the infrastructure condition in details along the route, examined the specific route, and successfully compiled a road book. The change of the route would also get the support of Bangladesh.[19]

Besides the Stilwell Road, many sections of the northern routes have worn down by the years without repair which are difficult to be reused. In addition, although this route can be built and repaired roughly along the Stilwell Road, actually most of the sections need to be measured and planned again. For China, most of this route passes through the remote poor areas of Myanmar and India, and it is also a route that is the slowest in reaping economic benefit and the has the smallest effect in promoting regional economy. But in the long run, the construction of northern route in the poorest and remote areas of BCIM will set up an example for the construction of other projects of BCIM Economic Corridor.

(iv) Implementing Early Harvest Programs

Not everyone has a positive and affirmative attitude toward the BCIM Economic Corridor connectivity project. Therefore, in order to boost morale and win over support, BCIM countries should implement some early harvest programs that have a quick and good effect as soon as possible, to arouse the enthusiasm and positive expectations of the people in this region for the construction of BCIM Economic Corridor, and to enhance the confidence of BCIM countries in the construction of Economic Corridor. For the implementation of early harvest programs, the early harvest plan of China-ASEAN Free Trade Area that was first implemented is a blueprint which can be used as a reference. The early harvest program is a tax reduction plan that was first implemented within the framework of the China-ASEAN Free Trade Area. It started on January 1, 2004. The plan was implemented based on the *Framework Agreement on Comprehensive Economic Co-operation Between the People's Republic of China and the Association of South East Nations* signed in November 2002. Even though China had not reached an agreement with ASEAN in connection with the tax reduction arrangement of all the goods, in order to make China and ASEAN countries enjoy the benefits of free trade area as soon as possible and build the confidence of establishing China-ASEAN Free Trade Area, two sides decided to choose some goods with strong complementary advantages and strong interest to implement tax reduction and to open the market in advance. Therefore, this early harvest program also becomes a fast track and test field for goods trade in China-ASEAN Free Trade Area. Through this early harvest program, the trade status between China and ASEAN countries has been improved to some extent, and the goods trade between both sides, especially the agricultural products trading, has achieved a rapid growth. The implementation of the early harvest program enhances the confidence of the China in building free trade area with ASEAN countries, which lays a good foundation for the successful construction of the China-ASEAN Free Trade Area. Therefore, the early harvest programs of BCIM Economic Corridor, should not only draw lessons from other early harvest programs of China-ASEAN Free Trade Area in agricultural tax reduction plan, but also should carry out some small projects with small investment to bring about quick effect and benefit for people. Particularly, due to the low degree of connectivity of BCIM region, carrying out the early harvest programs for some special and meaningful traffic nodes and bringing tangible benefits for local people can stimulate positive expectations of their masses who will become both the stakeholders as also constituencies for promoting the BCIM Economic Corridor connectivity projects.[20]

Endnotes

1. Qinghua, "China and India Propose to Build BCIM corridor", May 21, 2013, http://epaper.jinghua.cn/html/2013-05/21/content_1990815.htm
2. Ku Huo, Tao To, A Tour in North Burma, (Hong Kong Freedom Press, 1954 Edition), p.44.
3. Zhu Changli, "South Silk Road and the Economic and Cultural Exchange among China, India and Myanmar", Southeast Asia, 3rd issue, 1991, p.8.
4. Qu Xiaoling, "Ancient Trail of Southwest China and Abroad: A brief Account of the Southern Silk Road and its Researches", North West Ethno-national Studies, 1st issue, 2011, p. 177.
5. Qu Xiaoling, "Ancient Trail of Southwest China and Abroad: A brief Account of the Southern Silk Road and its Researches", North West Ethno-national Studies, 1st issue, 2011, p.176.
6. M. Rahmatula, "Promoting BCIM Traffic Connectivity and Countermeasures-Thought of Bangladesh", translated by Zhang Lin, Southeast Asian and South Asian Studies, 3rd issue, 2010, p.73.

7. Xinhua News Agency, "Full Upgrade of Yunnan-Myanmar-Three Fields will Become the Cooperation Focus", June 10, 2010, http://www.gx.xinhuanet.com/dm/2010-06/10/content_20038326.htm.

8. The Ministry of Commerce of the People's Republic of China, "Signing the MOU on Muse-Kyaukpyu Rail Transportation System Project Between China and Myanmar", http://www.mofcom.gov.cn/aarticle/i/jyjl/j/201104/20110407525271.html

9. The State-owned Assets Supervision and Administration Commission, "China Railway Engineering Corporation Signing the MOU on the Burmese Muse-Kyaukpyu Railway Project Cooperation", May 12, 2011. http://www.sasac.gov.cn/n1180/n1226/n2410/n314304/13495987.html

10. Li Chenyang, "Development of China-ASEAN Connectivity", in Liu Zhi (ed.), Report on Greater Mekong Subregion Cooperative Development (2011-2012), Beijing: Social Sciences Academic Press, 2012, p. 25.

11. Ren Jia, "Review and Prospect of 10-year BCIM Regional Economic Cooperation Forum (2009-2010)", in Guo Suiyan (eds.), South Asian Report, (Kunming: Yunnan University Press, 2010), p.155.

12. Guo Suiyan, "The 11th BCIM Forum Opened in Bangladesh", in Guo Suiyan (ed.), Southeast Asian and South Asian Studies, 1st issue, 2013, p. 90.

13. Guo Suiyan, "The 11th BCIM Forum Opened in Bangladesh", in Guo Suiyan (ed.), Southeast Asian and South Asian Studies, 1st Issue, 2013, p. 90.

14. Communications Department of Yunnan Province, The Rapid Development of Yunnan International Road Helps the "China-South Asian Expo", June 14, 2013. http://www.ynjtt.com/item/14545.aspx

15. Liu Zhi (ed), "Report on Greater Mekong Subregion Cooperative Development (2010-2011)", Social Sciences Academic Press, 2011, p.60.

16. Zhu Tong, Zhang Yue, "American Foreign Trade Policy Change and the Rise of Regional Economic Integration New Wave", Asian-Pacific Economy, 2007, 2nd issue, pp. 34-38.

17. Lu Xin, "Analysis of India's Regional Economic Integration Strategy", Journal of Dongbei University of Finance and Economics, 4th issue, 2011, p.72.

18. ASEAN official website: http://www.asean.org/resources/publications/asean-publications/item/master-plan-on-asean-connectivity-2
19. Yunnan, "The First BCIM Car Rally to Start on February 22", February 22, 2013, http://yn.yunnan.cn/html/2013-02/22/content_2627420.htm
20. "Early Harvest Program", Contemporary Guangxi, November 2009, 21st issue, p. 25.

10

Scope and Promotion Mechanism of BCIM Cooperation

Yang Yishuang

This Chapter explores the scope and promotion mechanisms of the BCIM Economic Corridor with a premise that any such analysis must surpass the framework of both old and new frameworks of regionalism. In examining this proposition from aforementioned perspective the second premise of this chapter is that BCIM region needs integration impetus for common growth yet the existing conditions inevitably restrict the effect of Economic Corridor cooperation. The arrangements of promotion mechanisms in BCIM region, therefore, must begin from an objective understanding of its limitations and feasibilities. Especially, the regional public goods supply in BCIM region faces serious shortage, leading to the high cost and lack of realistic scope for expansion of cooperation. Providing urgently needed regional public goods, based on institutional environment, therefore has to be the priority in BCIM Economic Corridor initiatives. The stable supply of that basic institutional environment and regional public goods must remain the shared goal and primary aim of BCIM as a prerequisite for the BCIM Economic Corridor to become anideal platform for their long-term inter-state collective action.

Lack of Endogenous Forces

In 2013, China's prime minister, Mr. Li Keqiang and India's prime minister Dr. Manmohan Singh had jointly put forward the idea of constructing BCIM Economic Corridor, writing the idea of 'constructing BCIM economic corridor' into their India *and China Joint Statement.* Later, in December 2013, Four-country Joint Working Group meeting was held in Kunming, and the four-country government officials, scholars, representatives of financial institution, etc. studied the Four-country Joint Research Program, confirmed the Joint Research Framework and research schedule, and signed the "Summary of Minutes" and "Joint Research Framework" etc., which indicates to their shared consensus on meeting challenges of globalization by boosting their sub-regional cooperation. Based on the definition of Asian Development Bank, sub-regional economic cooperation is a mechanism by which one can contact production, trade and infrastructure in a special geographic area. BCIM needs such integration impetus for shared growth, but is facing five restricting economic characteristics. These are as follows:

1. In the past few decades, the region has never enjoyed the market and economic growth and expansion that Asian production networks have witnessed simply because of the lack of transportation infrastructure, fragmented market, and the low flow of trade and capital in BCIM region.
2. Although experts tend to link BCIM and Southern Silk Road together, but apart from a few exceptions in history, this area has always been far away from their country's central markets and main trade routes. Since ancient times, trade linkage between China and India and Southeast Asia have always been through maritime trade routes, rather than BCIM region. This is one of the main reasons that this region has not been part of any production network so far.
3. Also, it is a feature of this area that while the geographical distance is very short, economical distance remains very long. Complex political situations, unstable social environment and the already rugged terrain in these peripheral regions, makes

the cost and time spent on road transportation unusually too high to encourage trade and commerce.

4. This region consists of frontier areas which are now disputed borders. China's Yunnan, India's northeast, northern parts of Myanmar are all frontier areas. Firstly, these people and markets are artificially cut across by political boundaries. Second, the possibility of national interests and sub-national interests being inconsistent is greater.[1] Economic and social underdevelopment of these landlocked frontier areas is often attributed to inefficient policy of the central governments.
5. The trade structures amongst BCIM countries are both competitive and complementary, but the current intra-regional trade level proves that the trade potential of this region has not been developed. Compared with the economic growth and the total development level of trade and investment of these four countries, development of BCIM intra-regional economic and trade cooperation has been much lower. The intra-regional trade, investment of the four countries is negligible. It proves that the BCIM intra-regional development lacks market force.

Indeed, it is this lack of such endogenous force that has compelled BCIM to consider building of an Economic Corridor. Also, based on these above mentioned characteristics and the accumulative effect caused by resultant underdevelopment, that their regional cooperation will be triggered purely by market mechanism is hard to happen on its own achieve. This explains the limitationor gap between theory and practice of traditional regional integration pattern. Traditional regionalism proposes faith in trade development expecting it to play a significant part in cross-nation regional integration. Secondly, the occurrence of intra-regional trade creation is sure a critical mark to measure regional cooperation but the 'new regionalism' thesis now stress on the effect of production integration as well as transnational investment creation leading to integration further encouraging foreign direct investment and create growth effects. However, no matter whether it is the standards of traditional regionalism or new regionalism, there remains a large gap between the development stages of four BCIM nations and sub-regional integration calls for state intervention. In other words, in such an environment, the cooperation among these four nations can not comply with the pattern of traditional regional integration as it is hard to follow the road of traditional market integration of these developing and least developed countries. BCIM sub-regional cooperation needs to surpass the traditional regionalism framework of general sub-regional economic integration to enhance the cooperation of each party and expand the common benefit points of each nation. The same is true of new regionalism paradigm as these four nations have varying development levels.

The key point of this argument is to determine the promotion mechanism and scope of BCIM sub-regional cooperation by based on their unique regional conditions as well as learning from other similar examples of different regional cooperation for different cooperation sectors. It is from this perspective that this chapter examine how BCIM Economic Corridor can become a potent promotion mechanism to promote BCIM sub-regional cooperation, investigate what can make it a dynamic mechanism, constituting conditions and action logic, and defining each member state's role in building this lasting regional cooperation thereby facilitating the economic development of these peripheral regions of these four states.

Scope of BCIM Regional Cooperation

Actually, except the abundant resources and economic complementarities which can be exploited potentially, the base of BCIM sub-region cooperation in trade and commerce is not so solid. However, these characteristics of under-development in BCIM sub-region also highlights the urgency that this region must actively participate in larger regional cooperation and benefit from it. For their peripheral regions that form the core of BCIM sub-regional initiatives, it is their only hope to avoid being completely marginalised and make the region regain growth momentum. The very conception of this sub-regional cooperation in BCIM region was to raised the development levels of these pheripheries. This has remained the focus in all the BCIM sub-regional cooperation celebrations all this time. But, over the years, their promotion mechanism have not acquired essential development, which has remained at the level of merely "matching regional integration needs through facilitated policy of trade and investment", possibly ignoring the real key points of BCIM Economic Corridor initiative. In order to analyse the feasibility of cooperation among nations of the BCIM sub-region, it is necessary, therefore, to conduct detailed examination of its possible cooperation scope or limits.

The most essential factor for successful regional cooperation is common interest among regional nations. The more the common interests among the participating countries, the more likely the cooperation will occur and occur faster. But it is widely believed by the modern regional integration theory that the situation that all nations will benefit from customs union, common market, free trade zone or other integration process does not necessarily happen. BCIM region is still at the starting phase of regional integration. Foreign trade in this region mainly depends on the export of primary commodities or low value added products of each nation. The internal trade in this proposed Economic Corridor only occupies a small part of total volume of their trade. The complementarities in economic structure are not sufficient conditions for expansion of intra-regional trade an this is not an isolated phenomenon. Even in ASEAN, where the regional integration has become relative mature, the trade growth among member states has always been below their anticipation.[2] The occurrence of large-scale investments depend on whether the proposed Economic Corridor is effectively embedded into the value chain of global production and operations. But, achieving the most ideal value chain of division of responsibility in this BCIM Economic Corridor framework is not realistic based on the current institutions and hardware as its basis. The ideal value chain division means that the different links of one kind of product value adding will be finished by different companies separately, while these companies might distribute in different countries or regions. But for the current BCIM region, it is a hard condition to reach that level of co-production and marketing given high logistics cost, lack of capital and unskilled manpower as major hindrance that need to be addressed to make it to the satisfaction of investing companies. On the other hand, the experiences and lessons of regional integration of developing countries of recent decades indicate that the success rate for international production pattern to enable each party to obtain earnings through promoting industrial specialisation to achieve rationalisation of division of production patterns within a region. However, the usual result is to give up the production specialisation of agreement, returning to the traditional trade liberalisation path.[3]

To achieve market integration and industrial specialisation based divisions of production patterns in this region, BCIM must build mutual trust and be the negotiations platform firstly among these four states, and then amongst their respective companies and people. This means that under the current conditions, the number of multilateral and bilateral contracts signed by any participant involve long term investments that involve the costs in pre-phase inspection, investigation, supervision and implementation and so on.[4] This is a time-consuming and arduous process, and the trade cost of constructing various promotion mechanisms is very high. If the trade cost can not be lowered in the short span of time, then the expansion of cooperation can only have a rather limited scope. The expansion of the scope of sub-regional cooperation, therefore, calls for increasing consciousness of the four BCIM countries about the common interest in promoting their Economic Corridor. But even if overlapping interests of each of these four nation exists, the degree of making it a shared enterprise may not be the same. In spite of high academic conceptions on promoting peaceful relations and economic development of this region, therefore, it is not easy to make these common interests be recognised by their states, society and market at large. Meanwhile, the establishment of regional cooperation multilateral mechanism is based on the fact that the earnings from the BCIM Economic Corridor mechanism promise to be higher than logistical cost and governance cost. And if various stakeholders do not have a shared understanding on earnings and costs, then the motivation and scope of their participating in the region cooperation remains impaired.

Take the issue of interconnection and interworking issue in BCIM for an example. Interconnection and interworking are the key points for constructing BCIM Economic Corridor, and also its real bottleneck. What this means is that the scope for trade and investment development potential remains limited by inconvenient traffic and high transportation costs. But besides the limitation of administrative and material infrastructure, lack of investment funds, of mutual trust and consensus and the varying degrees of insufficient interaction of each of the four governments, their societies and companies, are the important factors to restrict the interconnection and interworking. To promote the transportation communication and other infrastructure in BCIM region, it is required not to establish interconnection and interworking of infrastructure only in terms of its limited technical understanding, but also to form these interconnection and interworking mechanisms amongst and within their government institutions and humanistic society of relevant parties. The accomplishment of transportation convenience and communication convenience can provide conditions for the occurrence of large-scale trade and investment. However, Myanmar and India have not displayed clear strong motives to participate in this regional cooperation. The northeast part of India and north of Myanmar that forms part of core of BCIM Economic Corridor are very sensitive regions for these two countries. India and Myanmar worry that once the Corridor is opened, the trade deficit to China of India and Myanmar will be further expanded, and will damage the economic interests of their own country. Meanwhile, for a long time, China has been doubting that its attempts to solve the port issues by participating in the building of transportation of this area are read in terms of its attempts to take the region as the 'buffer area' of China's geopolitics environment.[5] Persistence of such worries in both politics and security, impair the investment in the construction for transportation infrastructure in this region. This is the typical uncertainty caused by the participation of varying interests that flow from their varying levels of development that make them view their potential risks, and this uncertainty leads to the security anxieties and lack of mutual trust. This also leads to that the participants of this sub-regional cooperation not confirming their self prospective earnings for participating cooperation. Under such circumstances, the scope other cooperation tends to become far limited.

There are, therefore, several restraining factors in the current institutions and Pareto improvement in BCIM region. Few of these major restrictions can be listed like this:

> *Restriction 1:* First obvious restrictions comes from the uncertainty that exists in mechanisms of BCIM sub-regional cooperation. Although relevant countries and their respective regions have made positive responses to the BCIM Economic Corridor proposition and a four-party Working Group conference has been initiated, it is still in a low degree in formalising and authorising and still remains a non-formal agreement in international institutions based arrangement. To reduce such an internal uncertainty, BCIM Economic Corridor must rise to the next phase of self-implementation and then realised further to the level of becoming an international organisation. However, it is obvious that to achieve this BCIM needs lots of time for trust building among BCIM countries.

> *Restriction 2:* The cost of disadvantages caused by uneconomical distance within various contact points of the BCIM region present the second major restriction to Economic Corridor initiative. Distance

is the most fundamental influencing factor discouraging any industrial agglomeration. The regions involved in BCIM sub-regional cooperation are basically underdeveloped regions, with poor infrastructure, and the internal transportation cost is not favourable. The time cost and transportation cost caused by uneconomical distances is an inevitable limitation for decision making on trade and investment. This is the reason why the interconnection and interworking issue is hard to resolve in an effective manner for a long time. The insufficient investment are just its surface reason, its fundamental reason is still the lack of infrastructure, lack of trust and lack of consensus in this region.

Restriction 3: The high-level of socio-economic heterogeneity also hampers the effective cooperation of their internal and shared regions. The heterogeneity does not mean only their economic gap but that this region is not only the poorest region in the world but also the region which has great differences in the patterns of life in their internal regions. It is much more than saying there exist great economic differences among nations involved in the BCIM sub-region. Moreover, due to the differences in their histories and nature of their geographies, there are obvious differences in social formation, political institution, race, religion, belief and culture, etc. which make it hard to develop the uniform value and consensus.

Restriction 4: The transaction cost involved in building market integration institutions is also too high. The promotion of market integration in developing countries involves mainly has four paths and these are:

a) All-around trade liberalisation; that is, to promote regional work division through the power of market;

b) the establishment of complementation agreement for participants; achieve the industrial specialisation based division in production to reach the goal of achieving scales of economy and reduce redundant production capacity;

c) Establish planed industries and enterprises based on the agreements signed among governments, and ensure the implementation of the agreement by adopting customs duties and other facilitating policies;

d) Provide tariff preference for intra-region products or industries, but not carry out all-sided free trade.

All this shows that no matter which method is adopted, the accumulation of internal inter-industry or intra-industry connections in this region is needed urgently. On the other hand, because these promotion mechanisms are related to the internal interest allocation problems of integration, it will be a long-term negotiation process while these mechanisms are promoted alongside. Therefore, as to the existing BCIM sub-regions, it is not realistic to achieve integration and anticipate earnings right away through adopting an Economic Corridor mechanism, and it is important to address the persistent lack of the feasibility based policies.

Promotion Mechanism Based on Scope of Cooperation

(i) Institutional Innovation and the Expansion of Regional Cooperation

As the previous part explains, to practically promote the regional cooperation in BCIM region, it is a must to break through the current situation of lack of political trust, administrative and material infrastructure that limit the scope of their current cooperation. Under the circumstance dominated by these restraining factors, the only way to expand their scope for cooperation is for the BCIM to focus on institutional innovations. To enumerated some of the main limitations that hinder promotion of BCIM sub-regional cooperation and decelerate expansion of scope of their cooperation are as follows: (a) there is obvious uncertainty existing in BCIM regional cooperation mechanism; (b) the scope cost disadvantages caused by the distance exist in

BCIM region; (c) the oversize gap of each party makes it hard to develop the effective cooperation within the region; and (d) the trade cost formed by market integration mechanism is too high.

It is important to understand that this BCIM sub-region does not only have such inhibiting factors but also lacks basic institutional environment for addressing these challenges for promoting sub-regional cooperation. Here, the institutional environment means a series of institutional frameworks which influence the international cooperation formed by the formal and informal rules and procedures. As the specific object-based institutions, the international mechanisms of regional cooperation needs to be 'embedded' into this framework to play specific roles, and the interaction of these two regional and international influences also impacts on the construction of promotion mechanisms streamlining the carrying cost as well as the effectiveness of the mechanism itself.

It is such promotion mechanisms of the macro institutional environment that is called regional and international public goods. The concept Regional public goods is derived from the concept of global public goods, and these can benefit all participating countries, their peoples in the region, as these are non-competitive in the nature.[6] If there are the common needs and common interests in one region, but the international public goods supply seriously missing or unable to meet the needs, then the region or a group of countries can work together to design a set of such arrangements, mechanism or institutions and share the cost of raising these. Due to the international and/or regional public goods have exclusive feature relative to the global public product, regional public goods are also often called as the regional club products.[7] As for BCIM region in particular, at present, the basic level institutional environment which the region lacks refers to the similar ideals and ideologies, the regional institutions with regionalisation as purpose. The regional organisation and groups produced by regional institutions as well as the effective communication and coordination methods or dialogue mechanism, such as the regular negotiation and meetings, regional safety and crisis management mechanism, infrastructure construction, knowledge dissemination and sharing and other regional public service. We can see that these are necessary public goods which BCIM region needs for achieving economic development and social stability. However, at present, the supply of all aspects is not enough yet. Indeed, the current situation of undersupply of public goods in BCIM region is can be seen listed in the table below:

Table 1: Regional Public Goods Supply in BCIM Region as the Basic Level Institutional Environment

Category	*Contents*	*Demand*	*Supply*
Regional dialogue and cooperative mechanism	cooperative organization and uniform administrative and legal platform	High	Insufficient
Traditional safety and non-tradition safety	Reduce the internal conflicts, increase political mutual trust and the treatment of cross border crime problems, etc.	High	Insufficient
Public service	Including the infrastructure construction, education, social security and communal facilities with transportation network included	Very high	Insufficient
Regional market	Manage or adjust the economic mechanism, including a series of measures such as, promoting the trade facilitation of integration, investment preferential arrangement and cross border economic zone.	High	Insufficient
Regional identity	participate in the foreign international affairs With uniform identity	Common	Insufficient

From the above analysis, it appears that BCIM region urgently needs the public goods, mainly including regional dialogue mechanism, the management of public service as well as traditional security and non-traditional security apparatuses. The mechanisms and institutions promoting economic cooperation specifically for the regional market and the institutional arrangement promoting economic cooperation need be evolved. The undersupply of basic level institutional environment of regional public goods leads to the long-term uncertainty, but more importantly, it leads to the high trade cost for maintaining and establishing the new institutions thus limiting the scope for any possibility of expansion of cooperation.

Because of the lack of public goods supply and basic level institutional environment, the promotion mechanism of BCIM Economic Corridor shall not be able to 'map out' an ideal regional integration picture. It will not be able to outline its short and long term objectives. This will only cause excessively high trade cost in constructing the promotion mechanism, leading the participants to lose their motivation for participating in sub-regional cooperation. Moreover, even if the relevant mechanisms can be set up successfully, its operating efficiency will be not satisfactory under such a situation that it has overarching conflictual environment.

The increase in the supply of regional public goods can mainly play the following roles: firstly, to reduce the cost for intra-region economic cooperation and integration through trade; secondly, to reduce the uncertainty which will benefit the seeking out of their shared interests for this sub-regional cooperation; thirdly, to reduce the internal developmental gaps through financial support and assistance. This means that the cost of institutional innovation can be reduced; due to the uncertainty and the narrowing of intra-region gap, the scope of their cooperation can be thereby increased. Hence, only when the situation of short supply of regional public goods is improved and the scope of their regional cooperation is enlarged, the increase of trade and investment will occur naturally.[8]

Therefore, the real key points of the construction of BCIM Economic Corridor as part of providing urgently needed regional public goods as basic institutional environment for this sub-regional cooperation. The stable supply of basic institutional environment and regional public goods shall be the common goal and primary income for each nation in BCIM region, making BCIM regional cooperation become the long-term inter-state collective action possessing self-lasting and running ability.

(ii) Key Issues Faced by Promotion Mechanism

If BCIM wishes to promote this sub-regional cooperation, it must improve the supply of regional public goods as basic level institutional environment in BCIM region, so as to make the expansion of scope of their cooperation possible. In any kind of mature promotion mechanism for regional cooperation, it is a basic requirement to steadily and effectively solve the institutionalisation issues for regional public goods supply. In terms of demand, some scholars think that the frequent intra-regional trade activities can facilitate the functional needs for building international institutions, the interdependency of economy is the basic motive to deepen ASEAN and EU international mechanism, and the political leaders just comply with such requirements under certain conditions.[9] The another opinion holds that the economic symmetry among stakeholders determines the effectiveness of any cooperation mechanism; that is, only when the economic symmetry among partners is higher, can the constant expansion of trade promotes the development of international institutions. However, the two conditions mentioned above, that is, the interdependency in economy and highly developed trade as well as the economic symmetry happen to be absent in the current BCIM sub-region.

While from the perspective of supply, we can see that though the status of BCIM region in regional geopolitics is becoming increasingly important yet, it is still not the primary interest of any regional great power or global powers. This can perhaps account for that the great powers led by China and India have not had the motive to establish and provide a highly cost multilateral institutions, though the BCIM sub-region cooperation that has been raised for so many years. On the other hand, the focus of BCIM cooperation, that is the cross border cooperation among regions, a new field for regional cooperation mechanism creation and construction, has not been fully explored, and there are no specific policy orientation and guidance framework of each nation for this.

Challenges Ahead

After the BCIM Economic Corridor is finally realised, the consensus on promoting interconnection and interworking of this region can be reached, and the needs produced, the participants had the higher supply motive than ever before, and the other hinderances dealt with the promotion mechanism. Therefore, in the process of promoting Economic Corridor, the real issues BCIM is facing are as follows:

(i) To Determine the Provider of Regional Public Goods

Traditionally, there are two kinds of the suppliers of regional public goods: the leading countries and regional cooperation organisations.[10] The former refers to a certain nation or group of national that undertake conclusive leading role to direct progress of integrative development; the second one refers to that the institutional improvement cost which is shared by all participating parties, thus being able to effectively prevent the product from being 'privatised'. However, there are difficulties for regional cooperation organisations to supply regional public goods in BCIM region. Firstly, such kind of regional cooperation organisations do not exist in BCIM region at present; secondly, though the neoliberal institutionalism thinks that as long as there exists correlative dependence relationship and common interests, the institutions and cooperation in the region will emerge at the right moment, in the process of cooperating, it is hard to overcome the common problems, such as prisoner's dilemma, etc. Meanwhile, because the BCIM region mechanism construction must meet multilevel requirements, under the circumstance of lacking of overall planning and coordination, it is hard to reach collective action technically, which is also the biggest difficult faced by BCIM sub-region cooperation promotion mechanism construction.

Under the current circumstances, it is relatively feasible to ask China and India to become the main suppliers of the public goods of BCIM Economic Corridor. It is generally acknowledged that the existence of regional dominant power has the positive influence on the formation of intra-region inter-state cooperation mechanism. However, on the one hand, at present, in BCIM region, though the regional cooperation of BCIM region is only involved with two nations, there exist two possible dominant powers and power centres. On the other hand, neither China nor India can play the unique leading role. Although the position of the BCIM region in the geopolitics has become increasingly important, it is not the primary interests region for China and India. This is why over the years, both China and India have the motivation to supply a costly multilateral institutions in this area.

Compared with other countries in BCIM region, China is a developed economy. The benefits China can obtain though establishing regional institutions, promoting infrastructure, constructing and integrating regional markets in the BCIM region is higher than other nations. Hence, China has more reason to become the supplier of regional public goods in this region. Being the first one to put forward BCIM Economic Corridor was a fundamental reflection of this perspective. However, the other three countries have had doubts for this line of argument for a long time, worrying that once China becomes the supplier of public goods for this region, the dominant power will lose its neutral posture, and the regional public goods might be privatised by China. In addition, though BCIM region is playing an increasingly important role in geopolitical environment around China yet, it is not the primarily for benefits for China only. Given that the phenomenon of 'The free rider' prevails in the international mechanisms and regional public goods, China will carefully measure the cost and benefit to be a supplier of regional public goods. Under such circumstance of uncertain prospects, the high cost and excessive obligations have lowered the aspiration for China to be the leader.

India also has the motive to provide public goods for this region, and have more advantages than China in building' regional consensus'. But, India is also unable to establish the basic institutional environment of higher level alone. India does not wish China to entirely lead the international mechanisms construction of this region, making the regional cooperation promotion mechanism of this region as these mechanisms may become the way to enhance China's power over this region. Therefore, India remains reticent and has been holding the negative response towards the construction of BCIM Economic Corridor for a long time. In a sense, the idea that 'ensuring other parties cannot obtain the dominant position' results into the low supply capability of China and India as well as the compatibility of willingness to work for each other, which is also the reason leading to the restriction of each kind of cooperation towards building mechanism and rules in this region on the one hand, but the seriously insufficient effectiveness of international mechanism on the other hand.

The mutual competition exists among main regional powers, while none of them has the willingness or capability to independently provide regional safety public goods, resulting into the decrease of regional public goods supply capability and efficiency as well as the serious lack of regional public goods. This makes the supply-demand relationship of public goods in BCIM region low supply and therefore not meeting the requirements for a long time. It is demonstrated that without cooperation, the construction of BCIM sub-regional transport network has been negatively influenced by lack of political mutual trust among participants.

Then, is there possibility of China and India becoming co-leaders for BCIM sub-regional cooperation. In fact, China choosing to put forward BCIM Economic Corridor idea along with India, and the expression of Premier Li Keqiang on May 29th 2014 to the newly elected Prime Minister of India, Narendra Modi over the phone talked how they could' together promote BCIM economic corridor construction', which again reflected China's hopes to surpass the dominant position issue to solve it for the construction of international mechanism and supply of public goods. This is how China seeks to promote the regional cooperation in BCIM region by jointly providing public goods or sharing leading role along with India. However, cooperation means self-identity, which means that both parties shall bring their own behaviours under a certain kind of rule or institutional arrangement. This, however, may also result in the BCIM sub-regional arrangements in the future improving China-India bilateral core equations as well. In addition, the premise of such model is to define precisely the constitution and use of international mechanism and regional public goods, and to make the both parties ensure that there is no possibility for this mechanism to be privatised by the other party. This means that in the process of constructing of BCIM Economic Corridor, China and India must make more efforts in building dialogue mechanisms, regional security and regional market rules, thus also negotiating on trade cost that will be higher than that expected.

Meanwhile, the roles of Myanmar and Bangladesh must also be carefully examined as they are also participating in decision making and supply of public goods. Bangladesh has demonstrated both the motive and willingness to actively participate BCIM regional cooperation. However, due to the nation's economic conditions and unstable political situation, its role in promoting the intra-region public goods and the construction of international mechanism has been rather limited. As for Myanmar, at present, it remains the 'weakest link' in BCIM regional cooperation. Though Myanmar government has expressed its support for the construction of Economic Corridor, on the whole, Myanmar is not very sure about what it can obtain from BCIM regional cooperation, and has had its doubts about security aspects as well. As regards its motive to participate in the supply of regional public goods and construction of international mechanism remains the most negative of all.

However, as a regional cooperation mechanism used for improving supply of public goods, the construction of Economic Corridor has its own particular characteristics. There are only four countries involved into BCIM regional cooperation. Naturally, this small number reduces the possibilities to negotiating cost as also of any 'free rider'. On the other hand, it makes the situation such that only when every nation lends a helping hand, the numerous regional public goods (including dialogue mechanism, interconnection and interworking and safety issues) can be provided fully. If one country holds negative attitude and is reluctant to bear higher regional international products costs while other countries can not surpass its sovereignty to intervene, or undertake the costs of being 'free rider', this will lead to the supply of public goods of this region always remaining at the lowest level. If this situation continues, it will make the promotion of regional cooperation nothing but an empty talk.

(ii) Ways to Determine the Mechanism Promotion

The difficulties of three aspects that exist in building promotion mechanism are namely, firstly, to settle concerns about one party gaining dominant position; secondly, under the circumstance of lacking the overall planning and coordination, how will multilevel needs be met; thirdly, in a situation that any one of nations becomes 'the weakest link' how that must be avoided? To solve these issues, BCIM Economic Corridor cooperation shall be divided into functional cooperation, which might be a feasible route to address these questions. Specifically, when BCIM sets the aim to constructing Economic Corridor this big aim can be divided into and refined into functional cooperation sectors. This may also help them address their concerns about one party gaining dominant position. Meanwhile, they must also more clearly define the rights and obligations as well as costs and incomes of participants in every sector. This method has proved to be a feasible way in the construction practice of regional foreign exchange reserve pool in East Asia.[11]

Firstly, the regional public goods which are needed in expanding the scope of the BCIM regional cooperation are at multilevel. To further subdivide it BCIM will find that the needs of members are diverse. This means that the supply methods of regional public goods by individual members using the Economic Corridor will be diverse. This provides solid basis for breaking up the promotion mechanism into functional cooperation sectors. To illustrate this point from the regional public goods perspective, this implies changing the way of promoting regional cooperation through starting with construction of free trade area, instead putting stress on making detailed division in dialogue mechanism, public service, border crossing points for transportation and other border cooperation channels. And, the other key to conduct these mechanism construction will be the basis for subdivision, such as the program coordination committee of infrastructure construction targeting at cross border transportation etc. Such sub-divisions will enable the regional dominant power to be effectively segmented, avoiding the hegemony by the dominant power which could hinder their deepening cooperation.

Secondly, focus on proper planning and coordination will make functional cooperation convenient to conduct. This is in line with clarifying authority-responsibility relationships, avoid 'thumbing a lift', prompting each nation to adopt corresponding actions to participate in the mechanism's construction, and construct specific development strategy and formulate targeted development pattern in different fields. Meanwhile, because the costs and earnings of each member state in each of the subdivisions are relatively easy to confirm, it can also enable them to change these earnings using the compute-mode of member states participating in regional cooperation, avoid member states' opinions that are of 'zero-sum game' nature and avoid regional cooperative mechanism becoming' privatized'. This will enhance incentives for cooperation as also discourage any member state to be seen as 'the weakest link' of BCIM.

Thirdly, thesis of functional cooperation favours seeking a calibration where common interests of all member states become integral to their cooperation paradigm and each party begins to look for effective paths of Pareto improvement, preferentially providing international agreement and enforcement mechanisms at least for their specific sectors. This will guarantee fairness in the regional cooperation income distribution. It also favours seeking out fields where trade costs are the least in constructing cooperation mechanism, through the method of 'small incision', pave the way for in-depth regional cooperation.

Fourthly, functional cooperation is also in favour of avoiding the situation where the discrepancy among participants is too large to reach an agreement and establish negotiation mechanism in gradual fashion. As mentioned above, in case of BCIM, there exists great difference in economic development levels, political institutions, social formation and religious culture etc. Accordingly, it is hard to establish a institutional integration at one stroke. It can, therefore, lower the difficulties in making each member state reach consensus in every field by subdividing sectors of their functional cooperation. Meantime, we can establish a secondary dialogue mechanism and negotiation mechanism, modify relevant policy and cooperation modes and enhance the force of constraint and coercive force.

Fifthly, functional cooperation not only avoids situation of one member state gaining a dominant position it also avoids a situation of excessive competition that will lead to failure of deepening of sub-regional cooperation. Functional cooperation also helps make controversial areas separated and/or merged with other conflict-free sectors so as to effectively avoid part of intra-region conflicts, such as the intensification of border issues that can influence trends of cooperation and promotion in other fields.

Finally, the functional cooperation, especially the functional cooperation in public service, can produce the products which can specially improve the supply level of overall regional public goods. It also acts appropriately to the given situation in order to reinforce the support systems of participants which are 'unable to do what one hopes to do'. It also targets at providing greater chances and help in ensuring effectiveness of mechanisms, thus stimulating the enthusiasm of member states for participating in regional cooperation, making them join in the process of sub-regional cooperation after receiving extra assistance. Meantime, it can help to deepen the mutual trust of participants and enhance regional integration.

Conclusion

The reality of underdeveloped condition and larger gaps within the BCIM intra-region development reveal the characteristics of low degree of promotions mechanism in the BCIM Economic Corridor area. Especially, in this era of globalisation, the underdeveloped areas or countries lack regional integration, hence it is hard for them to obtain benefits from processes of globalisation. However, due to lack of development and accumulative effects of initial stages, BCIM region remains subject to obvious restriction, as it depends on traditional regional integration mode to promote the construction of its proposed Economic Corridor. Most experts only predict the benefits of different countries and regions from trade liberalisation or foreign direct investment through mechanism of their regional economic integration which in turn also promote regional cooperation. Such perspectives will not obtain ideal results for the construction of BCIM Economic Corridor. This calls for exploring alternative perspectives; to experiment with the participation methods and participation contents of BCIM regional cooperation and rethink the effectiveness and feasibility of regional cooperation.

The feasibility and effectiveness of regional cooperation depend also on the size and scope of cooperation. While in BCIM region, due to the lack of economic development and low degree of regional integration, it leads to the relatively narrower scope for economic cooperation, making the regional cooperation difficult. It is the aim and motive of the BCIM regional cooperation to avoid being further pushed into zero cooperation. Expanding cooperation through institutional innovations is the way to change the status quo. But, the analysis in this chapter show a remarkable degree of uncertainty that exists in BCIM regional cooperation mechanisms. This is primarily due to their lack of mutual trust, their disadvantages of costs that are hard to be controlled. Also, large developmental gap of participants and high trade costs produced by lack of market integration mechanism further limits any possibilities of institutional innovation. On the whole, the regional public goods in the BCIM region remain seriously insufficient, resulting into the high costs of expanding cooperation through establishing regional integration institutions as well as its lack of realistic feasibility of their mechanisms.

This study puts forward that the promotion mechanism of BCIM Economic Corridor is not likely to 'map out' an ideal regional integration prospect, based on which they can plan region cooperation path and design relevant institutions. The current format of Economic Corridor not only causes excessively trade costs while in the process building promotion mechanism, it also is likely to result in participants losing the chance to achieve regional cooperation. Moreover, even though relevant mechanism of Economic Corridor gets successfully established, even under the circumstance existing in too many 'conflicts' with big institutional environment, its running efficiency will not possible to make it satisfactory promotion mechanism. Only when the supply of regional public goods is in place that the boundaries of their shared interest can be expanded outside they current imaginations and allow their regional cooperation to fall into free cooperation and naturally achieve growth in trade and investment. Therefore, the real focus of BCIM Economic Corridor shall be to provide urgently needed regional public goods which are based on institutional environment for the region. The stable supply of basic institutional environment and regional public goods must be the common goal and primary objective of each country in BCIM region, making their regional cooperation experiment become source of their long-term inter-state collective action with a self-running ability through supply of regional public goods to lower the costs of institutional innovation.

And finally, to improve public goods and basic institutional environment in the BCIM sub-region, their promotion mechanisms will face three main difficulties, namely, firstly, to determine benchmarks for the dominant position which they seek to avoid going to any one party; secondly, in spite of them lacking the overall planning and coordination, the given circumstances would still require them to provide for multilevel needs; thirdly, they must also avoids situation where any one of nations becomes 'the weakest link'. To address these fundamental challenges, BCIM Economic Corridor mechanism may be broken up into functional sectors thus surpassing the competition for dominant position. Meanwhile, they have also to continue building consensus in defining more clearly the rights and obligations as well as costs and benefits for participants in every specific sector of Economic Corridor related initiatives.

Endnotes

1. Li Tieli and Jiang Huaiyu, "Sub-regional Economic Cooperation Mechanism Research: the Analytical Framework of a Border Effect", Northeast Asia Forum, May 2005, the third phase of 14th volume.
2. Nie Wenjuan, "Symmetry and Development mechanism of ASEAN", *World Economics and Politics*, 2010, Vol.2, p. 35.
3. Peter Robson, The Economics of International Integration, (London: Psychology Press, 1998).

4. Dreher & Axel, "Does Globalization Affect Growth? Empirical Evidence from a new Index", Applied Economics, 2006, Vol.38, p. 10.
5. Yang Siling and Gao Huiping, "Discussion on BCIM Region Cooperation and the Shape of China's Geopolitics Environment", Indian Ocean Economic and Political Review, 2014, Vol.2, p. 9.
6. Li Zenggang, "Global Public Goods: Definition, Classification and Supply", Economic Review, 2006, Vol.1.
7. Fan Yongming, "Regional International Public Goods - Analysis of Regional Cooperation Theory", *World Economics and Politics*, 2008, Vol.1.
8. Gao Chen, "Supply-Demand Relations of Regional Public Goods and the Shifting Regional Order: A Case Study of Evolutional Paths to the East Asian Order", World Economics and Politics, 2012, No.11
9. Helen Milner, "International Theories of Cooperation among Nations: Strengths and Weaknesses", *World Politics,* Vol. 44, No. 3, 1992, pp. 466-496
10. Chen Fengjun, Qi Jianhua, *New Regionalism And The East Asia Cooperation,* (Beijing: China Economy Press, 2007), pp. 234-235
11. Wang Yuzhu, "Surpassing of Regional Public Products Supply and Issue of East Asia's Cooperation Dominant Right", *Contemporary Asia-Pacific Studies,*, 2011, Vol.7, pp. 75-94

11

Locating BCIM-EC in India's Sub-Regional Diplomacy

K. Yhome

In March 2014, Prime Minister Manmohan Singh had visited Myanmar to attend the third summit of the Bay of Bengal Initiative for Multi-Sectoral Technical and Economic Cooperation (BIMSTEC), a sub-regional grouping of which India is a founder member. The visit underlined not only Delhi's continued commitment to its Look East policy (LEP) but also its growing interests in its peripheral sub-regions in the east. Media reports before, during and after the visit rightly focused on the significance of the LEP and Myanmar did not seem to attract much attention. A fundamental question that needs an in-depth examination is how New Delhi views its sub-regions and where do they fit in the overall sub-regional diplomacy of India? This also has clear implications for India's approach to the BCIM-Economic Corridor.

That New Delhi lacks a well-defined neighbourhood policy has been well-documented.[1] Until a few years ago, India's policy towards its immediate neighbourhood had largely been framed by its civilisational linkages and the colonial legacies as the inheritor of a territorial space that has, for over one hundred years, been ruled from the city of Delhi. However, independent India seems to have lacked the strategic vision that can articulate its interests and strategies and tie these to its diplomacy around its surrounding sub-regions. India's central location in the subcontinent with strong cultural ties with its periphery seems to have been replaced by policies somewhat similar to the British Raj's imperial send of entitlement reflected in its creating of concept of suzerainty. Successive leaders in India have viewed the subcontinent as India's backyard, and assumed it to be its sphere of influence. However, this conventional wisdom has been challenged with the entry of extra-regional powers. This has occurred because of their own strategic and commercial interests as also for India's smaller neighbours' strategy to balance India's predominant regional position reflecting their smaller power syndrome.

This is not to say that New Delhi had no vision of its role in providing regional leadership. In the face of rapid geopolitical changes in recent times, India's has been reframing its sub-regional approach as also its policy responses albeit slowly. Indeed, soon after independence, India's first Prime Minister Jawaharlal Nehru had initiated the Afro-Asian Solidarity to garner support for anti-colonialism. Nehru, along with several other world leaders from the so-called "Third World" had led the Non-Aligned Movement (NAM) with the aim to stay out of the bipolar world during the Cold War. But this also led to perceptions that perhaps New Delhi was far too ambitious and focused more on larger Asian and global issues while completely neglecting its immediate neighbours. It was felt that in its initiatives New Delhi took its smaller neighbours for granted and presumed that they would support it as the unchallenged regional leader.

This chapter contends that India's regional economic and strategic diplomacy has undergone critical transformation in the recent years to address its rising global ambitions as also in face of its increased consciousness of is developmental needs and its compulsions to respond to its increasing domestic and external security challenges. It is in this backdrop that the logic of twenty-first century geo-economics and geo-strategic imperatives has compelled New Delhi to rethink its approach towards its immediate peripheries including BIMSTEC or BCIM. One of the most visible outcomes of this rethinking has been its manifest re-imagining of its peripheries into sub-regions. This chapter explores the factors that have been shaping India's regional diplomacy and locates the significance of sub-regions in India's new regional approach. In doing so, the chapter examines both the prospects and pitfalls of sub-regional forums in India's emerging new regional diplomacy. India's new regional approach and the growing regionalisation of foreign policy have gained much currency in India's neighbourhood policy.[2] In this new narrative, the significance of sub-regions is discussed with a particular focus on its economic dimensions. The chapter finally examines the significance of the BCIM sub-region in India's regional policy from both geo-economic as well as geostrategic perspectives.

Factors Shaping India's Regional Diplomacy

India is both a continental as well as a maritime nation. In the subcontinent, India occupies a unique position where no two of its immediate neigbours share common land borders but is linked to each other through India. However, this unique position of India in the region changes drastically when one considers two more immediate neighbours sharing land boundaries with India namely, China and Myanmar (***See Map below***). A view of India's maritime boundaries with Southeast Asia makes the regional picture still more complex. In the case of China, three of the six sub-continental countries (Pakistan, Nepal, and Bhutan) share common land boundaries with China along with India and, in the case of Myanmar, Bangladesh share they both land and maritime boundaries with India. But while Myanmar shares land borders with China, Bangladesh enjoyed not border but strong physical proximity to China which is separated from China only by a slim corridor called 'chicken's neck' that connects India to its North Eastern Region. In maritime

India, the Andaman and Nicobar Islands makes India as much a Southeast Asian nation with the islands located closer to Myanmar, Thailand, Indonesia and Malaysia than to mainland India and making India a stakeholder in South China Sea region.

Recent geopolitical changes have prompted New Delhi to revisit colonial imaginations about its strategic location in South Asia and to relook at the 21st century ground realities and these have borne fruit in obtaining India new success in its LEP. On the one hand, factors of geographical realism have also opened new economic opportunities though these are also simultaneously creating strategic challenges. This mix of potentials and concerns has been prompting New Delhi to reframe its regional approach as also explains slow evolution of its sub-regional policies and initiatives. Despite its central geographical location as the connector in the subcontinent, India has failed to envision the larger Southern Asian region as a whole within its policy parameters. This is clearly reflected in the fact that the first idea for regional integration in the form of South Asian Association for Regional Cooperation (SAARC) was proposed by Dhaka in the mid-1980s and kept restricted to seven South Asian countries. But there is also a counterview that perhaps India allowed it to be Dhaka's initiatives simply because initiatives from New Delhi may have been suspect amongst its smaller neighbouring countries. But either way, progress in SAARC has remained intermittent and rather slow by any reckoning owing to the political tensions between India and Pakistan. This has perhaps also pushed New Delhi to explore LEP for the larger East Asian region as also sub-regional initiatives like BCIM as possible alternatives.

Another critical factor that has played a role in prompting India and other South Asian nations to exploit sub-regional initiatives has been the successful achievements demonstrated by comparatively compact smaller regions in growth triangles in Southeast and East Asia including sub-regions like the Johor (Malaysia)-

Singapore-Riau (Indonesia) (JSRGT); the South China Growth Triangle comprising of Hong Kong, the Guangdong, and the Fujian provinces of China and Taiwan; Brunei Darussalam-Indonesia-Malaysia-Philippines East ASEAN Growth Area (BIMP-EAGA); Greater Mekong Sub-region (GMS); and Indonesia-Malaysia-Thailand Growth Triangle (IMT-GT).[3] India and few other South Asian countries have also adopted this sub-regional concept as an alternative to SAARC cooperative framework in order to address their economic and security concerns both at the domestic as well as regional levels. The ideas behind setting up sub-regions were aimed at strengthening regional economic cooperation by improving cross-border connectivity and facilitating trade and people to people contacts. An important Indian policy objective in sub-regional initiatives has been to open up border trade points and to encourage its immediate neighbours to take advantage of the opportunities from India's faster economic growth. This has had its appeal amongst India's immediate periphery though scepticism also remains amongst few of its neighbouring countries.

There are two factors that have been shaping India's strategic thinking towards its immediate neighbourhood. First is the recognition that a peaceful periphery is a precondition for a sustained economic growth and second is China's growing presence in the region. The geo-economic imperative has been to ensure that India's economic development is not negatively affected by instability in the neighbourhood, and the geo-strategic imperative has been to ensure that India does not lose its traditional influence in its backyard to rising China. Explaining the logic of the new approach Indian strategist C Raja Mohan has observes that without a peaceful periphery India cannot "realise its global aspirations" and "failure to re-integrate the subcontinent around India would cede India's natural hinterland to a rising China."[4] The challenge of course is how India can encourage its "neighbours to see the possible gains from a more active engagement" with India.[5] India's strategy has been to provide "growth opportunities for the neighbours" and by using its "new options" provided by its economic growth, India could "leverage its own market for diplomatic gains on the regional front."[6] A major departure from the past has been that the regional policy is driven by India's self-interest as C Raja Mohan has observed: "India's new regionalism is focused on self-interest, rather than mere sentimentalism that favours good neighbourly relations, and therefore is likely to be more effective."[7] One of the key objectives of India has been to share its increasing prosperity with its neighbours thereby deepening regional economic integration.

At the domestic front, the rise of strong regional political parties at the national level in the era of coalition politics since the late 1990s has also brought in regional/provincial interests to the fore both within the nation as also in India's neighbourhood diplomacy and foreign policy. This has also presented its own strengthen and challenges.[8] The central issue that dominates the current discourse is New Delhi's growing inability to take strong stands in its neighbourhood policies is partly due to these increasing pressures from powerful regional parties in the coalition era. Examples of Tamil Nadu in the case of India's relations with Sri Lanka and West Bengal in the Bangladesh's case are often cited to support this line of argument. Even as this debate continues, there is growing recognition of federalisation of India's neighbourhood policy and the need to accommodate these interests of India's provinces in India's regional diplomacy has come to be paramount and essential. As former Indian foreign secretary, Nirupama Rao, rightly puts it:

While traditionally, foreign policy is the sole purview of the Centre, we are now entering an era where the word of the State governments and the parties that run them is increasingly weighing in on the moves that New Delhi can make....we need to develop a "whole of government" approach that enables a concerted approach of consultation involving all the States that border [our neighbours], so that a critical balance of interests is evolved without sacrificing national interest.[9]

For a long time, particularly since the launching of India's LEP, state governments, trade bodies and civil society from India's Northeast have been demanding the reopening of border for trade with the neighbouring countries.[10] India's North East region has wide-ranging linkages with the frontier regions of Myanmar, Bangladesh and China that include informal trade, narcotic trafficking, gun running and so on. They also have overlapping communities and cultures which have been divided by political boundaries. These issues have often created both traditional and non-traditional security threats in the region and also in shaping relations between the governments of these nations. These linkages also mean that the geographical advantages of this sub-region could be tapped for greater trans-national collaborations to tackle security as well as development issues in the border areas. Some of that has also been happening over the years.

Sub-Regions in India's Regional Diplomacy

In the recent decades, India has initiated and joined several sub-regional groupings with the aim to address both its economic and security interests of its adjoining domestic regions. That these initiatives have witnessed mixed results in achieving the stated objectives continues to confound experts. The question that confronts New Delhi is as to what is the best approach to move forward in redressing the persistent trust-deficit and for bringing development in its often underdeveloped peripheral domestic regions? India has accepted the formulation that bringing development in India's peripheries would need regional cooperation. An important point that supports the idea is the fact that most of the countries in India's immediate periphery also suffer from similar challenges of poverty, ill-health, and illiteracy and hence cooperative approach holds greater prospect for everybody. Another obvious advantage of regional cooperation for India is in bringing development in its peripheries by leveraging the strengths of other regional players. Locating mutual complementarities remains the first step in conceptualizing sub-regional cooperation.

There has been a realisation in the subcontinent that it was necessary for the region to explore new ways of regional cooperation such as sub-regionalism.[11] For instance, due to the persistent hostility between Delhi and Islamabad over Kashmir, the South Asia regional grouping had long been a hostage to their mutual political tensions. Thus, sub-regions allow the region to circumvent the slow progress of SAARC. For a long time, Delhi's strategy to deal with the SAARC impasse had been to push cooperation through bilateralism as a way to bypass the SAARC. Going for a FTA with Sri Lanka was one such instance. However, Delhi has reviewed that strategy by adopting sub-regionalism concept, where sub-regional groupings are seen as complementing and supplementing the SAARC efforts for regional cooperation.

The concept of sub-region is primarily based on cooperation among geographically contiguous parts of the member countries. This brings border regions in the forefront of regional policies. These peripheral regions had remains negletion the conventional thinking of policy making by state that allowed their mutual policies to be guided purely by 'national' interests. By bringing the focus on frontier provinces and regions, mostly neglected in the development process, sub-regional initiatives have helped address the questions of equitable development. Sub-regional schemes also address another perception issue among India's smaller neighbours. Cooperation through sub-regions minimises the implications of India's overwhelming size as sub-regions gives a sense of dealing with equals. Most of the sub-regional initiatives have centred in India's eastern neighbourhood particularly following the launched of LEP.

Map I: Building Sub-Regions

In May 1995, at the meeting of the SAARC Council of Ministers in New Delhi, the idea of forming the South Asian Growth Quadrangle (SAGQ) comprising Bangladesh, Bhutan, Nepal and Northeast India was first mooted based on concept papers prepared by Bangladeshi and Nepalese delegations.[12] The proposed SAGQ did not receive much attention in India, let alone any serious political debate of its pros and cons. But the initiative generated a fierce political debate in Bangladesh between the then ruling party— the Awami League and the main opposition party––the Bangladesh Nationalist Party (BNP) as also amongst various experts. Examining BNP's opposition to the sub-regional grouping, MD Nuruzzaman, for instance, sums up the key points thus:

First, the proposed grouping [SAGQ] undermines the spirit, importance, interests, and functions of SAARC. As SAARC is the very embodiment of co-operation of all the countries of South Asia, the formation of a sub-grouping is likely to diminish its effectiveness and make it loose regional forum. Secondly, once the grouping is formalised, the BNP argues, India would demand 'corridor' facilities through Bangladesh in order to help crush armed insurgency in her North Eastern states, endangering Bangladesh's sovereignty and independence. And, in view of Sino-Indian hostilities, India would use Bangladesh territory for military purpose whenever any war situation between India and China arose. Thirdly, the proposed grouping would be superfluous paperwork. The key to regional development is the simulation of growth in the smaller nations, not initiatives and additional paperwork at a superstructure-level by a multilateral bureaucracy.[13]

After initial reservations, Bangladesh has come a long way in supporting sub-regional forums. In 2001, the SAGQ was further boosted when the Asian Development Bank (ADB) mooted a new development plan called the South Asia Sub-regional Economic Cooperation (SASEC) made up of the SAGQ countries. According to the SASEC project portfolio summary, the total number of projects funded so far is 32 mostly going into the transport and energy sectors at an estimated cost of $5.69 billion.[14] In fact, the inter-grid connectivity between India and Bangladesh became operational in October 2013 is one such example. According to an ADB study, the sub-region format has huge potential for energy trade with hydropower potential in Nepal and Bhutan, coal in the Indian states of West Bengal and Bihar, and oil and gas in Bangladesh and in the Indian states of Assam and Tripura.[15] The same study, however, also points out that the "SASEC's vision is to develop, utilize, and optimize power links, but there has been limited progress so far".[16] Similarly, SASEC in one of its reports observes that while the member-states have taken "the crucial first steps toward unlocking the tremendous potential of a more integrated subregion—but much remains to be done" underscoring both the potential as well as the need to do more.[17]

A year after SAGQ was proposed, a new sub-regional grouping was proposed by Thailand comprising the littorals of the Bay of Bengal. Initially, the new sub-regional grouping was proposed with four countries and named BIST-EC (Bangladesh, India, Sri Lanka, and Thailand Economic Cooperation). Subsequently, Myanmar was added as a member later in 1997 and in 2003 Nepal and Bhutan were also added a members and the name of the grouping was changed in Bay of Bengal Initiative for Multi-Sectoral Technical and Economic Cooperation (BIMSTEC) in 2004 with the key objective of reaching a free trade agreement for greater economic integration. In fact the declaration on the establishment of the sub-regional grouping in Bangkok in 1997 clearly spells out the aims and purposes of the grouping. Among other objectives, the grouping declared that it will "accelerate the economic growth and social progress in the sub-region through joint endeavours in a spirit of equality and partnership" and "cooperate in projects that can be dealt with most productively on a sub-regional basis among the [BIMSTEC] countries and that make best use of available synergies."[18]

In 2004 a framework agreement was signed for BIMSTEC free trade area (FTA). However, even after a decade, it is yet to be implemented. So, not all of the sub-regional groupings are able to take their agenda forward, even while they have an agreed agenda. This has often occurred because of the lack of political will or lack of political stability in some of the member countries particularly Myanmar but other member-states including Nepal, Sri Lanka, Thailand, all also had their share of political turmoil in the recent years. However, there is no running away from the fact that a over ambitious approach from the leadership of few member states to push the BIMSTEC agenda ahead also has to be blamed. During the third BIMSTEC summit held in March 2014, leaders of the BIMSTEC, recommitted to the founding aims and purposes of the grouping and decided to 'fast track' the finalisation of the draft agreement on trade in goods. In 2008, BIMSTEC completed a study to promote and improve transport infrastructure and logistics among its member countries with ADB as its development partner.[19] A BIMSTEC connectivity project to improve transport connectivity and to promote intra-region trade and tourism in the sub-region includes the Trilateral Highway project linking India, Myanmar, and Thailand. This is expected to be completed by 2016.[20]

BCIM and BCIM-EC Diplomacy

After several years of hesitancy, in the recent past New Delhi has been actively pursuing the sub-regional grouping known as the Bangladesh-China-India-Myanmar Forum for Regional Cooperation (BCIM) Forum. Especially, the proposed BCIM-Economic Corridor (BCIM-EC) project intends to develop socio-economic linkages among the four member-states. The roots of this idea go back to 1999, when the Chinese Yunnan provincial government proposed a sub-regional scheme called the "Kunming Initiative" as a Track II forum comprising the four contiguous countries. The ideas driving the BCIM-EC project are a combination of domestic and external interests of both New Delhi and Beijing who are major players though it is only their contiguous regions that are involved in BCIM-EC. Especially for China, a major challenge has been to address the economic imbalance between the coastal developed regions and the underdeveloped frontier regions. Given the continental size of both China and India, the interior regions have not benefited as much as the coastal regions that enjoy the geographical advantage of maritime connectivity.

The BCIM-EC project is an important part of New Delhi's and Beijing's strategies to open up their landlocked frontier regions to the neighbouring countries. This is to maximize advantages by reviving their historical commercial and economic interdependence and inter-linkages. Especially, the Yunnan Province of China is a landlocked region far-off from the booming coastal areas in the east. Regional cooperation in BCIM-Ec promises to obtain these landlocked provinces of China an easy access to too open oceans allowing them become what some Chinese scholars refers to as "from continental to maritime economies."[21] Since the launching of the "Gateway Strategy" in 2009, Yunnan has formally been made the gateway to Southeast and South Asia with several networks of road, rail, and air connectivity being planned to connect Yunnan with the neighbouring countries. An important part of this strategy is to revive the ancient "Southern Silk Road," believed to have connected China with India.[22] This has since come to be the favourite theme for President Xi Jinping.

Within the renewed China's 'Going Out' policy, Yunnan's geographical location that shares common borders with Myanmar, Laos and Vietnam is seen as a major gateway for this landlocked underdeveloped region of China. Similarly, India's landlocked and turmoil ridden North East Region has also lagged behind compared to other parts of the country. Within the LEP, New Delhi's strategy has been to encourage greater economic integration of the North East with the neighbouring economies of China, Myanmar, and Bangladesh through border trade and connectivity to provide sea access to the region.[23] Like Yunnan province of China, the North East Region of India also shares common borders with Bhutan, Bangladesh, Myanmar and China, making it the bridge between mainland India and its eastern neighbours. This is also in line with India's new approach toward its periphery that aims at creating a favourable regional environment conducive for India's overall economic growth and this especially applies in case of India's North East Region. In this special context of seeking peace and stability in India's North East Region through growth and development, the idea of sub-regional connectivity has since come to be seen as synonymous with New Delhi's new emphasis on pursuing sub-regional diplomacy as a new niche are in its foreign relations with India's immediate and extended neighbours.

New Delhi's official endorsement of the BCIM forum and the BCIM-EC explains the change in India's sub-regional diplomacy. It has been noted earlier that two factors – need for a peaceful periphery and China's growing regional presence – have prompted New Delhi to rethink of its sub-regional approach. One way of addressing the two concerns has been to engage Beijing in stabilising the shared periphery. This allows for building common stakes for both countries in the stability and development of their respective peripheries. Engaging Beijing in sub-regional projects also create opportunity for building piecemeal trust between the border communities of these two countries. This thinking is at departure from the past of adopting a purely national-capital driven and reactive approach to each other's initiatives in regional matters.

Secondly, another factor that has perhaps influenced New Delhi in endorsing the BCIM-EC is that there are mutual benefits in both political and strategic terms. Politically, India and China could work together in the development of the sub-region that has been the soft under-belly of both these countries. The traditional and non-traditional security threats emanating from the sub-region has been a major issue of instability and underdevelopment. The BCIM and BCIM-EC provides a platform for India and China to collaborate in dealing with these common problems and challenges. The strategic interest of both India and China with the BCIM and BCIM-EC is to open up their land-locked regions to neighbouring economies. Cooperation with the neighbouring countries also provides sea access to their landlocked regions thereby facilitating long-term development.

Sub-Regionalism: Pitfalls and Prospects

India's re-imagining of its immediate neighbourhood through sub-regions has provided new ways to accelerate the integration process in the form of BCIM-EC, BIMSTEC, SASEC, the Mekong-Ganga Cooperation and so on. An important policy objective of India in all these sub-regional initiatives in its diplomacy has been to encourage its neighbours to take advantage of the opportunities flowing from India's rapid pace of economic development. These sub-regional cooperative frameworks also allow India to overcome its weaknesses by capitalising on the strengths of other regional players. However, this sub-regional approach has its own complications. The mushrooming of sub-regional initiatives around India could mean prioritizing which make some of these have moved faster than the other. Each of these also pose their own set of political and security challenges. Gradual involvement of China – which is often seen as extra-regional power – in the Indian subcontinent creates its own implications. The increasing role of external powers in India's sub- region may compromise Delhi's preeminent position in the subcontinent. The challenge for New Delhi is how its plays a balancing-act in accommodating the competing strategic interests of major regional players while entering into cooperation for various regional and sub-regional forums.

Conventionally speaking, physical contiguity and connectivity have been the core elements of any regional and sub-regional integration process. Geographically, BCIM-EC presents itself as a contiguous space with shared history and culture. Historically, given the porous nature of these borders and because of certain special treaties, these sub-regions have always witnessed movement of people and goods from one country to another. Their overlapping communities were especially responsibility for this historical connectivity. However, because of political obstacles and limited transport and connectivity links in their post-colonial period, their limited interactions have not been able to propel these sub-regions for deepening their economic integration and development in their border areas. The sub-regional initiatives in diplomacy aimed at building new connectivity networks could meet the growing demands and expectations of the sub-regions that have been witnessing a new economic dynamism in the recent years. The BCIM=EC sub-region holds huge potential to re-define the economic geography of not only this smaller sub-regions but the larger subcontinent by connecting this BCIM-EC to the South, Southeast Asia and China.

India's peripheral sub-regions where India seeks to engage neighbouring countries are both landlocked and maritime in nature. Therefore an important element of this sub-regional cooperation includes providing sea access to landlocked regions of these neighbouring states. India's sub-regional diplomacy can surely leverage these advantages. Other geographical advantages like resources and terrain can also be counted that can be accessed by the landlocked sub-regions of neighbouring countries. For example, exploring potential for transit facilities and more effective transport corridors needs supporting architecture of rules and regulations to facilitate cross-country movements can be an attractive reason to strengthen sub-regional diplomatic initiatives. The existing linkages and possible economic corridors to link these sub-regions with the neighbours and extending ongoing and planned economic corridors such as the BCIM-EC are critical for making the idea of sub-regional framework more attractive and effective.

Perhaps the most critical question remains on the growing stakes of state governments and other stakeholders. New Delhi will have to deal with the growing role of the states in its sub-regional diplomacy. All such cross-border cooperative initiatives are likely to be conceptualized by the national governments but implemented primarily by the sub-regional principalities and this has been the track record in case of China and could be the trends in future in other three participating countries. As India catches up with the concept of sub-regional cooperation where smaller compact geographical regions seek greater economic integration through growth triangles and quadrangles, the significance of the role these sub-regions for State will see them becoming the key stakeholders in India's neighbourhood diplomacy. Rather than resisting the role of States in national development and sub-regional diplomacy, finding ways to accommodate their interests and concerns of sub-regional stakeholders and integrating these with the country's larger interests is the way forward. The role of the States in foreign policy-making has so far been framed narrowly as a zero-sum game – one's win, another loss, where the national and the regional are often juxtaposed as two parallel interests with no meeting point. There is need to reconsider this thinking if India were to take full advantage of the sub-regional cooperative frameworks like the one developed through the BCIM-EC.

Conclusion

The growing recognition of the centrality of their security and development challenges in the peripheries would need India and China to focus on regional and sub-regional solutions and to evolve cooperation which has been well-accepted. China's as also India's economic rise has benefitted not only their peripheries but also these two countries. BCIM-EC has clearly added a positive spin to the complicated equations between Beijing and New Delhi as also amongst all the four participating countries. One of the key objectives of their sub-regional diplomacy has been to take the lead and share their prosperity with neighbours by deepening their sub-regional economic integration. This has led to evolution of new diplomatic trends in their overall regional engagement with each other.

As BCIM-EC experience makes India begin re-imagining its peripheries and makes their needs and concerns integral to its conduct of inter-state diplomacy there remain several challenges. BCIM-EC has been one step forward in this sub-regional approach yet it remains slow and some other such sub-regional initiatives remain even standstill. This lack of momentum can be explained their past colonial legacies as also in terms like China's growing economic footprints which sometimes generates concerns in its immediate periphery. But, be that as it may, the new sub-regional approach to India's diplomacy has surely injected some new dynamism in its sub-regional diplomacy both in ideas as well as its experiences that is expected to guides its strategic planning and approach towards its peripheries.

Endnotes

1. See for instance Ashok K. Behuria, Smruti S. Pattanaik and Arvind Gutpa, 'Does India have a Neighbourhood Policy', *Strategic Analysis*, 36(2), March 2012, pp. 229-246.
2. Kripa Sridharan, 'Federalism and Foreign Relations: The Nascent Role of the Indian States', *Asian Studies Review*, 27(4), 2003; 463-89;
3. Isher Judge Ahluwalia, "Economic Cooperation in South Asia" (date and pleace not found) at http://jica-ri.jica.go.jp/IFIC_and_JBICI-Studies/jica-ri/publication/archives/jbic/report/paper/pdf/rp16_e09.pdf
4. C Raja Mohan, "Exponential Advantages," *Himal*, February 2011.at http://old.himalmag.com/himal-feed/53/3633-exponential-advantages.html
5. Ibid.
6. C Raja Mohan, "Peaceful Periphery: India's New Regional Quest," Centre for the Advanced Study of India, University of Pennsylvania, 23 May, 2007 at https://casi.sas.upenn.edu/iit/crajamohan
7. Ibid.
8. See for instance Smruti S. Pattanaik, "Federalising India's Neighbourhood Policy: Making the States Stakeholders", *Strategic Analysis*, Vol. 38, Issue 1, January 2014, pp. 31-48.
9. Nirupama Rao, "India in a tough neighbourhood", *The Hindu*, 20 December, 2013 at http://www.thehindu.com/opinion/op-ed/india-in-a-tough-neighbourhood/article5479263.ece
10. See D. Nath (ed.), *Reopening of the Stilwell Road : Prospects and Problems*, Maulana Abul Kalam Azad Institute of Asian Studies, 2004 Delhi.
11. MD Nurizzaman, "SAARC and sub-regional co-operation: Domestic politics and foreign policies in South Asia", *Contemporary South Asia*, November 1999 at http://sga.myweb.uga.edu/readings/saarc.htm
12. MD Nurizzaman, "SAARC and sub-regional co-operation: Domestic politics and foreign policies in South Asia", *Contemporary South Asia*, November 1999 at http://sga.myweb.uga.edu/readings/saarc.htm
13. Ibid.
14. For details see SASEC official website at http://www.sasec.asia/index.php?page=projects

15. *Infrastructure for a Seamless Asia,* A Joint Study of the Asian Development Bank and the Asian Development Bank Institute, Tokyo, 2009, pp. 34-35 at http://www.adbi.org/files/2009.08.31.book.infrastructure.seamless.asia.pdf
16. Ibid.
17. See "South Asia Subregional Economic Cooperation", SASEC Secretariat, Asian Development Bank, 2013 at http://www.sasec.asia/dl/SASEC%20Expanded%20Brochure.pdf
18. See BIMSTEC official website at http://www.bimstec.org/about-us.php
19. The final report is available at http://www.adb.org/sites/default/files/projdocs/2008/38396-01-reg-tacr.pdf
20. "India, Thailand hopeful of trilateral highway by 2016", *The Hindu*, 30 May, 2013 at http://www.thehindu.com/news/national/india-thailand-hopeful-of-trilateral-highway-by-2016/article4766782.ece
21. The remark was made by some Chinese scholars during the third RIIO International Conference on International Relations in Indian Ocean Economies held on December 1-2, 2013 that was organised by Regional Institute for Indian Ocean Economies, Yunnan University of Finance and Economics, Kunming, China.
22. "China wants to revive 'Southern Silk Road' with India", *The Times of India,* 9 June, 2013 at http://timesofindia.indiatimes.com/business/international-business/China-wants-to-revive-Southern-Silk-Road-with-India/articleshow/20510534.cms and "China to revive 'Southern Silk Road' for regional prosperity", Xinhua, 9 June, 2013 at http://english.people.com.cn/90778/8278986.html
23. See for instance "North Eastern Region Vision 2020", Ministry of Development of North Eastern Region, Government of India, 2008. The full report is available at http://www.indianchamber.org/northeast/Vision2020.pdf

Index

C

N

O

P

R

S

T

■■■